GROWING UP
YANOMAMÖ

PRAISE FOR
GROWING UP
YANOMAMÖ

It is excellent, a great read and unique insight into a culture and upbringing that are cinematographic, to say the least. The descriptions of growing up with the Yanomamö remind me a bit of Huck Finn, with an Amazon twist. The story about hunting for tapir is wild—it makes a deer hunt, or even an elk hunt, seem tame by comparison.

—SIMON ROMERO
Andean Bureau Chief,
The New York Times

It is a book you will enjoy reading while learning about the problems of preaching the gospel to a people with a different worldview.

—DUANE STOUS
New Tribes Mission missionary
and trainer, Retired

Mike Dawson is an awesome story teller! Having lived and worked cross-culturally with indigenous peoples in numerous parts of the world, in both my youth and adulthood, I am "right with" Mike as he so openly and effectively relates his social and spiritual story! The challenges and truths that he experiences will equip and encourage you in your faith, even if you've never had the privilege to live in another land.

—ROGER KRENZIN
JAARS missionary pilot to Africa,
South America, and Asia, Retired

Michael's sense of humor, wit, and caring come through the pages. It is like sitting down with a good friend who is ready to surprise you with a true story of an amazing adventure. Imagine a white boy, in "the hood" of this jungle tribe, living, playing, and growing up Yanomamö.

—CHRISTOPHER BESSETTE
Writer/director of the feature film,
Yai Wanonabälewä: The Enemy God

The beauty of fiction is that it allows the author to create characters that are uniquely designed to elicit the full range of human emotions. In nonfiction, only rarely does one find a range of characters we can not only admire, but best of all, root for, and even dream of a better world for their children. Such are the characters about whom Mike Dawson writes in Growing Up Yanomamö, a story of life with Stone-Age people, guaranteed to expand the mind of even the most experienced. Nothing demands a self-review like a trip through another time and culture. Dawson provides just this sort of trip in his special book.

—MARK ANDREW RITCHIE
Author, *Spirit of the Rainforest*

Growing Up Yanomamö

Missionary Adventures in the Amazon Rainforest

Michael Dawson

Sketches by Ruben Pintor

Foreword by Larry M. Brown
New Tribes Mission

GRACE ACRES PRESS

CULTIVATING JOY

Grace Acres Press
P.O. Box 22
Larkspur, CO 80118
888-700-GRACE (4722)
(303) 681-9995
(303) 681-9996 fax
CULTIVATING JOY www.GraceAcresPress.com

Library of Congress Cataloging-in-Publication Data:
Dawson, Mike, 1955–
    Growing Up Yanomamö : missionary adventures in the Amazon Rainforest / Michael Dawson; sketches by Ruben Pintor
    p.   cm.
    ISBN: 978-1-60265-009-1
    1. Yanomamö Indians–Venezuela–Amazonas–Social life and customs–Juvenile literature. 2. Yanomamö Indians–Missions–Venezuela–Amazonas–Juvenile literature. 3. Amazonas (Venezuela)–Social life and customs–Juvenile literature. 4. Dawson, Mike, 1955–Juvenile literature. 5. Children of missionaries–Venezuela–Amazonas–Biography–Juvenile literature. I. Pintor, Ruben. II. Title.
    F2520.1.Y3D39   2008
    987'.64– dc22   2008032955

Printed in Canada

12 11 10 09   01 02 03 04 05 06 07 08 09 10

DEDICATION

This book is dedicated to the memory
of Reneé Pintor Dawson.
She lives in our hearts as a
penetrating reminder that
not only is Christ worth living for,
He is worth dying for.

"She was a woman of uncommon beauty,
a fiercely loyal friend,
a compassionate critic,
a doting mother,
the perfect wife ..."

—JOHN GRISHAM, *A Time to Kill*
(foreword)

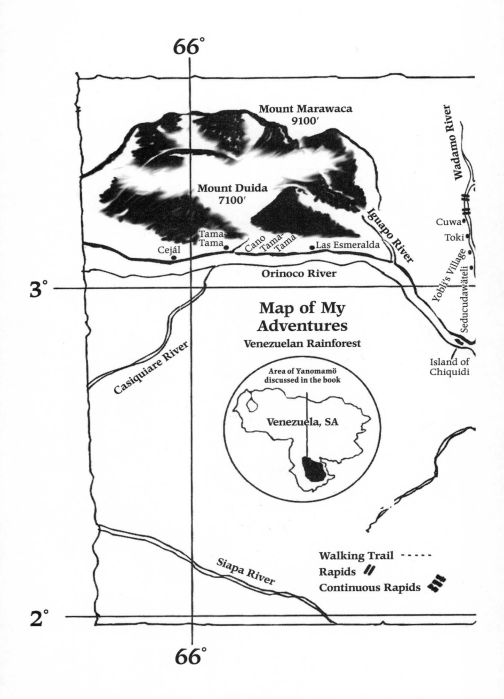

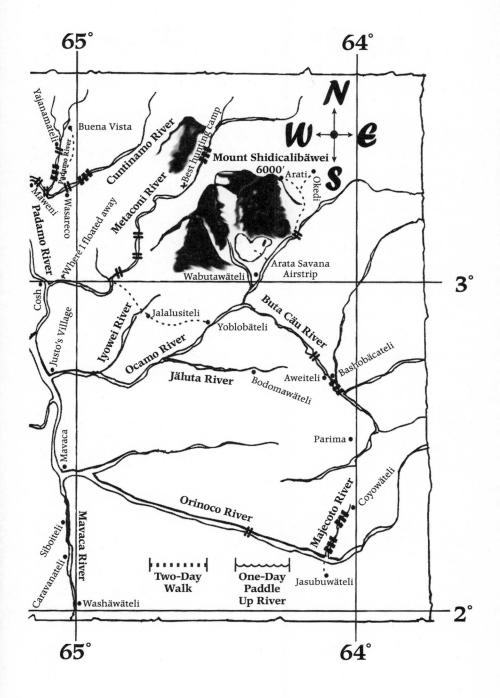

ABOUT THE AUTHOR

Born in a small missionary base, TamaTama, on the Orinoco River, Mike is the fifth of ten children of Joe and Millie Dawson, who were among the first missionaries to the Yanomamö tribe. His first language was Yanomamö and he learned English when he was seven years old.

After high school, Mike worked in remote villages along the upper Orinoco River system to determine the understandability of a translation of the New Testament. He returned to the United States for Bible School in 1976 and finished missionary training in 1979. He married Renée Pintor in 1980 and left for Venezuela in 1981, discipling new Yanomamö believers and traveling with them to show how to evangelize their own people. Mike and Reneé had three boys: Joshua, Ryan, and Stephen.

In June 1992, Mike and Renée both contracted cerebral malaria and were evacuated to Caracas. Renée did not recover; she is buried in the village of Coshilowäteli. Her headstone reads: "She lives in our hearts as a penetrating reminder that not only is Christ worth living for, He is worth dying for." Because of the delay in Renée's treatment, Mike dreamed of having an airplane based in the jungle to handle medical emergencies.

Mike and his boys continued working with the Yanomamö. In October 1994, he married Keila Cornieles, with whom he had two daughters, Mikeila and Mia. On January 12, 2006, Mikeila went to be with the Lord. Again, the need to have an airplane based in the jungle was forcefully brought home.

Michael is executive producer of *Yai Wanonabälewä: The Enemy God* (www.theenemygod.com), a feature-length movie based on the true story of how the Gospel of Jesus Christ has affected the life of a Yanomamö shaman and his village.

CONTENTS

CONTENTS

FOREWORD

I had the privilege of meeting Mike Dawson and some of his siblings when Mike entered Bible School around 1975. Mike's passion was very evident even way back then, and as we were both missionary kids—MKs—I made an immediate connection with him. It was during those years that the Lord challenged our hearts to give our lives to reaching peoples and groups who still lacked the knowledge that Christ made a provision, through his death, for them to stand justified in God's presence. I was blessed have spent this time with Mike.

New Tribes Mission has similarly been very blessed to have many of our MKs complete our training and then go back into the fields where they already know the culture and language. They are able to bring the church planting work to a deeper level because of their understanding of the people they have grown up with. Reading *Growing Up Yanomamö,* you'll discover the challenges of presenting the precious truths of God's Word in a culture and language that are so different from our own.

I had the opportunity to read *Growing Up Yanomamö* straight through and thoroughly enjoyed it. Mike's story of the close friendships that he developed with the Yanomamö as he grew up with them is refreshing; it's also a suspenseful adventure story of growing up in a very different culture. These great stories of what it was like to grow up in a tribal setting are just plain fun to read, and they will captivate you and your children. (I definitely would have read this book to my son, but now that he's in college, I guess I'll just recommend it to him!) It is full of cultural insights, and Mike's heart to see the Yanomamö reached with the precious gospel is very evident. Great job, Mike!

—LARRY M. BROWN
New Tribes Mission USA Chairman
MK from Brazil

Acknowledgments

Of course there are too many people to thank, and you all know who you are . . . but special mention does have to be made of the following persons since, without them, this book would never have been written.

First of all, my dad and mom, Joseph and Mildred Dawson. Mom, you wrote your book, *All the Day Long*. While reading this book to my little boys, I realized through this what a gift you and Dad had given to us all, and it gave me the push I needed to put my personal experiences down for my own children. Thanks!

Secondly, Dad and Mom, you brought us to the jungle and lived your lives in such a manner that you demonstrated to us God's love and concern for a lost and dying world. This was so engraved in my early life that I grew up knowing I wanted to serve the Lord, exactly as I saw you both doing.

Special thanks to my wife, Keila. She hates sleeping with a light on, but since I could only work on this project at night, she had to put up with a lot while I was writing. Her love has so filled my life with song again that it will take another book to document it.

Acknowledgments

Last but not least, to Joshua, Ryan, Stephen, Mikeila, and Mia. This book is for you, my children. I hope it gives you a better understanding of what my early life was like, without my having to give endless recitals of "walking to school, uphill both ways, barefoot in the snow."

1

MEMORIES

A long time remembered,
are the memories we shared through the years;
the good times are cherished,
the bad times forgotten with the tears.
With friendship and laughter,
we've walked hand in hand along the way.
Yesterday's memories still linger in the memories of today.
Tomorrow's making changes;
our lives aren't the same anymore, but the
echoing laughter is still heard from our open childhood door.

Time can't erase all the dreams that we shared along the way
and we're making new memories
to add to the ones from yesterday.
Yesterday's memories still linger in the memories of today,
with friendship and laughter,
we've walked hand and hand along the way.
The good times are cherished;
the bad times forgotten with the tears.
A long time remembered,
are the memories we've shared through the years!

—Velma Dawson Griffis

Upon reflection, my earliest memory is one of being hurried down a jungle trail by a Yanomamö woman. I am snuggled inside her arms and quite comfortable riding in her *yalinata* (a type of tree bark) carrying strap . . . my face

1

protected from the vines and thorns by her arms as she hurries down the narrow, overgrown jungle trail . . . her bare feet making scarcely any sound in the soft, humid, rotting leaves.

During the long day I got thirsty and began to root around to find something to eat, with the dedication that only a hungry baby can muster. I was facilitated in my search by the fact that this lady was not wearing any clothes, and the way she was carrying me placed my head in a good position to satisfy myself. If the Yanomamö woman was surprised to find herself suddenly suckling a *nabä* (Yanomamö word for any non-Yanomamö), she gave no indication of it, but kept her gait steady, hoping to arrive in her village before nightfall. She was probably just as happy as I was that I was content, as it kept me from crying as she hurried along.

There were quite a number of Yanomamö in the party hastening down the shadowy trail back toward their village — shadowy not because of a pending storm, but by virtue of a jungle canopy so thick it barely let in sunshine even at noonday. The travelers had all trekked down to the river from their village, a hard day's walk away, to help the missionary family (ourselves) move to their village. This effort consisted of their dividing up amongst themselves baskets of hammocks and blankets, some foodstuffs, and five small children.

Adept at their task, they quickly reduced the pile of stuff to manageable loads. They then made straps out of *yalinata* bark to transform the bundles into packs, each of which they carried with a strap across the forehead and the pack resting on the back. They worked to make the bundles as comfortable as possible. The long day's walk down to the river from their village would turn into a two- or three-day return walk. This was partially due to the fact that they were now burdened with heavy packs, but more to the fact that the funny-sounding white people did not know the first thing about walking in the jungle and were forever tripping over the smallest root or vine along the trail.

The two oldest boys, my brothers, possibly eyeing the naked Yanomamö, decided they would walk. I was too small to care if they wore clothes or not. All I cared about at the time was that I was dry and well fed. Breakfast, lunch, and supper were bouncing just a couple of inches from my face, so I was as happy as a pig in slop! It just doesn't take a lot to make you happy when you are less than one year old.

But things change. That evening Mom noticed sores all along my diaper line. She faithfully doctored them every time she changed me, but they only got bigger. She was quite concerned. That night Dad heated up some water in an old pot and Mom bathed me. Still, during the couple of days on the trail, the sores became worse. After a while my crying became almost nonstop, so, during one of the rest stops while Mom was changing my diaper, one of the Yécuana guides (named Velázquez) walked over, possibly to see why I was crying so much. Mom pointed out the large sores. By that time there were about eighteen of them. Looking intently at the sores, he spoke gravely.

"Those are not sores, but *gusanos del monte.*" Mom had no idea what a *gusano del monte* was, but figured it was not good. The next time we stopped, Velázquez said something to the lady who was carrying me. She disappeared into the jungle, and a short time later returned with a branch with some leaves on it. She broke off a leaf and allowed the milky sap to drop down on each sore. Before long a large grub worm began making its way out of my flesh. *Imagine my mom's horror!* Her baby was being eaten alive. Not quite, but I'm sure that's what it seemed like to her at the moment. In all, the lady extracted eighteen of the loathsome things. By the time we arrived at the village of Calijocos, I was as good as new.

Actually, to be honest, I don't think these earliest memories are *my* recollections at all, but I heard the stories so many times as I was growing up that they seem to be my own. When I decided to write a book, I figured I would have to start with this story, or someone else would put it in, possibly as the fore-word to the book or on the back cover. Anyway, I figured it would be better if I told it (kind of like damage control) because—take my word for it—whenever anyone else told this or other stories, I always found myself cast in a rather uncomplimentary light.

When I got a bit older, I hated having to hear and rehear this particular story. The Yanomamö tell it best and, with typical Yanomamö logic, always say, "Yes, and that is why you talk Yano-mamö so well. Your tongue was washed by Yanomamö *suje u* [mother's milk]." I won't even bother with what they have to say about the *moshas,* as there is just no way to spin that story to make it OK for the Western reader.

I especially wanted to run and hide, during the time I was in Bible school in the United States, whenever I heard that some of the old missionaries from the Venezuelan field were coming to visit. Every one of them delighted in making me squirm by telling and retelling these stories. The worst one for recounting them was Jim, the mission field chairman. He had worked with my parents up on the upper Padamo River and had been on those first trips inland with us. He was an eyewitness, so to speak, and would really ham it up, making me wish I could call in sick on the days he spoke during our Bible school chapel hour. So, now that this embarrassing story is out of the way, I can dive right into those stories that I most want to tell.

2

BORN TO LIVE ON THE EDGE

I was born on August 2, 1955, right out in the middle of the jungle, in a tiny clearing that had been hacked out of the dense Venezuelan rainforest. A collection of five small palm-leafed huts stood nearby, like guards against the encroaching jungle. You hear a lot about how great quantities of the rainforest are being chopped down, but what no one ever mentions is how much of the crazy thing quickly grows back! Why, half of my childhood was spent trying (without much success, I might add) to keep the jungle at bay. But I'm getting ahead of myself.

The mighty Orinoco River flowed close by. On this river, the supply boat had just left to head back down to Puerto Ayacucho. It was the last and only link with the outside world that anyone had, and it had just disappeared around the bend. My parents, Joe and Millie Dawson, had arrived on it with their four small children and their meager horde of supplies. The supplies they had brought were supposed to last them for the next four to six months. The children were Steven, age five; Gary, four; Faith, three; and Velma, almost two—and any onlooker could see that Mom was great with a fifth one on the way!

5

If my parents felt any fear at being left up here with no way out, they did not show it. Actually, they had volunteered to come. Dad and Mom were saved in October of 1951, and two weeks later sent in applications to the New Tribes Missionary Training Center to begin training to work with primitive peoples. Dad remembered some tribesmen who had helped him while he was fleeing from the Japanese on a Philippine island, so he had a desire to return there and tell them about the saving love of God. But while he and Mom were finishing up missionary boot camp training, the Venezuelan field wrote, asking for a family with young children. With a young wife and several small children, Dad felt they met the qualifications for that job pretty well, so here they were. Everything was not easy, though. To start with, the leadership was not exactly thrilled with the fact that Mom wanted to go with and do everything *with* Dad. They wanted Dad to go up by himself and let Mom stay out in town with the children.

Their being able to be on this trip together was a big deal, especially as the mission leadership wanted Mom to wait in town for my birth. A little more than a year earlier, Mom had given birth to my sister Velma in that same hospital, and had then had to return there to have her appendix out. If she *never* saw that hospital again, it would be too soon, she said. She'd decided she would rather take her chances giving birth out in the jungle. Still, the leadership insisted that she stay and have the baby in the hospital, as they felt responsible for her safety.

One day, one of the Venezuelan Christians, a member of the church the missionaries had started in the town of San Fernando de Atabapo, suffered some form of medical mishap. Some in the church wanted to take her out to town for treatment, but she was adamant about not going. "No, I am trusting the Lord. If I die, I will die here. God is able to take care of me. He is faithful. He is able to take care of us regardless of who or where we are."

6

The next day, in early morning prayer, the mission leader commented on this woman's faith. "What a testimony for the protection of the Lord," he said. "I sure wish we had missionaries like this family; ready to trust the Lord wherever they are. Now we Americans would run out to town like a whipped dog, trusting in our doctors and hospitals instead of trusting the Lord! How I pray the Lord would raise up missionaries who were ready to put it all on the line for Him!"

When the mission leader finished and sat down, Dad rose slowly to his feet. This was the exact issue he had been arguing with mission leadership! Had the man forgotten? Anyway, this seemed like the perfect time to bring the subject up again.

"Carl, I am so happy to hear you say that. Millie and I are going to trust the Lord for the birth of our child. We would like permission to head up to TamaTama with the rest of the team."

What could Carl say? He stared at Dad, but reluctantly had to nod his assent. As soon as they could get ready, they departed San Fernando for TamaTama, called TT by the missionaries. It could be argued that they left as quickly as possible because they were afraid that this leader would change his mind, but after ten long days on the river, there they were in TamaTama. They continued staring at the bend that hid the supply boat. *What will happen now? What if there are problems with this birth?* But there was too much to do to sit around worrying.

During the men's last trip up here, they had managed to make five little palm-leafed huts. Now Mom had to make this dilapidated little hut into a home for her four small children and her husband, who came home each evening so tired he could barely stay awake. They needed to chop the jungle back further to try to keep the snakes and other uninvited guests away from the house. What with palm walls and roofs on these huts, it was far too easy for snakes to push right through the palm and slither into the house.

Indians arrived by the boatload, all wanting machetes and cooking pots. This was the only place with *nabäs* within weeks of travel on the river, and they wanted to make sure they were able to talk the funny-sounding white people out of one of their possessions before something happened and they left. Up to this time, any contact with the *nabäs* had been sporadic at best, as most people unfamiliar with the harsh life of the rainforest never lasted very long.

No outsider as yet spoke the Yanomamö language, but the missionaries were trying desperately to learn it. They were so limited in the language that it was a challenge just staying ahead of the mob in trying to communicate. Still, these were exciting days, as well, because as each new word was learned it enabled them to develop new lessons—lessons that one day would give them enough of the language to tell the Yanomamö about a God who really loved them.

From babyhood, I grew up speaking Yanomamö, so I cannot appreciate the difficulties involved in trying to learn the language of a monolingual people. Mom and Dad and the rest of the missionaries struggled with the simplest concepts. The Yanomamö delighted in having as much fun as they could wring out of whatever situation these tongue-tied, funny-looking, white people were always getting themselves into. One of the easiest ways to have fun with my parents and the other missionaries, the Yanomamö learned, was to "help" them with language. The Yanomamö were fascinated by how the missionaries could stare at this white leaf and repeat back what they had been told even days earlier. It became a competition of sorts to see who could make them repeat and write down the most obscene words on the little white leaves they carried.

For instance, let's say you wanted to learn the word "tree." You would point to a tree and ask for the word.

"Wedi? Wedi?" (You had learned earlier that *wedi* meant *what.*) When you got a word, you wrote it down. The next time you

were with someone, you would try to use the word. There is a bird in the tree, you would say, putting together the series of foreign sounds you had been told meant this. If the whole village about died laughing, you scratched out that word, and possibly even that informant—except that they were *all* like that, so it was not long before you were back with the ones you had fired.

The grammatical challenges of trying to learn a monolingual people's language are difficult at best, but trying to learn it one word at a time, never quite being sure your informant was giving you the right word, made it almost impossible. Words and meanings of words in Yanomamö are changed just by adding prefixes or suffixes to the word. Mom remembers one of her fellow missionaries coming over and saying that Jim had just finished up a lesson to teach the passive voice.

"Jim has worked up a lesson that is cuter than a little red wagon," he said. They eagerly began to study this lesson with a new informant. Thankfully, this guy seemed to want to help.

"Aiwänöpaluli a niamaje." They thought the *-je* on the end of the verb showed the passive voice. They knew *"Aiwänöpaluli a niyama"* meant "My older brother shot a turkey."

They were trying to say, "The turkey was shot by my older brother." For some reason, though, their informant would not accept it. He kept trying to tell them something, but the language barrier was too great for them to understand what he was saying. They repeated the phrase again. Again he shook his head in the negative. This time he held up one finger to indicate only one. He had just learned a word in Spanish. "Uno. Uno," he repeated. *"Niyama,* uno. *Aiwänö paluli a niyama*—uno." He held up more fingers. *"Aiwä bänö paluli a niyamaje, bluca.*

"Joe, do you think he means putting *-je* on the verb pluralizes the doer? Instead of teaching passive, maybe Jim found the suffix that means more than one is doing the action?" They were excited, and thought of different phrases they had learned to try it on. Sure enough, now they understood the man's insistent gesturing and attempts at correction.

Time passed swiftly, and soon it was time for my arrival. Thankfully, mine was an easy birth. Soon the quiet of the small jungle clearing was shattered by my shrill cry, but mother and baby were both fine. My oldest brother, Steve, says he remembers me being born and their placing me in a cardboard box. So much for the silver spoon! I wasn't even given a simple crib, but had to spend my first weeks in an old cardboard box.

Then, as if this were not humbling enough, when I was about a week old my three-year-old sister Faith got me out of my box and got me up in the hammock with her. There she proceeded to feed me some manioc. We call it *mañoco*. It is made from the yucca root. Although the Yanomamö love it, most missionaries only tolerate it, and even the Yanomamö won't give it to a baby, as it is very rough on the stomach. My older brothers even say it had soured, so I got a double dose of the stuff. Personally I don't remember it tasting that bad, but then again I was only about a week old, so my memory is going to be questionable, after all.

Living life on the edge was rough, but that was before the days where everything in your early life supposedly traumatized you. My goodness, if that were to happen today, I'm sure I could make a good case for anything I wanted to do now by explaining that when I was born I was placed in a cardboard box. But instead of being traumatized, despite my rough, humble beginnings, I grew up relatively normal. Yet even from my earliest days, I felt compelled to live life on the edge; thus, the adventures that follow . . .

3
FIRST FRIENDS

I once read a book in which the author began his story by saying something about his first friend being a Zulu and his first enemy being a Zulu also. That was true for me as well.

Not a Zulu, of course, since I lived with Yanomamö, but my first friend was native. I didn't have any enemies; we were missionaries and were not allowed to have enemies. I had lots of friends, though!

My best friend was a skinny little kid with big eyes who went by the name of Yacuwä. We were inseparable. His little loincloth barely covered what it had to in front, but the tail of it hung all the way to the ground behind him. His mother was the daughter of the head man of Coshilowä, but his father was from a different village, so when he wanted to go home with his family back to his own village, the grandfather kept Yacuwä, as was his right in Yanomamö culture. I remember his mother crying and crying as she and her husband made ready to leave. She begged her father to allow her to take Yacuwä with them, but the old man would not change his mind: Yacuwä was staying with him. I stood with Yacuwä on the riverbank as he sobbed, watching the little dugout canoe his dad had built disappear from sight around the bend in the river. Soon enough, though, we were cheerfully playing in and around the river. Since we lived right on the river, we could all swim like fish, and this was our chief enjoyment.

The old man wanted to keep Yacuwä, but I never understood why. He didn't do a blessed thing with the boy, and the poor kid about starved to death. He was so skinny and yet his belly was large and distended from the effects of malnutrition. He was always naked, except for his very brief loincloth. Looking closely at it, I could tell it had at one time been the bright red color that is so prized by the Yanomamö, but now it was just plain *dirty*. I really believe that if we hadn't been there, he would have starved to death. But we were so poor back then that we were barely able to keep body and soul together, so he almost did starve, even with us there.

One day Yacuwä was so hungry he went down into our garbage pit to try to find something, *anything,* to eat. While rummaging around, he startled a squirrel that was also down there trying to find food. The squirrel reared up in fright! Little Yacuwä screamed, thinking someone's *boleana* (spirit), which the kids were told to watch out for, was about to grab him. He madly dashed out of the hole. Still hungry, he came around to our house.

"Let's go swimming," I said.

"No, I am too hungry. If you want me to go swimming with you, you need to bring me something to eat. I am so hungry I will drown."

"I can't; the last time I brought you food, I got a spanking, as we don't have enough even to feed ourselves, my mom told me," I replied.

"Just bring me some bananas," Yacuwä said.

"No, I'll get a spanking; can't you hear?" We argued back and forth.

Finally I compromised. "OK," I told him, "I'll go in and steal you one banana."

"No, I want enough to make a drink. If you bring one, I won't take it," he insisted.

"Look, if they catch me with one, I can say I was hungry. If I have a bunch, they will know I came in to take them to give away, and we just don't have enough. I'll be spanked again, and I refuse."

I walked in and picked the largest banana I could find. *He will be happy with this one,* I thought. *It's big enough that we could both make a drink out of it.* I took it out to him, but instead of saying "thank you," Yacuwä looked for another banana. When he realized it was the only one coming, he threw it down on the ground in disgust. Picking up a stick that was lying there, he beat the banana into a squishy pulp on the ground.

"*Bei!*" he said, and walked away, the little tail of his loincloth bobbing along behind him.

Another time Yacuwä, Däduwä, and I decided to go fishing. Däduwä was Yacuwä's cousin. Their mothers were sisters. Däduwä's father was one of the better hunters in the village, so in contrast Däduwä was in better shape. Although younger than Yacuwä, he was already as big as his cousin. He also was dressed only in a loincloth, although his was much shorter than Yacuwä's.

We wanted to be at the best fishing place just at dawn, so I got permission to leave at five o'clock in the morning so we could be up to the good fishing spot by daybreak. They agreed to call me at the right time. None of us had clocks, but I figured they would tell the time by the different birds and animals that call at different hours of the night and in the early morning. I was awakened during the night by the low whistle we used to call each other. Recognizing it as our whistle, I sprang out of my hammock. I had just slept in my clothes, since I did not want to take time to find my clothes and put them on in the darkness. Grabbing my stuff, I fumbled my way through the blackness to the door and stepped out.

Boy, was it dark! I jumped a bit when Yacuwä materialized right beside me.

"Come on," he whispered. I was sure he must have been motioning, but it was so pitch-black I couldn't see anything. I tried to follow right behind him in order to stay on the trail. Except for the stars, there was not a light to be seen. I never cared much for the darkness and was grateful for the stars, but I sure wished the moon were out, though it was the wrong time of the month for the moon. I wished more that I had one of those fancy flashlights I had seen someone with a couple of times; then I wouldn't have to worry about the moon. But wishing wouldn't take me to the canoe, so there was nothing to do but grope my way behind the boys as we felt our way along the trail to where they had the canoe tied up.

I remember wondering for a brief moment if my friends had gotten permission from the owner to borrow his canoe. Many a fight had been started over canoes! I started to say something, then realized that all it would do if I asked was to make me an accomplice. There was no way we were going to go up to the owner's hearth and ask him for permission at this time of the night. Also, one of the biggest reasons very few people asked for permission was because the owner almost always said no. So, my safest position was to *not ask*. That way, when we got home I could always say, "I thought they had permission to use the boat; it was their trip, and all I did was go along."

"I thought it would be lighter at 5:00 a.m.," I told them.

Däduwä glanced at me over his shoulder. "It will be light soon," he said. "Let's hurry!"

Back in those days I did not have a watch and had to take his word for it. Still, I had been trying to learn the different birdcalls and what time of the night the birds normally called. All of a sudden I heard a *jashimo* (a large dove). I remembered my two older brothers saying that this particular bird always calls right around three o'clock in the morning.

"It's the middle of the night," I hissed to them.

"Oh well, we might as well go anyway since we're already up," Yacuwä answered.

I shrugged my shoulders. *He's right,* I thought to myself. We kept walking until we reached the canoe by the river.

We took our places in the canoe. The canoe they had borrowed was a nice one. It was about twenty-three feet long and about twenty-four inches wide at the widest point, and set low in the water. With the three of us in it, we had about three inches of freeboard.

The dugout canoes the Yanomamö make are not like the canoes Americans make. They are hollowed out of a tree and then burned out inside to cure them. The canoe is then placed up on a platform and a fire is started outside along the entire length of the boat. The builder then puts himself inside the boat; he judges the heat on the wood by the heat on the bottoms of his bare feet. When it is hot enough (and I mean *hot*—you can watch the steam boil out of the wood!), he slowly begins to spread it open. Carefully he spreads first one side, then the other, until the whole canoe is beautifully and evenly formed.

A well-made canoe is a thing of beauty and art and, for its size, is incredibly stable in the water, not tending to roll over as American canoes do at the slightest provocation.

Yacuwä sat in front, as he was the oldest and knew where we were going. I was the strongest paddler, so I paddled at the rear. Däduwä was the best storyteller, so he sat in the middle and told us jaguar stories, occasionally paddling a stroke or two. He was in fine form that night.

"My uncle Lecima almost got eaten by a jaguar the other day," he told us. I quit paddling to pay closer attention.

"What happened?" asked Yacuwä.

"He was hunting up the *yalacabuwei* [Minnow Creek] when he became aware of something stalking him," continued Däduwä.

I glanced over at the shoreline, glad we had some water between us and any potential threat that might be lurking over there. Däduwä went on.

"He decided to return to his boat and try and put some distance between whatever was making him nervous, because he was afraid it was a jaguar!" He paused, and I glanced over at the shoreline to make sure we were not getting too close.

"The further he went, the more convinced he was that it *was* a jaguar. He finally made his way to the canoe, and as soon as he got in it, he shoved off. With a loud roar, the cat sprang at him, but he was already out in the current. He figured he was fine at that point, but the next time his canoe came close to shore to get around the rocks there, the cat lunged at him again . . . scared him so badly he almost fell in the water! Now he was *really* frightened, he had never figured it would keep chasing him—with him out in a boat. The jaguar had by this time abandoned all attempts to hide his intentions, but would roar and lunge every time his boat came close."

Däduwä stopped and took a halfhearted swipe with his paddle.

"What happened then? How did he get away?" I demanded.

"Oh, he finally got the attention of some other hunters, and when the jaguar saw there were too many hunters, it left him alone, but my uncle is still really worried. He is afraid that the next time he goes out of the village, the jaguar is going to be waiting for him." Däduwä paused again. "He even told me to be careful today, as he thinks the jaguar might know our family's smell and be waiting for me."

Boy, I wanted to hear that! Come to think of it, the shoreline was awfully close!

I looked at the jungle looming over us as we paddled along the dark shore. In my mind's eye I could see a large jaguar crouching, ready to spring and just waiting for us to paddle closer. I steered the boat a little farther out. The farther we went, the more stories Däduwä told. The more he told, the farther from shore I steered the boat. If the others in the boat noticed that we were paddling up the middle of the river, they didn't say anything. Possibly they had pictured the same jaguars I had imagined crouching along the shore. By dawn, we were paddling as hard as we could, but making very little headway, as the current is much swifter out in the middle of the river. As it became lighter, I slowly allowed the canoe to drift closer to shore.

We were all still nervous from Däduwä's stories, but we finally found a prime fishing spot and pulled in. At first we caught baitfish. It was easy to catch these with the worms we had dug from the bank the day before. We then used these little fish to bait our big lines. We would throw them out and wait for something big to bite. Most of the time, before our lines could sink down to where the big catfish waited, the piranhas would attack. We didn't care; the piranhas were good eating, too.

It was good to be alive and ten years old in the jungle. At that time I had no idea of how privileged I was to live here. It was so beautiful. The peaceful stillness of the river always soothed me. We could hear monkeys and so many different birdcalls. Butterflies swarmed all up and down the river as far as we could see. The deep blues, greens, and reds splashed and collided with each other as the butterflies floated along on random paths crisscrossing the river.

Only the obnoxious gnats and bumblebees spoiled the splendor. The gnats just bit you and you knew there was no getting away from them, so you tried to put them out of your mind, ignoring them as best you could. The bumblebees, on the other hand, had these loud, irritating, buzzing sounds. They would swarm around your head for who-knows-what purpose, until you were beside yourself. We cut branches and had them ready just for swatting at the bees. Why, on some of our trips we spent more energy trying to swat bees than we did paddling.

But the fishing was good, and except for the bees we lived in a pretty good world. The piranhas were biting well, and we caught a lot of them. Now, normally we each had a small club to whack them over the head. They have wicked teeth, and the last thing we wanted splashing around near our bare feet was a bunch of live piranhas!

Piranhas are a fish that run in schools. So when they're biting, they're biting like you wouldn't believe! One right after another . . . as fast as we could throw our lines back into the water. Excitement ran high as we tried to catch as many as we could before the school moved on.

Yacuwä's line grew taut and he quickly pulled in another piranha. He carefully removed the hook and tossed the flapping fish into the canoe.

"Kill your fish before you throw it into the boat!" I screamed. We lifted our feet from harm's way until Yacuwä could club the offending fish in the head. I must have gotten distracted, as the next thing I knew the piranha, seeing his chance at revenge, clamped down on my too-slow pinky toe. Mercy, I don't think I cried, but I didn't come up with a comically droll statement, either. I was scared, though, and with as much blood as I was losing, I was sure he had bitten off my toe. We carefully pried the fish's mouth open. I still had a pinky, but it was hanging off my foot by only a thin thread of skin.

That was it for fishing, I can tell you that! On the long way home, I was more interested in keeping my little toe attached than I was in looking at the butterflies, the birds, or anything else along the way. Believe me, when you are coming home in pain, the way is a lot longer than when you were going out in fine, good spirits. As an outdoor person, I've always known the value of coming up with a sarcastic statement to belie my pain and suffering, but by the time I thought of something funny to say about getting my toe bit off by a piranha we were a couple of years older and no one cared much to hear it, so I kept it to myself.

Dad and Mom were great. I've seen Mom panic at little things, but when there was a real crisis, she always rose to the occasion and took charge. She cleaned my foot off and gently aligned my toe back in place at the spot where it belonged. My folks didn't know how to put in stitches, but they knew how to put on butterfly bandages. These were put on, and Dad held my foot between his work-hardened hands while we all bowed our heads as he prayed. His faith in the Great Healer was rewarded, because my toe grew back in place and was none the worse for wear.

During my growing-up years, I drove my folks to their knees too many times to count. Remember, depending on the boat, we were anywhere from three to ten days' canoe travel from the nearest hospital. There *was* no medical help available other than what they themselves could provide. This tended to keep us reliant on God. Along with all the various times I got cut (I was forever cutting myself!), there was the time I stepped on an alligator spear and drove it clean through my foot, from bottom to top. Then there was the time I came sliding down the bank, right foot forward, and ran it right over Bautista's machete, which was sticking in the ground blade up. Boy, *that* got my attention in a hurry! My foot kinda just *flopped* as I hobbled home, leaving a trail of blood like a stuck hog. Not to mention the different times I was bitten by spiders and vampire bats . . .

I was only one of ten children, and actually was relatively accident-free. Now Gary, one of my older brothers, was a different story. Why, he was so accident-prone he needed a full-time church praying for him—and even then he barely made it. He once fell from a tree while climbing after a monkey. He was about eighty feet high when the whole top of the tree broke off—with him in it, careening to the jungle floor. All told, it would be easier to list the bones he didn't break. He regained consciousness to find his head in Bautista's lap and Bautista crying. There was blood everywhere.

"Leave me here and go and get my dad," he told Bautista.

"No, you have too much blood on you. If I leave you here, there will be a jaguar here before I could get back," Bautista told him. He gently lowered Gary down and began to cut a trail back to the boat. He would cut trail for about fifty yards and then come back to pick up Gary. Gary is way bigger than Bautista, so Bautista had to really work to carry him. Bautista would leave him leaning against a tree and cut more trail. He would then return and Gary would drape himself over Bautista, who would carry him down the trail and lean him against another tree.

"I don't know how we ever made it down the side of the mountain to the boat with me bleeding as hard as I was," Gary told us. They finally made it back to our village. Frantic efforts were made to contact the mission plane, but we could not reach them by radio. A quick decision was made to take Gary out by dugout canoe. My dad and others traveled with him day and night for almost forty hours before getting to the nearest hospital. The hospital was not that big of an improvement over the dugout canoe, according to Gary.

"I woke up and my foot hurt like you would not believe," Gary told us later. "I looked down and my foot was covered with roaches, which were busy eating at the wound where the bone of my ankle had come out. My foot was in traction and I couldn't move it. I twisted myself around, trying to get at the cords that were holding the weights. I finally reached one and pulled it down, then started gnawing on it. I had tried to call the nurses, but no one answered my frenzied calls for help. Finally I gnawed one of the cords through and started on the second one. With a large crash, the weights fell free. When the weights fell off, they jerked my ankle in such a way that it opened the large wound. Blood spurted all over, drenching me and everything else. Hearing the commotion of the weights falling finally brought a nurse to see what was happening. Walking into the room, she took one look at my blood-covered body, screamed once, and promptly fainted."

To make matters worse, the doctors began talking about having to amputate his foot. At the first opportunity, Gary stole a pair of crutches and snuck out of the hospital, making his way to the mission compound. There he made my oldest brother, Steve, promise not to let them take him back to the hospital. Dad had left to go back upriver to get the rest of us, so as soon as he arrived back in town a decision was made to take Gary to the United States, where he spent the next eleven months in and out of hospitals. I'm sure his guardian angel asked for—and was probably given—a transfer after that incident. It must have caused quite a stir trying to find him a replacement angel, however.

The Yanomamö are a verbal people. I guess that's how you would say they love to talk and tell stories, because they really do. A good storyteller on a trip is almost as important to them as someone who is a good hunter. Storytellers who could keep the camp laughing on our outings were in hot demand. We had some of the best right in our village. I've already mentioned Däduwä. He was good, but the best one for scary stories was Ramon.

(You might wonder at the Spanish-sounding names, but I can't tell you Ramon's Yanomamö name, even in a whisper.

Here is what happened with the Yanomamö names. When the missionaries came in, the people were surprised to hear them call each other by name. They were even more surprised when whoever was called answered the caller and did not show anger. Why, any Yanomamö knows that your name is a secret! To use someone's name is to invite swift retaliation upon yourself. To use someone's name gives you tremendous power over that person. But the *nabäs* were different. Names did not seem to have any meaning to them. Perversely, it seemed, every time the *nabäs* did anything with someone, they wanted that person's name. To make matters worse, every time they got someone's name from someone else, they wrote it down. Later on they would look at their little pieces of what looked like smooth white bark and repeat the name they had scratched there. The bad thing was, most times they never even thought about who was listening when they did it. Finally noticing the Yanomamös' discomfort, the missionaries began to give them names that sounded like their own. That was fine with the Yanomamö. So, slowly, over time, most of them took on the foreign names, each also retaining his or her own secret name.)

To continue, as a kid out hunting and fishing with them, I listened in fascination as Ramon told story after story of things that had happened to his people. He also knew all the legends. These legends are best told around a fire at night. As the story-teller drones on, your ears begin to pick out sounds in the surrounding jungle. It is amazing how many little rustlings you hear. I have seen people almost put their necks out of joint swiveling around to see if anything is creeping up on them. Come to think of it, my own neck still has a crick in it.

The firelight flickered on his face as he paused in yet another one of his stories. Ramon looked around, making sure he still had everyone's undivided attention. He needn't have worried. He continued.

"Yes, this being lives in the jungle. People have only seen it when they hunt by themselves. This thing has the ability to turn into anyone. If you are out there and hear someone fall from a tree or in some other way be hurt, don't go and help him or her. This is what this thing does. It hurries to some place ahead of you on the trail, and once it is in a good position, it then makes a loud noise to get your attention.

"When you come running up, you'll see maybe your father, or maybe your brother, or someone else you really love. You'll see their suffering, and your heart will be saddened that they are suffering so.

"'I am here; I will carry you home. Where are you hurt?' you will say. You might be shown what looks like a broken leg, or the pain may be in his back, so you will quickly make a carrying strap of *yalinata* bark. You will carry this person, who you think is someone you love, down the trail toward home. Here you are—hurrying, and crying for your loved one, who is moaning in pain on your back.

"What you do not know is that you are no longer carrying your loved one. It has changed into its normal shape and it is so ugly . . . with great, long fangs, huge ears, green-colored skin, very wrinkled. Ugly wisps of hair straggle down its misshapen skull. It grins wickedly and sinks its long razor-sharp fangs into your skull . . . and begins to suck your brains out. *You* are what it feeds on.

"You continue to hurry home. Suddenly you feel your head itch. This is the last thing you feel, as this thing pulls its teeth out. You reach up to scratch your head and your hand crumbles

23

your scalp. You trip over your own feet and fall down dead. What we know for sure is that it always picks its victim out from the camp the night before. It is probably out there right now watching you. Some nights it even comes and tries to slowly worm its way into your hammock. Keep your ears open, and if you hear anything moving around, be careful."

Boy, as if I needed to be told that! Every branch that moved out in the jungle was suspect from then on. Thankfully, I never found my brothers or Dad out in the jungle hurt, because if I had, I would probably have run screaming in the opposite direction.

A funny thing did happen, though. I had a book on *Star Wars* and was showing the pictures to my friends. Upon seeing a picture of Yoda, they all agreed that this was exactly a picture of the *Jao* the brain eater and then, on the very next page, there is a picture of this thing on Luke Skywalker's shoulders. That picture was the clincher.

"See, I told you this is how they do it," said Ramon. "This is exactly how they ride. If we had more pictures I am sure you would see it eat this man's brains out."

I don't think I ever convinced them that this was just something made up for the movies. To be honest, I was not that convinced myself that there might not be some spiritual connection that *I* could not see, but was maybe clearer to my more spiritually attuned Yanomamö brethren.

Some of the best stories were about missionaries. Remember, in the early 1950s the Yanomamö still thought they were the only people in the world. Missionary Jim Barker was one of the first men to start working with them. As I think of what it meant to go into these villages, not speaking a word of the language, not being able to understand a word they were hearing, I have to take my hat off to these dedicated people. They really had it rough.

During the first months he was up with the village of Maje-codoteli, one of the warriors got really upset with Jim. Jim had caught the man going through Jim's bag and made him stop. The Yanomamö was very upset and felt he had been humiliated. He ran over, grabbed his machete, and came back over to where Jim was lying in his hammock. Yelling loudly, he jerked him by the arm. Jim got up. A crowd quickly gathered. With everyone yelling, pointing, and jabbering at Jim, he could only shake his head. He could not understand a word.

Many people were actually yelling at the man who still had Jim by the arm, but whether they were telling him to stop or egging him on, Jim could not tell. He had no idea what they had planned for him. Although he towered over the short, angry Yanomamö, he went with him meekly, not really scared, but not sure what was going on. The Yanomamö led him out to the center of the village. He motioned for Jim to assume the pose for being whipped with a machete. Still thinking the angry warrior was bluffing, Jim assumed the pose.

Paao! The machete left an angry red welt down his back. It was not a chop, but a slap with the flat side of the machete. Jim staggered back to his hammock, with the whole village laughing at him. He lay there quietly trying to get his breath back. *What was happening? Was his life in danger? How was anyone going to work with this tribe?* Suddenly he realized that this might be the test for all future missionaries.

What should he do? Thinking quickly, he prayed he was doing the right thing. Grabbing his own machete, he ran over to the still-smirking man who was lying in his hammock, basking in the praise of the rest of the village. He took him by the arm and indicated it was his turn. The Yanomamö could not believe it. He stared at Jim's massive build. Culturally, he was obligated to give Jim his turn. The crowd formed again; this time they were all yelling at the man who had hit him, and Jim figured he knew what they were saying. They were telling the man he would be a coward if he did not let Jim have his turn.

Jim led him out, giving him a whap that the guy probably still feels. This time it was the Yanomamö who staggered back to his hammock amidst everyone's laughter. No one offered to avenge him. They realized their white giant had a good hitting arm and was not afraid to use it. From that time on the missionaries were respected. This incident set the tone for many years of working with the tribe.

Another time, Jim was awakened in the middle of the night. He was not allowed to even put his clothes on, but was marched out of the village in his underwear by a group of very angry Yanomamö warriors. It was pitch-black, and he couldn't see his hand in front of his face. It's hard enough to walk in the jungle in the daytime; in the dark it is a nightmare. Jim felt he crawled as much as he walked upright through the long, black, endless night. No one said a word. Finally they came to a small clearing.

"*Waje!*" they told Jim. "*Waje.*" From the hand motions that he could just barely make out in the predawn light, he figured they were telling him to stop. Gratefully, he sank down to sit on a log. His skin, unprotected by clothes, was scratched and bleeding in a dozen long, jagged scratches from thorns and vines. All the warriors left, except for a couple who stayed behind with Jim. *Probably my guards,* Jim thought.

After a brief time the warriors materialized soundlessly out of the jungle, startling him. Every one of them was covered in black war paint, making it hard for him to recognize any of his traveling companions. Jim thought he recognized the husband of a girl who had been kidnapped by a different village a couple of days earlier. He hoped they were not somehow blaming him and taking him out to punish him. They had marched all night. Now, at dawn, Jim realized they were right outside the village that had kidnapped the girl. *What are they doing? Why am I here?* he wondered. He found out soon enough.

The husband of the girl led him right to the front of the warriors.

"Listen, you in there who have my woman," he said to those who had kidnapped his wife. "Let her out now, or I'll turn this white spirit loose. Look at his size! If I turn him loose, no one will be left alive! Decide now whether my woman is worth your whole village being wiped out by my giant white spirit."

The girl was returned. Of course, Jim could not actually understand what was being said about him, but since the warrior had him out in the middle and kept pointing to him, and shortly after that, they brought the girl, he assumed that is what had been said. Sure enough, years later, after he had learned to speak Yanomamö, he asked one of the men who had been with him that night so long ago what had happened.

"Well, you have to remember, at that time most of us Yanomamö had never seen a white man. We knew they would believe anything we told them, so we made it really good."

Ramon paused. "You know what is funny about the whole thing? If they had realized how effective Jim was for getting women, they might even have gotten more of the village's own women thrown in for good measure. But they were happy getting their girl back, so they took Jim back to their village. And for days he could hardly walk as he was so scratched up, and his bare feet had so many thorns in them. Slowly the *nabäs* learned the language, in spite of the 'help' we Yanomamö gave them."

He looked over at me. Even in the firelight, my white-blond hair stood out in stark contrast to all the other heads around the fire.

"Don't you listen to these stories of your people and think you have to avenge anything. Remember, you might be a *nabä,* but you are a Yanomamö like us. We are of the jungle; we drink the same water."

I nodded. More than anything else, I wanted to be considered one of them.

By then I was getting my own reputation of being a good storyteller. I remember telling them about man walking on the moon. We happened to be outside, and there was a beautiful full moon. The tropical moon is huge and seems to hang above the jungle.

"Right now," I told a group of guys with me, "right now, some of my father's people are up there walking around on the moon. They're up there. It took them three days of travel to finally arrive there, and one guy is flying around the moon to be ready to help them make it home. The other two are up there walking around right now," I said.

Every one looked up in awe. I listened as they all clicked their tongues in amazement at what a feat this was.

"Yes," I told them. "They are up there right now, walking on the face of the moon!"

One old guy looked up, and then looked back at me. I could tell he was having a problem.

"What is it? Why are you looking at me like that?" I asked him.

"You have told some big stories before," he replied, "but this is the worst you have ever told. I can see, you can see, everyone can see that that moon is not big enough for two men to even stand on, let alone walk around on."

My explanation of distance fell on deaf ears. Finally I gave up.

4
FRIENDS AND
ANACONDAS

I n 1960 we moved to the village of Coshilowäteli. It's located on the Padamo River, just where the Metaconi River flows into it. I would have to say that most of my childhood memories actually begin at "Cosh," since I was five years old when we moved there.

We had been working up at Calijocos, but the trip up to that village was brutal, especially for my mom, now with so many little ones. By this time, along with the first children mentioned (Steve, Gary, Faith, and Velma), there was also Susan, Sandy, and me. Just a short way upriver from Cosh, the river becomes very rough, with lots of whitewater. Navigating this requires many hours of portaging your boat over the rapids, which means you have to be in and out of the canoe, walking around the rapids dragging your canoe. Some of the rapids require you to run them in the boat and motor. While quite the adventure—something like a roller-coaster ride—it was not something Mom enjoyed doing with seven small children, the oldest not yet nine years old. So, when Paul Dye volunteered to work up in that area and leave the downriver villages to my parents, my dad readily accepted. Paul was a single man, and though I'm not positive how old he was at the time, he couldn't have been much older than twenty. So, that decided, we moved to Cosh.

I was just the right age to thoroughly enjoy everything that happened there. One night Mom and Dad woke us up saying we had to leave the house because the river was flooding. The darkness was complete; it was utterly, pitch black. I don't remember who carried me, but I could hear the splashing of the water beneath their feet as we made our way to higher ground. The water was high enough that Mom did not want to wade in it while carrying my baby sister Sandy. So, a small dugout canoe was brought along to transport her and my infant sister to safety. Mom grabbed up an armload of washed diapers, not having any idea how long they were going to be forced to live as refugees from the flood. Meanwhile, the rest of us were getting farther and farther away. Possibly because she was afraid of being left by herself, Mom hurried, trying to get into the boat. Suddenly, with a much louder splash, the canoe flipped over, with Mom in it, tipping her, her infant baby, and those precious dry diapers into the inky black water. The canoe just happened to be straddled over a prickly pineapple plant, further aggravating my already thoroughly miserable mom.

We spent the night in a smoky Indian hut. The Yanomamö use open fires in their houses, so the smoke is so thick many times it feels like you could cut it with a knife. It makes your eyes water and your nose run and it sure felt like high adventure that night. The next day was even better. We went back over to the house and Dad made us a sleeping place up in the loft. He stayed downstairs and cooked food, then passed it up to us. I remember sitting on the little ladder Dad had made with poles, watching Yanomamö kids (as well as adults) paddle their small dugout canoes in through the front door, then out the back door. It really seemed like a fine place to live!

Dad and Mom did not share my sentiments, however. A couple of days later Dad went downriver with some Yanomamö and found some dry land. Dad had the men build him a little leaf house in a small clearing there. This clearing had been slashed out of the jungle by the head man of our village for a garden. Dad, in his desperation, paid for the prepared clearing so we could go ahead and start building down there. The head man gladly accepted the machetes, axes, and cooking pots for it, but continued planting his garden all around where we were building our hut. I might add that, over the course of the next thirty years, any time the head man needed something, he was right there reminding Dad that the clearing the house had been built on was actually his, and he sure could use a machete, a cooking pot, or whatever.

Despite all the machetes and cooking pots he received over the course of that same thirty years, it did not change the fact that the old man always claimed any fruit on any tree growing there in "his garden." But Dad was always gracious about it and, in spite of this, Dad and Old Luis became very good friends . . . still are, for that matter. At first, though, we were all alone in our little clearing. Dad would go upriver every day and bring down the natives who were studying literacy. While he was traveling to bring them down, Mom would frantically clean up our breakfast things. Hammocks and cots were stowed away and our kitchen table became a schoolroom. Slowly, the Yanomamö began to move down to our clearing and build themselves houses.

This is where I really made my friends. They would come downriver with their fathers to work on their houses and we would spend all day exploring and hunting lizards. The small Yanomamö boys pretty much had to fend for themselves, so we would hunt small birds and lizards. We all had bows and arrows. I was a pretty good shot by then. We would hunt, always hoping to find a fine turkey or something, but usually settling for small birds and lizards. We would shoot them, then cook them. If you were hungry enough, they tasted pretty good, but you did have to be *pretty* hungry.

The sun browned my skin from hunting, swimming, and playing outside all the time, until I almost looked like a Yanomamö. The only thing I couldn't hide was my white, sun-bleached hair. How I hated my hair! It stuck out like a cotton ball in a pile of black beans. All my friends had coal-black hair. They teased me, saying I looked like I was "always ready to run into some village as a visitor." (They plucked the snow-white down off the harpy eagle or the king vulture and put it in their hair as a decoration before going into a village as visitors. According to them, this is what my white-blond hair made me look like.)

As we got settled in and developed friendships with the Yanomamö, we went on outings with them. Every time we went anywhere as a family, each of us had our special friends along with us. One day Dad and Mom decided to go for a picnic lunch up the Metaconi River. As usual, we each brought our friends. My two older brothers and their friends started to swim across the river. Unbeknownst to them, I decided to join them. They were already swimming, but I jumped in and began to dog-paddle as hard as I could behind them. They got to the far shoreline and walked along it, ready to jump in the river to swim back. (If you didn't walk upriver far enough, you could be washed far down the river from where you wanted to get out. You had to walk up along the bank to place yourself farther upstream, as the current was quite swift and would carry you downriver.)

I finally reached the far shore and, while crawling up the bank, noticed everyone already jumping in upriver to swim back. I was probably as brave as any seven-year-old alive, but I knew there were all kinds of jaguars and snakes waiting to eat me over on this side, so, without bothering to walk up along the bank, I jumped back into the river. The current immediately grabbed me and began pulling me downriver at an alarming rate. I kept swimming as hard as I could, but was losing ground fast.

I could see that I was now very far downriver from where everyone else on the beach stood. The riverbank across from where I was rapidly being carried away by the current looked forbidding and dangerous. Trees that had at one time looked friendly and inviting now seemed dark and menacing. It was also prime habitat for the huge anaconda snakes that just might find a small boy a delicious appetizer for some of their larger prey. Boy, I did not want to go into the shore now! I bravely kept swimming right up the middle of the river.

As I swam, a terrifying recollection filled my mind. A couple of days earlier I had gone with my dad and the Yanomamö to try and kill a giant snake, a huge anaconda that was big enough to represent a couple of days' eating for the entire village. It lay stretched out on the beach by our village. A real giant! In my boy's memory, it seemed it must have been fifty feet long. In reality, even recalculating for a boy's exaggerated recollections, the snake was probably about thirty feet long and about the size of an eighteen-gallon barrel. It was huge!

Dad had a large alligator spear made out of three-quarter-inch rebar, with a barb made from a piece of half-inch rebar welded onto it. On the stem of the spear was a welded-on eyelet. Dad tied a large rope to this eyelet. He gave the other end of the rope to one of the guys and asked him to tie it to a tree. This way once, the spearhead was in the snake, the rope should hold it fast until it could be finished off, guaranteeing that Dad would not lose his spear if something unforeseen happened.

Dad crept forward and plunged the spear into the snake's body, just behind his head. The skin of the snake rippled up and down his extensive length, as if he was testing to see what parts of him were still responding. Majestic in size and in the sheer volume of his own mass, he began to move forward. The rope stretched and twanged like a banjo string. The tree shook, but the rope held. By this time most of the Yanomamö were up in trees yelling at Dad to *run*. I was quite a ways back myself, encouraging the Yanomamö to help him: "Climb down out of your trees and quit being such cowards!" I screamed.

I didn't think the rope could get any tighter, but the snake never even slowed down. With a loud popping sound the anaconda snapped the half-inch rebar like a piece of balsa wood, then disappeared into the river, leaving an astonished missionary standing on the bank with his mouth open. The Yanomamö quickly shinnied down from their trees, and I joined them as we rushed up to Dad. In stunned disbelief, we inspected Dad's twisted and broken spear.

The memory of these events, just days earlier, was fresh in my mind—and now I was swimming in the river! I just knew that snake was right over in the jungle by the shoreline, madder than a hornet, waiting for me to swim by! In case you don't know, let me describe how powerful an anaconda is and how it eats. The anaconda's feeding strategy is ambush. Its prey is seized with powerful jaws, suffocated, and then consumed. Once the prey is dead, the anaconda unhinges its jaw and swallows it; they can eat an animal, or person, the size of a large pig. We once killed one that had a six-foot alligator inside of it!

With this vivid imagining in the front of my mind, I kept gamely fighting the current. I was getting really tired by this time. Finally, those on the shoreline noticed my struggle. "Mike, get out of the current; swim over to the shore!" someone yelled.

I kept swimming. *Fat chance!*

A couple of Yanomamö teenagers jumped back into the water and began to swim down toward me. Their approach made me feel a lot safer! I figured a snake as big and as angry as the one we had stabbed in the neck just a couple of days ago would surely want to eat a bigger person than scrawny little me.

At last the rescuers reached my side and helped me keep my head above water. Dad had jumped into the boat, started the motor, and was steering his way down toward us. One of my friends grabbed a line and helped me into it. Climbing into that boat ranks as one of my more salient memories. I lay gasping for breath. My vision swam and my chest heaved, but oh how good that rough dugout canoe felt against my back, so firm and comforting after the dark and brooding river I'd been swimming for my life in! That place, interestingly enough, was later named in Yanomamö, "*Where Mike floated away*." That was more than forty years ago, and it's still called that today. It brings a smile to everyone who recalls the incident—that is, everyone but me!

But I'll tell you, that was nothing compared to the time I went fishing with my oldest brother, Steve. We finally talked him into taking me and three of my little friends on a fishing trip, way downriver to the Orinoco. We got up early and the day was gorgeous, the fish biting really well. We fished until we'd had enough. The day was almost spent and we faced a long trip back upriver with our little three-horsepower motor.

The motor refused to start. *Can you believe it?* It just refused to start. We tried and tried but to no avail. To make matters worse, as we were pulling on the pull cord it pulled out—and refused to go back in. We had no tools. So, now not only would the motor not start, but with the cord hanging out, we had no hope of ever getting it started, either. A motor not starting is ten times better than a motor with *no hope* of starting.

"Start paddling, boys. It is a long way home," Steve said, picking up his paddle.

Personally, I hate paddling on large rivers. The bends on the river are so long that it seems as if you paddle forever and still see the same scenery stretching out perpetually in front of you. Long stretches define paddling on the Orinoco, but on we went, paddling gamely against the current. We finally arrived at the mouth of the Padamo River, our river, and continued paddling. The day was not getting any better, either. We had not brought any food, or anything to cook it with, as we'd intended to be home before dark. But it was getting too dark to see now, so we finally pulled over and made camp. And we were *hungry!*

How we got a fire started I don't recall. There are quite a few tricks you can use. The Yanomamö use fire sticks, but normally it is quicker to take the shot out of your shotgun shell and pour a little gasoline on your firewood. You then take the shell you removed the shot from and shoot the fire with just the powder. That old black powder the Venezuelans use would send a three-foot blast of fire out of the gun muzzle. This was normally all you needed to start a fire, but another fine way, if you didn't mind getting shocked and scared to death, was to take a spark plug out of your motor. Then use a cloth rag (one of your socks will do, if anyone in your party is wearing any; if they are not, cut your shirttail off), soak it in gas, then place it next to the spark plug you removed from the engine. Have one of your friends give the motor a sharp pull. The spark plug should then make a spark, igniting the gasoline-soaked rag. Voilá, you have fire! Be careful, though: I have seen people accidentally set the motor on fire. If you think you had trouble before (which, if you are trying to start a fire using this method, goes without saying), it pales in significance to burning up your dad's boat motor!

But I digress. . . . We got a fire started and made a smoke rack to try to preserve our fish. Alas, the hot tropical sun had taken a toll on more than just us. Our fish were very *ripe,* to say the least. If we had had any idea of just how long we were going to be without food, I think we would have tried to eat them, spoiled or not. But we didn't have any clue, so we threw them out. By the next day, we wouldn't have been so picky. I tell you, we were *starving!* But we labored through the hunger pangs and kept paddling. We eventually beached our canoe and stopped for rest. I climbed the embankment to find some shade to sit in. When it was time to go, while climbing back down the bank, I was so dizzy from lack of food that I slipped and fell down headlong. I staggered back to my feet and made my way to the boat. The rest were already aboard waiting for me. We kept paddling.

We were halfway home when we finally heard a motor coming downriver toward us. Knowing we were the only ones on that river with a motor, we knew it had to be Dad. When we failed to return home that night, he'd figured out that we must have broken down and had come looking for us. Mom had even sent some food down for us, and it was about the best-tasting food I have ever eaten!

Death

One day, shortly after we returned from our ill-fated fishing trip, Shoe-foot, Yacuwä's uncle, ran into our house, with extreme urgency marking his features. "My father is really bad off," he panted. "Come quickly!"

We all ran over to their house. Even as a child I wanted nothing to do with medicine, but I could not stay away, because the sick man was Yacuwä's grandfather, the old man who had insisted that Yacuwä stay with him. We pushed through the ragged palm fronds that were supposed to be the door into the dingy, smoky hut. It was so dark that it took a short while for my eyes to adjust enough for me to see anything. I noticed Yacuwä standing, crying, near the old man's hammock, so I pushed my way through the keening, chanting throng of people to stand beside him. As the women wailed, they took their tears and rubbed them on their cheeks, making a thick, black, crusty sign of grief on their cheeks. I stood beside Yacuwä as he cried and tears streaked down my own face. I began to cry with him. The grief in the small hut was suffocating.

Dad knelt in the dirt beside the vine-strung hammock of the old man. He almost had to shout to be heard above the wailing.

"Father," he shouted. The old man feebly opened his eyes. "Can you hear me, Father?" Dad shouted again. The old man nodded. "Father, when you said you believed on Jesus, were you sure?" Dad was almost yelling right in the old man's ears. Slowly the old man nodded again.

"Yes," he said in a voice so low I could barely make out what he was saying. "When you told me about a man who was God that had made a way to save me from the fire, I hung my desires on Him, and they are still hanging on Him."

A short time later the old man died. I stood with Yacuwä watching the men build the funeral pyre. Carefully selecting logs that would burn hot and long, they placed them on the bottom. They built up the sides the same way my ancestors had built up the sides of their log cabins. They started a fire in the center of the pyre while they worked. While it was being fanned into a roaring blaze, they built up the sides. By the time the sides were finished, the fire was burning hot. The cries of the mourners were such that I could barely hear myself think. Suddenly the wails rose even more in volume. I looked over to the house just in time to see people coming out with the old man's body suspended from his ragged vine hammock. They ran up to the fire and threw the deceased man, hammock and all, onto the fire. Quickly the body was covered with firewood as mourners continued to dance and scream around the fire.

Yacuwä wailed his grief, his face screwed up, his eyes closed tightly, as if he could shut out the sight of the burning body. The heat from the fire was intense. I put my arm around his skinny little shoulders and cried with him. As the fire died down we moved over to an old guama tree. Climbing the tree, we sat on a branch watching the fire burn down until there was nothing left. This was the first death I had experienced, and I was saddened beyond words. I had called the deceased old man "father," just as Yacuwä had, and he was now gone. Yacuwä and I were as close as brothers, and I was afraid that now the old man was gone, Yacuwä's parents would come back down and take him home.

Yes, this was the first death and cremation I had ever witnessed but, so sad to say, it was not going to be my last. The Yanomamö's infant mortality rate was—and still is for the most part, where help is unavailable—horrendous. Normally, though, with simple first aid and sincere trust and faith in the Supreme Healer, Mom and Dad could take care of most medical emergencies the Yanomamö came up with.

And they came up with a lot! Especially when it came to wounds from fighting! My goodness, the fights the Yanomamö were always in would have kept a good-sized emergency room busy. One fight in particular that still sticks in my mind was when the village of Seducudawäteli came down to try to get Dimiyoma back. When Seducudawäteli and Cosh were one group, they had taken her from another village when she was a young girl, but due to a disagreement, Seducudawäteli split off and did not take any of the people that were captured. When Dimiyoma reached puberty, the question of who she belonged to surfaced again.

One man in Seducudawä felt that he had the most right to her. Dimiyoma did not want him, nor did she want to go to his village. Dimiyoma was in love with Lesima (thin man), and wanted to stay with him. Lesima was willing to fight for her, and since he had a lot of brothers who were also willing to fight, they told the Seducudawä to forget it. One morning, right at dawn, the men from Seducudawä stormed into the village. Rushing in a mass to the hearth where Dimiyoma was sleeping in her hammock, they jerked her out of the hammock and began to make their way out of the village. Alerted by her screams, Lesima threw himself into the swirling mass of humanity and grabbed her by her other arm. His shrill cry for help instantly awakened the rest of the village, and people quickly ran to join the fray. A violent struggle ensued, with Dimiyoma finding herself the unwilling rope in a very serious game of tug-of-war.

The village of Coshilowäteli outnumbered the others, so because of the sheer weight of numbers against them, the village of Seducudawä had to admit defeat. Not being good losers, the village decided that if they could not have her, no one should. Grabbing up his machete, the warrior who wanted her as a wife ran into the swirling mass surrounding Dimiyoma. Slashing his machete down in a swinging arc, he chopped her right below the knee. She screamed, but before anyone could do anything to stop him, he raised the machete and swung down again, slicing through the bone on her other leg, also below the knee.

Cruelly satisfied that they had ruined her for life, the sullen warriors threw a few more insults at everyone and made their way out of the village, leaving Dimiyoma a bloody heap on the ground. Someone ran to call Dad and Mom.

I don't remember all that my dad and mom did to treat her, but I know back then, with the very limited amounts of medicines available, it consisted mostly of just lots of TLC and prayer for her. Her legs had to be cleaned daily. Infection in the tropics is a given, but slowly she began to improve. Her legs healed up completely and today she can walk as well as I can. For that matter, considering how much older Dimiyoma is than I am, she can walk all day through the jungle, carrying a much greater burden than I can!

Word soon spread to the surrounding villages of my parents' healing abilities. We, of course, knew it was not the feeble amounts of medicine Mom and Dad gave, but the power of *Yai Bada* that made the difference. Time after time we watched God do a miracle of healing when all else failed. Still, the times that we did not escape the bitter taste of death are forever burned into my memory. One stands out in particular.

For some reason we were down in TamaTama. Antonio, Däduwä's older brother and another of my best friends, was down with us. He had accepted the message of a Savior who loved him enough to die for him, and just could not get enough of the story. I was twelve years old at the time, and he was probably fifteen or sixteen, but looked my age.

One day someone came running in with very disturbing news. Measles had been reported on the Ocamo River at the village of Iyoweiteli. TamaTama is a center of a lot of comings and goings, so we felt it would be safer if we just quarantined Antonio in our house. Mom explained to all of us how serious this could be for Antonio, so we all agreed to make his time of quarantine as pleasant as possible. Dad was working on bringing supplies up the river, and Mom hoped he would get home so we could take Antonio home. If there was going to be an epidemic, we needed to be up in Cosh anyway, just in case the people needed help.

Unfortunately, our efforts at keeping Antonio quarantined were in vain. One day he woke up sick. Quickly the sickness ran though his body. Not having any immunity against measles, he was quickly debilitated. Everyone did all they could, and at first it seemed he would recover. He asked my brother Steve to kill some meat, telling Steve that he was *naiki* (meat-hungry). While Steve was still gone, though, Antonio took a turn for the worse. He asked my mom to read the story again about all the mansions in heaven. He motioned my mom to lean closer.

"Milimi," he whispered, "make sure you tell my parents that I am going on to *Yai Bada's* land, and I want them to believe on Jesus and follow me." He struggled for breath. "Tell them not to be angry, and don't drink my bones. I am going to be with Jesus." He quietly died.

We were devastated. We also had a very big problem. Our hearts were breaking for our friend, and yet we also knew the way the Yanomamö feel about their dead. Somehow we had to be able to take him home without infecting the whole village. I don't remember who helped us, but I do remember gathering firewood, a huge amount of firewood. We built the pyre up, as we had watched them do, and fanned the fire until we had a roaring blaze. Weeping for our friend, we covered his body in his blanket and committed it to the flames. Writing these words now, even despite the amount of time that has passed, my heart remembers that time of Antonio's passing and I have to blink away the tears. *What a loss!* A loss to the work, because he was so on fire for the Lord but, on a more personal note, a loss to us as a family. He had become just like one of the family. And now our friend was gone.

After the ashes cooled down, we carefully sifted through the ashes as we had seen them do, painstakingly and gently gathering up every piece of bone fragment we could find. This took hours. Finally we were convinced we had them all. Tying them up in a basket, we waited until first light to head upriver on our sad journey to take the basket and our sad news home.

Back in those days, when the people heard a motor coming upriver, they knew it would be us, as there were very few motors on the rivers back then, and fewer still on the Padamo. Everybody from the village was standing on the bank to watch the boat arrive. Seeing Antonio not in the boat, and realizing everyone in the boat was crying, the people immediately grasped what must have happened. Steve gently carried the basket containing the bones up the bank. The whole village began to wail. Antonio's father, Lobema, ran up and grabbed the basket. Clasping it to his chest he began to sway and wail, calling to his son to come back to him.

"Don't have left for good! Don't have left for good!" he kept pleading. When the Yanomamö people wail their grief, it is not simply a sound of crying or deep sobbing. The death wail of a grief-stricken Yanomamö is vocal, accented by a look of unimaginable loss. Tear-stained faces—deep with grief and fear—send a trembling throughout the mourner's body and also that of any observer.

While the family was gathered around the basket, the mysterious measles epidemic was explained. Steve told them how difficult it was for us to burn Antonio's body without letting them know anything. Steve explained our love and concern for them and our fear of what the disease would do to them. Lobema carried the basket with his son's bones around the entire village. Everywhere his son had gone, he took the basket. He and his family wailed until their voices were worn out—and still they wailed their grief. By this time we were just as worn out as they were.

"Watching Lobema and his wife Yadoima carrying that basket around had to be one of the hardest things I had ever done," Steve told me. I had to agree.

I have never forgotten Antonio, his cheerful smile, and always-sunny disposition. Although, after that day, I never heard Lobema speak of him again, I really doubt if he has ever forgotten his son, either.

5

A YANOMAMÖ EDUCATION

There was so much to learn in a Yanomamö village. As a young boy, it was expected by all that I would learn how to make my own bow and arrows. We used these daily. Normally one's dad would teach him. Mine was busy trying to learn a language, and I don't think he knew the first thing about making a bow and arrow set anyway. But Däduwä's father, Lobema, was an expert bow maker, and as he was teaching his son this skill, Yacuwä and I tagged along with them on their various journeys out to the jungle to find the special *bayowali* tree that was used for a small boy's bow.

Contrary to my fears, Yacuwä's parents had not come down to get him, so we were still together. Every trip to the jungle with Lobema was an adventure. He was famous in the whole Jayamo River basin for his speed and ability to track animals, especially the armadillo. I have seen him chase one out of a hole, run it down, and catch it.

One time Lobema climbed down a giant armadillo hole. He knew the animal was down there sleeping. Quietly he felt around. Suddenly his hand brushed against the rough skin of something. Gently he let his hands explore. *It did not feel like an armadillo. What was it?* Suddenly he froze. The hair on the back of his neck that had been trying to get his attention was suddenly screaming at him.

"*Snake! Snake!*" He had been rubbing the back of a bush-master snake—the deadliest snake in our part of the world!

Slowly he withdrew his hand. Carefully he backed out of the hole. Emerging from the hole, he quickly found and cut a forked stick. Carefully and quietly, so as not to awaken the deadly reptile, he crawled back into the hole, braving the pitch-black darkness. Ever so slowly, he hooked the snake's body with his forked stick and backed out of the hole, pulling the still-sleeping snake behind him. Emerging from the burrow, he drew the snake out and promptly killed it. Now, even if the armadillo somehow managed to escape, Lobema at least had supper.

Crawling back down into the armadillo's burrow, he located the sleeping giant. In the pitch-black darkness of the burrow, he had to determine exactly where the head was. Finally satisfied, he drew back his spear, and with all the power of his sinewy frame plunged his spear into the back of the beast's head.

Like I said, it was always an adventure. By the way, *Lobema* in Yanomamö means "fast man." He *was* fast. In fact, I remember always running when trying to keep up with the ol' guy.

Anyway, back to making our bows. We would each get enough branches to make two or three bows, as you always goof *one* up. Next we'd begin to shape them. This would require at least one trip to our house to let Mom put a Band-Aid™ on a cut. (I've got more scars on my hands than a fish cleaner.) Then Lobema would give us some bark off a *shiqi* tree. We would use this for our bowstrings. Earlier we had gone out to his garden and gotten some of the smaller *sheleca* (arrow shafts) that were growing there. He showed us how to hold them over a fire to cure them. We heated them up, carefully turning them so they would not burn. When they were hot enough to be pliable, we began the long process of straightening them. After that, we placed them out in the sun to further cure and lighten them up. When out getting the wood for the bows we also got some of the little *antali* stick. They used that to make the arrow nock. He let us take his *tomu naku*—the tooth of the paka—and we used this to shape the nock. The tooth cut into the wood in the perfect shape of the bowstring. We further shaped it until old Lobema was satisfied.

He showed us how to cut into the tip of the arrow shaft, and then how to wind a string around it, squeezing it till it came to a point. Then we carefully placed the wooden nock we had made into the arrow. We had the *paluli* feathers ready, and as soon as we had the nock placed to Lobema's satisfaction he allowed us to start tying the feathers on. It was a matter of honor that your arrows fly straight, with the high-pitched whistling sound that is so prized by the Yanomamö. But it was a lot of work making those arrows, and what was sad was how easy it was to lose one. Many times our hunts consisted of one hour of hunting prey and three or four hours of hunting for our arrows.

I think because I did look different I tried harder. It was good that I did, and it stood me in good stead. Years later, after my wife Reneé and I came back to Venezuela as missionaries, we were asked to go work with the Sanama for a year. They are the same culture as the Yanomamö, but the language is a lot different. When we got there, the people had no idea that I had grown up with the Yanomamö and knew the culture intimately. The Yanomamö always give new people a hard time. I knew the Sanama would do something similar to me, so I kept my eyes open in order to stay ahead of them. The second evening we were there, a large flock of birds flew in and landed in a tree right above us. I watched as they quickly sent a little boy running home. I figured out what they were going to do. I had watched the Yanomamö do this to many green missionaries. I decided to play along. Sure enough, the little boy came running back with a bow and arrow set.

They gave it to me and, pointing up into the tree, let me know they wanted me to shoot the birds. I acted like I did not know how to nock the arrow; they quickly showed me how. I fumbled with it for a minute in order to string them along, and then, catching them off guard, I swung the bow up and let fly an arrow, shooting fast without seeming even to aim, just like they would. Imagine their surprise when the arrow hit not one bird, but passed on through and hit another one. Two birds with one arrow!

Imagine *my* surprise! Thankfully, I had read a book by Patrick McManus where he mentions something about making a fantastic shot, and instead of reacting like a crazy idiot, which was his first thought, he nonchalantly walked over and picked up whatever he had shot. I decided to try it. I casually handed the bow back to Koli, who had given it to me, instead of running whooping over to the arrow with the two birds, as had been my first impulse. As it was, seeing my look of calm indifference, I was branded as a shot to be reckoned with. From then on we were accepted in the village and had a wonderful year with them until their regular missionary could come back.

But again, let's go back to our arrow-making story and my learning to shoot. The Yanomamö were always at war, so it was imperative that they learn not only how to shoot but also how to dodge an arrow. The only way to learn this was to practice it. How do you practice being shot at? The Yanomamö use a blunted arrow for practice sessions. Does it hurt? Very much!

What they do is take the point out of the arrow shaft and tie leaves around the stub where the point is. This serves to blunt it a bit more. Then the village divides into two parts and one group goes out to set an ambush. After waiting a short period of time, the other group sets out up the trail. Tension is high, because even though the arrows are blunted, they hurt—plus it is a matter of honor not to be hit. You walk along, trying to spot the ambushers before they can shoot.

But suddenly, *tak! tak! tak!* Bowstrings are popping all around you. It is amazing to watch the older men whirl around, making the arrows miss them. One minute there is a man standing there; the next minute the place your arrow passed through is empty. To make matters worse, that same man is shooting back! Did I mention that the arrows hurt when they hit? I speak from experience. I have shot . . . and been shot at!

One had to be careful, too, as the Yanomamö are very poor losers. More than once I watched as our boy's game turned into a man's fight because some father thought his son was shot unfairly. As a matter of fact, I remember the day Dad told me I could not participate anymore. Our last couple of games had ended in nasty fights, and it was obvious that hard feelings were growing in the village over them. Many of the guys had begun putting on fewer and fewer leaves to blunt their arrows, and guys were getting hurt with the arrows. So my brothers and I had to quit. At the time I was very disappointed. It was great fun! By the time the day was over we were pumping pure adrenaline.

Thinking back, I'm surprised that no one got hurt more than they were, what with arrows flying and warriors getting angry—and really letting loose! Proudly, but with disappointment, by the time we had to quit I sure knew how to dodge an arrow. I can still remember the "*tak*" sound of a bowstring and the thud of an arrow when it hits.

So what other games could we play? Since we had to quit playing with arrows, we graduated to throwing embers of fire at each other. Sounds crazy, I know, but it was a riot! It worked like this: You built a big fire and let it burn down to coals. You then grab handfuls of coals and throw them at the opposing people. *Wow!* It was beautiful, as this was always done at night and you could watch the coals arcing toward you like so many tracer bullets. We would go home with welts all over us from the embers hitting. Thankfully, I never got one in my hair. It's a wonder we didn't burn the village down! Actually, a couple of kids *did* burn the village down one day, but my brothers and I were not in the village at the time.

We had gone out in the jungle behind the village to hunt. We came home tired and hungry, only to find the village *gone*. There was nothing but embers standing where all the Yanomamö houses had been. Looking down the long row, the only one left standing in the row was our house, way down on the end. We could not believe it. The whole village was in shock. Slowly the story came out.

Up at the far end of the village, some little boys had started playing with fire. Most of the houses had mud walls, but in the house where they were playing the palm came all the way down to the floor. The palm caught fire and quickly engulfed the entire house. A wind sprang up, as winds perversely do whenever a fire wants to get out of hand. The fire was in fine form that day and quickly jumped to the next house in line. It jumped from house to house so quickly that the villagers had no time to get out their hammocks and other belongings. There was no stopping that fire! It ate house after house. Mom and Dad's first indication of anything being wrong came when they heard everyone yelling and screaming. Their first thought was that the village was being raided by enemies, *but who?*

"No, no. You must leave your house!" someone called out to Dad. "The fire is coming. You must leave."

My parents were entertaining missionary friends, Jake and Freda Toews. Frantically they tried to decide what they could get out of the house, but the Yanomamö urged them to leave. The fire was at the next house. Then, fearlessly, Tomas climbed up on their roof. As the wind blew embers over to our roof, he beat them out with his bare hands. It was a losing battle!— but suddenly the wind changed and blew the other way. Our house was saved. There were a couple of other houses still partially standing, out of the row of houses that had burned, but most of the village was in ashes.

Poor Carlos! His house, or rather his brother's house, had been the third house to go up in flames. (Actually, I never knew Carlos ever to build a house; he always just lived with his brother. This was his downfall, however, as he never could keep his hands off his brother's wife. There was many a fight in the village over his behavior as I grew up.) The day before this, he had gotten paid for something he had done for Dad. The gnats are very bad in the jungle, so he had asked that his pay include, along with a bright red loincloth, new pants and a shirt, of which he was very proud. He looked forward to the next time his village entertained guests so he could show off in his new clothes. At the same time, he had talked my mom out of one of her empty cracker tins to use as a place to store his treasure. We called them *latas*. He'd carefully stored all his possessions in this *lata*.

When the fire subsided and the ashes had cooled to the point where they could start poking around, the first thing Carlos found was his cracker *lata*. Boy, was he relieved that he had had the foresight to insist on the *lata*! It had not burned, and actually, aside from being a bit scorched-looking, it was OK. He pried the lid open and found his precious clothes safe. The only problem was that where the legs of the pants had touched the sides of the can, the cloth was burned through; the can had gotten too hot. He very sadly brought his possessions back over to our house.

"My pants are ruined," he said sadly. "All my work is for nothing."

"No, they are not," my mom told him. "Look, all I have to do is to sew two patches on and they will be as good as new."

He looked up excitedly. "Can you do that? Can you make them new?" He was so happy!

A couple of days later, when it was time to wash his pants he took them down to the river. *Boy, I sure am glad I had that lata,* he said to himself, dipping his pants in the river and beginning to scrub. Suddenly he noticed something that didn't look right. He held the pants up to get a better look. Almost before his eyes, his pants were disintegrating, literally coming apart in his hands. The only thing remaining when he left the river were the two patches Mom had sewn on. Poor Carlos! He was so sad. But others had lost even more to the fast-moving flames.

6

THE HEAD MAN, THE GATOR, AND THE UFO

An old alligator took up residence about two bends of the river below our village. The sight of it alone was enough to chill the heart of even the bravest Yanomamö warrior. One day it almost swamped the boat of the head man of our village as he was paddling home from his garden with his wife. Thankfully, they were close to shore, so they got out of the boat before it sank. They were so badly frightened, according to some eyewitnesses, that the head man actually screamed like a woman.

True to the Yanomamö tendency to ridicule others, these eyewitnesses beat the unlucky pair back to the village and told the story (with all the appropriate mimes), finally screaming loudly and acting like they were dashing out of a boat, almost trampling the wife in the process. By the time the head man and his wife finally walked home, the whole village was laughing. Old Spear was upset enough by his near-miss with being gator lunch, but when he got home and found out he was the butt of everyone's jokes, he was furious! Spear vowed to avenge himself on the offending caiman. Despite many trips downriver to waylay him, though, the old alligator proved to be more than a match for him. Spear just could not maneuver enough to get a good shot at the alligator.

My brother, Gary, figured *we* could do better. He thought that if we went down late at night we could possibly catch the gator up on land resting, and then finish him off before he had a chance to get back to the river. So, one night at about 10:00 p.m. we paddled downriver. Our group included my brother Gary, Tommy Melancon, and myself. I was pretty young, but Gary always let me tag along—as long as I could keep my mouth shut.

Gary sat in front with the shotgun and Tommy paddled at the rear. I sat in the middle, swiveling my head around, trying to see through the darkness, certain the old gator was sneaking up on us. I wished Gary would just go ahead and turn the light on, but he figured that if we didn't turn the light on until we were right at the place the old gator hung out, we would have a better chance of surprising it. *What if the gator wants to surprise us?* I thought. But I loved going out with them, so I kept my head swiveling and kept quiet.

We finally arrived in the darkness at the place the gator was known to lurk. This was a large backwash area, and to be honest it was spooky there—even in the daytime. The water was deep and murky, with trees growing right out over, and even draping their branches in, the water. A family of freshwater dolphins lived there, and one of these almost made me jump right out of the boat, coming up alongside of us in the darkness and blowing loudly. I think by that time even Tommy was feeling a bit spooked, because he climbed down off the stern, where he had been sitting in order to paddle better, and got down a bit deeper in the boat.

"Go ahead and spot him, Gary," he whispered loudly, "I want to get back and get some sleep." I squinted as the light stabbed through the darkness, illuminating the jungle at the river's edge.

The small white beach lay empty in the harsh light of the spotlight. No alligator! *If he wasn't there, where was he?*

I had heard stories of a huge caiman down on the Orinoco that would swim up alongside boats at night and, with one swish of its mighty tail, knock some unsuspecting Indian into the water, where the clever gator could grab him and kill him at leisure as the unfortunate fellow tried to figure out what had happened. I hunched myself lower in the boat to make a smaller target. My twisting neck ached as I kept a sharp lookout for anything coming up on us. Gary continued shining his light around, but no alligator. Suddenly he turned his light off.

"Look over there," he told us, pointing in the direction of the village. We looked and were amazed to see the heavens glowing as if the moon were rising.

"There's no moon now. What's happening up there? I'll bet the village is burning down again!" Gary's voice was frantic. We had just rebuilt the village and had no desire to go through *that* again.

Grabbing our paddles, we began to paddle as hard as we could back upriver toward the village. I looked up and, simultaneously, all of our paddles stilled. The light's intensity had grown so bright it hurt our eyes to look at it, and it was no longer hanging over where the village was, but had drifted down the river toward us. We stared at it, hardly breathing. The light continued hovering downriver until it came to rest sitting right across the river from us. I noticed the light was swirling in a circling motion around a central point. We continued staring, hardly breathing, afraid the light would try to get closer to us. Until then, I had never heard of a UFO, but if I had, I would have been sure we were about to be abducted by some space alien. The object hovered over the trees across the river from us for what seemed like an eternity. Even as many years ago as it has been, I can still remember the light being so bright it brought everything out in vivid detail, from the greens in the trees to the yellowish-white foam floating in the water. Suddenly it rose even higher and shot away from us with a high-pitched sound. Then it was gone!

Our eyes fought the darkness. After the brilliant white of the light, the darkness was even blacker than before. I couldn't see anything. Gary fumbled with his light to get it turned back on. Even Gary was spooked now! We began paddling really hard. We were going full bore when I noticed Gary dodge a low hanging branch ahead of him. I dodged it too, never thinking that Tommy wouldn't notice and dodge it as well. I jerked around as I heard Tommy grunt loudly, and then we heard a loud splash! The canoe swerved hard, as there was suddenly no one steering it. Gary grabbed for his flashlight as we heard a frantic yell in the darkness behind us.

"It's got me. Wait for me! Help!"

We had quit paddling, but the boat kept going forward under its own steam. In the blackness I could hear much frantic splashing behind us. We got the canoe stopped and backed it up to where we could hear the splashes. Gary finally got the flashlight to work and we shined it toward where we could hear Tommy calling out. He literally *levitated* into the boat. His shirt was ripped where the branch had caught him. Tommy's eyes were even bigger than my own. He spit out a mouthful of water, wiped his mouth with the back of his hand, and grinned sheepishly.

"Whew, I thought for sure that thing had come back and grabbed me," he said.

We kept paddling as hard as we could to get home. Finally, we arrived at our port and dashed out of the boat. Gary's light had quit again, so I just assumed he was running ahead of us. Tommy and I were in a full panic. Thankfully we had a straight shot up to the village. It was all I could do to make my short legs keep up with Tommy's older and stronger ones. Tommy must have looked behind us because all of a sudden he shouted, "The light is after us again." I looked back and saw this weaving, bobbing light behind us, coming on fast.

I was last in line, so I knew I would be eaten first. I don't know where the energy for it came from, but suddenly, with a burst of speed I never knew I had, I shot past Tommy. Still running full bore, I slammed through our front door, barely coming to a stop before ricocheting off the wall. Dad jumped up from where he was having his quiet-time devotions, almost spilling his coffee.

"What on *earth?*" he shouted.

Tommy dashed into the house with his mouth open. We both looked around for Gary.

His hair disheveled and his eyes wild with panic, Gary burst into the house behind us. "Why did you all run off and leave me?" he demanded. "I stopped to tie the boat, and the next thing I know I'm down there all alone."

Tommy and I exchanged sheepish glances. "Well, we thought you were ahead of us, and when we saw your light, we panicked, I guess," Tommy volunteered. I nodded in agreement.

Dad looked first at one, then another of us, searching for answers. We tried to tell him what we had seen, but even in the small, feeble glare from the kerosene lantern it was easy to tell from the look on his face that he didn't believe our account. What could we say? By that time my heart was almost back to beating normally, and if it hadn't been for Tommy's ripped shirt, it might have just been a bad dream. *What had we seen?* To be honest, I have no idea.

That was my first experience with panic. Since then I have experienced both group and individual panic, and while neither is to be sought after, if you have to panic, I'd say go with group frenzy. Having company is always better than going it alone!

7

FIRST TAPIR

I n the United States, kids dream of their first deer. They await with eager anticipation the day of their first hunting season. For us growing up in the Amazon rainforest, the animal to cut our teeth on—to prove our manhood, so to speak—was the tapir. This is the largest South American land animal. A large one might weigh in between four hundred and six hundred pounds. Some people, perhaps because they have only seen tapir in books or maybe a zoo, think they are very ugly. I do not share their view. Out in the wild where they belong, a tapir is a thing of beauty and grace. If you catch one swimming in the river, you are struck speechless by their speed and effortless motion through the water.

And taste? Why, it is the best eating animal you have ever tasted. According to Louis L'Amour, western novel writer and expert on the American frontier, the American Indians favored horsemeat over beef. In our science books, we were told the tapir was a member of the horse family. I don't know if that's the truth (and I am not saying it is, our science books being what they are today), but I know one thing: If horsemeat tastes like tapir, it's no wonder the American Indians preferred it to beef. Why, I would pull up a chair right there with them if it tastes anything like tapir.

I remember the first one that was killed when I was along. As mentioned earlier, Gary always let me tag along as long as I kept quiet. On this occasion, I had talked him into letting me go with him and Tommy again. In the boat were Gary, Tito, Tommy, and myself. Tommy was driving the boat.

Gary spotted a *malashi* (turkey) way up in a tree a ways back in the jungle. Tommy slowed down and eased the boat to shore. We all got out and quietly made our way through the jungle till we were standing under the tree the turkey was in. The vines and middle canopy were so thick we couldn't spot him. Tito was whistling like the *malashi,* and we could hear it answering, but still we just could not spot it. Finally the crazy bird got tired of answering a bird that just sat on the ground and whistled and never came up, so it flew away in disgust. We began walking back toward our boat. Suddenly Gary pointed down at his feet. We all looked down and saw a fresh tapir track that had been made just a couple of minutes earlier. A little blade of grass was trying to stand back up where the weight of the tapir had bent it down.

Looking up, Gary gave the whistle that sounds exactly like the sound a tapir makes. We all listened but heard nothing. Tito began to work out the trail. We moved in single file, as quietly as possible so as not to startle it if it were still really close.

Suddenly a *jelamö* (tick hawk) came flying over us, making the shrill call that they make. These birds are awful pests, because they are so meat-hungry they will rob anything out of your camp or canoe if you leave it where they can get at it. But they have one redeeming feature: They love to eat the ticks off of tapirs, and the tapirs love to have the birds eat their ticks off. So, whenever a tapir hears a *jelamö* call, it will whistle right back as loud as it can. I have seen them practically climb trees trying to get the attention of the bird so it will come down and groom the ticks away. It must feel good to a tapir to have the bird walking up and down his back; probably scratches him or something.

Anyway, this *jelamö* was making a racket above us. About fifty yards away we heard the tapir whistle. The *jelamö* answered and took off flying in his direction. Well, so did we! As we got closer, Tito motioned to Tommy and me to wait. He and Gary went on ahead. We waited, hardly breathing. With a boom so loud it almost made Tommy and me jump out of our skins, the gun went off. We waited, breathing even less, wondering if Gary had hit it. Sure enough, we heard him call to us. We made our way over there and looked down at this magnificent animal lying there. Wow! This was a lot of meat for the village and would guarantee that we all ate better for a couple of days. But it was much too heavy for us to drag to the boat. Gary felt he should go and get Dad and Steve and some help from the villagers. I don't remember why, but Tommy and I were told to stay there with the tapir.

We waited and waited. Time moves slowly when you have nothing to do but wait. Time moves slowly, but your mind speeds up. It was probably my fault, as I have always had a more-than-active imagination. I asked Tommy, "What would happen if a jaguar was attracted to all this blood and came over to investigate?"

"Well, I would just have to shoot it," he said. "Gary left us here to watch this tapir, and darned if I will let some cat come over and take it. But keep your eyes open," Tommy told me.

I could almost see a big cat smelling the blood and start heading our way to see what it was. "What if it comes up behind us?" I asked him. By this time Tommy's mind was taking over his good sense. I noticed his head swiveling around, his eyes glancing this way and that.

"Let's move over and place our backs against that huge tree," Tommy suggested. "That would at least keep him off our backs."

We had been pumping quite a bit of adrenaline earlier from the excitement of the hunt, but now the levels of adrenaline began to rise past our eyeballs, as our minds—ever quick to jump out of control—went wild. We sat with our backs to that tree, but then it about drove us crazy wondering what was sneaking up on us from behind the tree. Every so often one of us would peek around the tree to see if anything was there.

"Jaguars can't climb trees," I remember suggesting. We looked around.

"It has to be a small tree, though," Tommy told me, "something he can't get his arms around."

A bit away from where the tapir was lying was the perfect tree. Up about twenty feet high was a branch just perfect for sitting on. We walked over to it and began to climb. We got out on the branch and sure felt safer. Suddenly Tommy noticed the gun he had left leaning against another tree.

"If a jaguar comes and starts eating the tapir, we won't be able to do anything," he told me. "Climb down and get the gun."

By that time, I had allowed my mind to run so rampant I was positive that as soon as I climbed down from that tree, I would be face-to-face with a jaguar. But that was the problem with being the youngest: You either did what the older guys said, or you could forget about coming again.

"Keep a sharp lookout," I told him, and began working my way back down the tree to retrieve the gun. Running over to it, I grabbed the gun up and ran back to Tommy's tree. Dragging it up behind me, I finally got up high enough to pass it to Tommy and climbed back up to sit beside him on the limb. There we sat until we heard Gary and a gang of people coming back.

Panic can hold your attention as well as a circus act, but as soon as it realizes there is no longer any chance of scaring you any further, it leaves, and you suddenly look around and realize you are going to look awfully silly sitting up a tree with a shotgun when everyone gets there. We made a mad scramble to get out of the tree before anyone could catch sight of us. Thankfully, we made it back down in time and were standing there waiting nonchalantly when the reinforcements came into view.

As a first tapir that was fine, but it still was not *my* first tapir. It seemed like every time we turned around Gary was getting another one. It must have been the way he smelled or something, because he could literally step out in the jungle to dig worms and walk up on a tapir.

Gary had terrible allergies while we were growing up. They would make him deathly ill. When these hit, he would lie in the bottom of the boat groaning and moaning . . . or throwing up as if he would throw his stomach up next. Many a time we came home from a trip early because he was just too sick to last another day. On the way home, I would whistle for tapir from up in the front of the boat. When one would answer, we would paddle as quickly and quietly as we could to shore, and get out on the bank. Gary would sit up and look around. The pain lines that had been etched along his face would disappear as his body began to pump adrenaline in preparation for the hunt. He would grab the gun from me and disappear into the jungle before I could even get the boat tied.

It seemed like this was always at night, when the jungle was pitch black. Frogs would be croaking and you'd hear a myriad of little scurrying sounds that lend the jungle the ambiance it is known for. We would turn off the light and whistle again to see if the tapir would come to us, or whether it would just sit out there and wait for us.

By that time, you'd be pumping about 80 percent adrenaline, waiting for the inevitable *boom* of the shot. Your eyes would be staring because of the pitch-black darkness when suddenly, right in front of your face, you'd feel and hear the rustling wings of some stupid bat, then feel the air fanned by his wings blowing by your nose, causing you to gag at his smell. You could almost see the evil little smirk on its face as you jerked back in fright. I don't know why bats get their kicks out of this, but they sure seem to enjoy scaring the bejeebers out of people. By that time you'd decide *the heck with it,* and turn on your light. Finally, with a boom, the gun would go off, and Gary would come staggering back out of the jungle.

"It is right over there," he would moan, pointing in the direction from which we had heard the shot. There was nothing left to do but go in and pull the tapir out to the boat. Meanwhile, Gary would be back in the bottom of the boat, moaning and holding his stomach.

The Yanomamö loved Gary and the vast quantities of meat he brought back to the village. Meanwhile, I kept trying to get my first shot at a tapir. Finally I got my opportunity.

We had built a houseboat in TamaTama and were taking it on its maiden voyage up to Coshilowäteli. I was standing in front, guiding the guys who were driving the boat around the many sandbars. The boat was very wide, and the temporary motors to push it had been placed so that it was impossible to see around them from where the drivers were sitting; thus, they depended on my directions to keep them off the sandbars.

Something swimming in the river caught my eye. Leaning way out to see around the curve of the boat, I hollered to Gary. "*Shama, shama,*" which means, "Tapir, tapir," in Yanomamö. Quickly Paul Dye untied his speedboat that was being used to help push us, and I grabbed my .22 rifle. I jumped into his boat, and we veered off to intersect the route of the swimming tapir. The Orinoco is big and broad at this point, and there was no way the animal was going to get to shore before we did.

We did have one obstacle, though, and that was the fact that the river was in flood stage and was very deep where we were. If you shoot a tapir in deep water, it will sink until its stomach fills with gases that cause it to float back to the surface. This normally takes four to six hours. We did not have that kind of time to wait. Paul hollered at me, "Don't shoot him yet; he's going to sink."

I looked down at my feet. There, lying on the bottom of the boat, was the ski rope we had been waterskiing with the day before.

"What about I lasso him?" I yelled back.

"Go ahead and try it," Paul shouted above the roar of the forty-horsepower engine.

I got the rope ready. Meanwhile, the tapir continued swimming strongly for shore. Every time we approached close enough for me to throw my lasso, he went under. These animals can hold their breath for a long time, so it was always interesting trying to guess where they would come up for air.

I had the rope ready. I'm sure some of my ancestors were cowboys in the Old West, and probably could swing a rope pretty well. If that were the case, they would have laughed themselves silly watching me trying to rope that crazy tapir. I had watched enough television cowboy shows to know how a rope is supposed to look as it goes floating out, then drop like magic around the neck of whatever the cowboy is trying to rope. My rope not only would not catch anything, it just would not float through the air! The loop wouldn't even open up in flight. I figured I would either just spank the tapir to death or it would die laughing at my attempts.

Finally, though, I did manage to get a loop around the tapir—around his nose! Not his neck, but around his nose. Well, let me tell you, he liked that a whole lot less than he did when I was just hitting him with it.

He dove deep, almost pulling me out of the boat in the process. I quickly discovered why in all the pictures I've ever seen of cowboys, they are wearing gloves. I thought it was just part of their attire; I mean, part of their image. In fact, it's really hard to hang on to a rope when it's trying to burn a deep furrow through your hands. Thankfully, the tapir got off the rope, and

I regained my balance in the boat. Dipping my hands in the water to cool them off, I tried to regain my breath.

At this point the tapir was far ahead of me, doing funny things he could tell the next gathering of tapirs. All I'd gotten so far was a busted shin where I banged up against the side of Paul's speedboat—and rope burns on my hands!

I shook out another loop. This one I made even bigger. Paul ran the boat in close and, just before the tapir went under water, I made my throw. I watched in amazement as my rope floated out and settled down like magic around the tapir's neck. *Wow!* My ancestors could be proud of me after all.

Meanwhile the tapir was heading deep. I think old-time whalers called it "sounding." I braced myself better this time and hung on. That tapir was not happy. Never have I had a fish give me such a fight. Finally, figuring he couldn't pop the rope, he decided to see if he could bash the sides of the boat in and maybe swamp us. That got our attention like nothing you have ever seen. Especially Paul's, since it was his boat!

Tapirs have huge heads, and this one was swinging his back and forth against the side of the boat with a vengeance. *Wham! Wham!* I wasn't sure what would give first, the rivets in the boat or Paul's and my teeth! I cringed again as he bashed his huge head against the side of the boat, jarring me to my knees.

Paul threw the motor in reverse in an attempt to put some distance between us. My body was tight and ready against the tug of the tapir, but I was *not* ready for the boat to be violently pulled in reverse. Again I almost found myself swimming with the tapir.

"Don't let him get close again," Paul yelled at me. "Shoot him!" Taking up my .22, which I had forgotten in the excitement, I took good aim.

You know what? I think the American Indians have a good point. If tapir is related to the horse, horsemeat must taste pretty good! As a matter of fact, I say horse would have to taste awfully good to compare to tapir. Especially your *first* tapir.

Speaking of my cowboy ancestors, we also are cattlemen of sorts now. I think the operational phrase here is "of sorts," though. Like the American Indians and the buffalo, we could read the handwriting on the wall: We could see that with the village populations growing like they were, the natives would soon be running out of meat. The jungle just cannot support that large a population. The game thins out or moves away. Our Yanomamö were having to go farther and farther afield, trying to find enough meat to feed their families.

Also, the definition we use for an *indigenous church* is that it should be self-governing, self-propagating, and self-supporting. Well, without any form of an economy, it doesn't take a rocket scientist to tell you that they cannot be self-supporting. We had to give them an economy. We needed meat; they needed an economy. Why couldn't two needs be met with the same solution? We decided to try to introduce cattle to them. The Yanomamö greet most ideas with a certain amount of dangerous exuberance. They were, of course, ecstatic!

We went up to some old gardens they had abandoned and cleaned them out so that the grass would start growing. We dug out all the stumps and made it so we could mow the grass and maintain it. We lovingly built a corral and then started looking around for some cows that could call the place home. We knew the Yécuanas (another Indian tribe) down by the island of Chiquide had mentioned they wanted to sell a big bull. Now, they had wanted to sell us the meat, but we figured if we got down there we could buy it on the hoof and maybe talk the owner into selling a couple of his cows, too. We got down there and, sure enough, he was not only willing to do business, but he wanted to sell us his whole herd of one bull and eight scrawny cows. We dickered back and forth for a bit, but by the time we shook hands we were cattlemen. Now all that remained was to figure out how to get our herd from Chiquide to our base camp in Cosh.

We returned to our village and got our huge, dugout canoe. Quickly building a corral in it, we headed back downriver for our first cattle drive . . . but then, since they were going to be riding in our dugout canoe, it could hardly be a drive now, could it? Excuse my excitement, but the cowboy blood runs deep in my veins, and I was really beginning to get in the spirit of this fine adventure—so much so that I even brought my three-year-old son, Joshua, along. He and his cousin Donny were as excited as we were to be going down to pick up these cows.

My brother Gary had a guest from the United States who he said had been raised on a farm. "Oh, yeah," he told us, "you just have to show those cows who is boss. If they get too cantankerous, you just belt them between the eyes with your fist. That will show them!"

This I have got to see, I thought to myself, remembering the size of Fortunato's bull. His cows were a scrawny lot, but boy, his bull was a sight to behold!

Three hours later we tied the dugout canoe and started up the hill to find old man Fortunato. I looked behind me. Half the village was tagging along, as no one wanted to miss the excitement.

"Stay right with me, Josh," I told my son. "With a crowd like this, it could get very interesting. I don't want that bull to start running wild and trample you."

"Dad, just belt him between the eyes," answered my wide-eyed little boy.

"I am not going to belt anything," I replied. "Just stay close, so I don't run you over if I need to get away," I told him with a grin. We walked on around the house, then came face-to-face with that old bull. If anything, he looked bigger than I had remembered him. The bull snorted and pawed the ground at the large crowd that had suddenly materialized in front of him. "Well, Roy, just belt him between the eyes," said my brother Gary to his friend, not taking his eyes off the bull. I turned to see his reaction and was surprised to see Roy at the front of a mass exodus back to the boat. *Oh brother, it is going to take a lot to turn this bunch into cowboys,* I thought.

We finally got a rope on the bull and worked our way down to the boat with him. He was not excited to see the boat and, frankly, he wanted no part of it. We insisted, and finally maneuvered him into the boat, then into his corral. Believe me, that was a lot more difficult to do than it sounds on paper! The old bull was getting madder by the second. He began to lunge against the poles of the corral. The boat began to tip and rock dangerously. The more it rocked, the more he lunged. By this time, all our Yanomamö would-be cowboys had abandoned ship with, once again, our friend "just-belt-him-between-the-eyes" leading the way.

It was obvious to us that our boat was doomed. It just couldn't hold that big an animal lunging from side to side as the bull was now doing. Suddenly it tipped too far over—and the next thing I knew we were swimming . . . and the boat was upside down. I looked around. There went the bull, swimming slowly to shore. He climbed up the bank with a disdainful look back at the boat. Shaking his horns at us, he disappeared over the bank, the lasso still around his horns. Gary ran after him and grabbed the rope. Quickly we all ran over and grabbed the end with him, meanwhile keeping a close watch on the bull so we would know when to let go and run for it if we had to.

While we held him, some of our "cowboys" turned the boat back over and began to bail it out. I realized we would need something to balance our boat and stabilize it.

"Let us borrow your canoe," I asked Fortunato. He agreed. We sent some guys into the jungle to cut some long poles we could use as outriggers so we could tie his boat alongside ours. Slowly we worked the bull back down the bank. We wedged him back in the boat, this time with the outriggers on it. Finally, with the bull worn out, we managed to transport him to his new home.

Over the next few weeks, we slowly repeated this process until we had the rest of the cows collected in their new home. Never in the history of livestock raising have any animals been watched over so carefully. Every evening the whole village would go down and lean or sit on the corral and watch those animals. There was a story behind every one of them. Each head we had gotten here had been an adventure, but the worst one was a great big old cow we had bought from Toki. When we went up to get her, it took forever before we finally got a rope on her. We must have had fifty people on the rope, and even then it was all we could do to get her down to the boat. We finally got her on — and she jumped back off.

We got her on again, and that time she capsized the boat, even with the outrigger on it. We finally got her out, bailed out the boats, and got her back on board. By this time she was so worn out she didn't give us much grief. We got her secured in the boat, quickly said our farewells, and took off downriver as hard as we could go. I'm sure everyone was thinking what I was: *Let's get this cow down to our village before she gets her second wind back.*

Too late, I remember thinking as she lunged to her feet. The boat rocked violently.

"Whoa, Boss," Gary kept repeating, hoping, I'm sure, that calling her "boss" would put her in a better frame of mind. It works with some women, but it sure didn't work with this ol' cow, because with a twist of her head she flopped herself out of the corral — and right out of the boat! Talk about "out of the frying pan into the fire!" The cow was a whole lot less happy, if you can believe that, in the water than she had been in the boat. And the way the rope was still tied around her crazy head, she was now being pulled under water. *Great,* I remembered thinking. *My ancestors drove thousands of head of cattle for thousands of miles, and we are going to drown one lousy cow before we can get it home.* Gary grabbed a machete and cut the cow loose. Keeping just a short rope on her, he directed me to head downriver to a cleared spot we could see on the bank. We got there and tried to coax the cow up the bank. She lunged against the rope, promptly getting stuck up to her belly in the soft mud. She was already so exhausted that it was all we could do to hold her head out of the water and keep her from drowning.

Hours later, muddy and exhausted ourselves, we pushed the boat out into the current and admitted defeat. The cow was still on the bank. We had at least gotten her out of the mud, but by the time we did, nightfall was approaching and we were too exhausted to do anything else.

"You did *what?*" my dad asked us, when we arrived home, muddy and shivering from the cold. "You all left that poor defenseless cow *where?*"

"That old cow might be a lot of things," I told him, "but it sure is not defenseless." Dad was insistent, however, so we found someone who would head back upriver to spend the night with the cow to keep the jaguars off of it. By that time I figured the jaguars were welcome to her!

Dad went back upriver with us the next morning. Taking a handful of salt, he walked up to the old cow. We watched with amazement as he held out the salt to the cow and she started eating out of his hand. While we built a wooden rampway for the cow, he kept talking to her and she kept licking that salt. When we were finished with the ramp, he took a rag he had brought for the purpose and tied it around her eyes. Taking the lead rope we still had on her from the night before, he calmly walked her up the ramp and into the boat. *Well, at least one of us was a cowboy!* I figured.

8

BOARDING
SCHOOL DAYS

During my teenage years, my brothers and sisters and I
went to a mission boarding school in TamaTama. It was
located about eighty miles downriver below our village. When
the school year was ready to begin, we would all head downriver by dugout canoe, usually pushed by a thirty-five-horsepower
outboard motor. Teary-eyed, we would be dropped off down
there, with Dad and Mom normally being the most teary-eyed.
They hated to leave us and, to be honest, we hated to be left,
but Dad and Mom explained to us that sacrifices had to be
made to reach the Yanomamö with the gospel. This was something we could do to help. So, with trembling lips, we brushed
the tears from our eyes and kept trying to tell ourselves that
it was worth it. This in itself is another story, which I'm going
to leave alone right now, as someone will probably psycho-
analyze it and try to use it as the reason for all of my problems.
Instead, after just this one story from school, I want to talk
about our many trips going to and coming home from the school.

I had some fine adventures in that school, but most of
them I can't write about yet, because even if I changed the

names there are too many people who would know exactly who I was writing about. As I said, though, I *would* like to tell one story. I don't believe it's derogatory, and as it will reveal that we engaged in bold-faced lies, I'm hardly condoning our behavior. But it was humorous at the time, gave us much pleasure, and really didn't hurt anyone. So I had better just tell the story before I dig myself in deeper.

I started going to the dormitory in TamaTama when I was in the fifth grade. One of the things about the dorm was that we had work detail. I believe there must have been a course somewhere given to dorm parents that said they had to keep their charges busy 100 percent of the time, except for when they were sleeping, of course. Anyway, as soon as we got finished with school, we had to run home to the dorms and get our assigned work detail. The path home was well established and had been timed out, so our caretakers knew exactly when we would get there. Heaven pity the poor boy who was late!

We were soon assigned our jobs and, gathering our implements, went out and worked. Most of the time, this work consisted of trying to keep the ever-encroaching jungle at bay. What made this whole work thing so bad was that the kids of the school staff didn't have to do work detail at all. They were with their parents, so if their parents weren't concerned about their idle little hands getting into trouble, that was their affair. But we *dorm kids* . . . boy, they worked us like little slaves. I have always felt a real affinity with the children of Israel in bondage to Pharaoh, as I too have felt the burden of forced labor.

Did I mention Saturdays? Every morning, bright and early, we had to hit it, working our assigned tasks until noon. Then one of the school or dorm staff would take us on some kind of an outing or something. That was OK, but we sure preferred to go out on our own.

One year, about halfway through the school year, our dorm parent bought a three-horsepower outboard motor and found that it would not run. My best friend in the dorm was a kid by the name of Jonathan. Jonathan was a good mechanic for a kid his age. That particular Saturday, we were assigned the job of trying to fix the motor. Within an hour, Jonathan and I had the motor running: purring like a top, actually! We asked for and received permission to take the motor down to the river to test it. We put it on a boat and, while I paddled slowly upriver, Jonathan fiddled with the motor, acting like he was trying to get it started. In fact, he had the gas turned off! To anyone interested, it would look like the motor was not starting, and I was just trying to keep us heading a straight course. Really, though, I was slowly edging our way around the bend. As soon as we were out of sight of the port, Jonathan turned on the gas and gave the motor's pull-rope a sharp tug. We were gone!

We spent a pleasant afternoon fishing and lazing around, then headed home. While still out of sight, Jonathan turned the gas back off, and I paddled us back around the bend. To any on-shore observer, I would have appeared just exhausted from paddling this boat with the crazy motor that would not run.

While we were removing the motor from the boat, the owner of the motor came down. "Well, any luck?" he asked.

"Nope, sorry sir, we can get it to run, but I'm afraid it is only running on one cylinder," Jon replied with a straight face.

I bit my lip and looked away because my face would have given us away for sure.

"Okay, you all put it away and work on it again next week. I really want to get it running, as I would like to sell it," he told us.

After he walked away, I turned to Jonathan. "Well, no one can say you lied," I told him, "at least not in words. In spirit, I guess it would be a different story."

He had not lied because, in truth, the motor only had one cylinder! We kept the story under wraps for a long time, continuing to enjoy our outings.

One day I thought we were goners. We had just come back into port, with me paddling. While coming down the river under motor power we had been passed by Paul, the field chairman. He was still fiddling with his motor when I paddled in. If he was surprised to see us arrive under paddle-power instead of using the motor, he didn't say anything.

"Well, how is my motor doing?" we were asked. *Jon, be careful. Paul is a good mechanic,* I thought to myself. But with the straightest face in the world, Jon came back with his same line.

"I'm sorry, we just can't seem to get it to run on anything but that one cylinder."

I saw Paul glance quickly at the motor. The one spark plug sticking out was unmistakable. I saw him bite his lip, then turn back to his motor.

Paul was a missionary kid (MK) from Bolivia and knew what things were like. I never asked him, but I'll bet they had pharaohs down there, too. We kept that motor project going the rest of the year. Although we weren't permitted to work on it *every* Saturday, we got it enough that we grew to love that motor as if it were our own. We finally took it in on one of the last weeks before summer vacation and gave it back to its owner. "Look, I fixed it," said a beaming Jonathan. Mr. Dorm Parent was happy, and we were tickled to death.

During our vacations, we Dawson siblings would leave Tama-Tama as soon as school let out on Friday afternoon. While we were young, Dad would motor down by dugout canoe to pick us up. Our school only went to eighth grade, so not too long after I started school, Gary and Steve graduated to doing correspondence studies at home, and they would come down to pick us younger ones up to take us home. During the dry season, we always planned to spend the night on sandbars and get home the second day. Our motor broke down more times than I care to remember, and it seemed like most of the time we were right outside the village of Chiquiri when it did. I've often wondered if there was not some old Yécuana witch doctor sitting there cursing us as we ran by. Anyway, whatever the reason, we spent an awful lot of time broken down, waiting for someone to come down and get us.

We had so many adventures on the island of Chiquiri that I have to slowly sift through the many to winnow the good experiences from the disasters. The one thing I do remember is that if we were broken down, it was raining. That was a given. This always added to the sense of impending doom. Also, one sure way to invite a breakdown was not to have any food with you. At any rate, we broke down one day, and of course, it started pouring down rain. We were cold and hungry, trying to get a fire going. We thought that if we could start a fire maybe we could catch a fish or something. We tried all of the many different ways of starting fires that I had mentioned earlier. Nothing worked.

I walked back down to get some more gasoline out of the tank, belatedly realizing as I cautiously made my way back up the slippery muddy bank that the can I was using had a hole in it. I was leaving a trail of gasoline behind me—a trail the fire would be only too happy to run back down, engulfing me rapidly, if we *did* get the fire to start. Telling everyone to watch out and not stand where I had walked, I instructed the guy who was in the position to shoot the stack of firewood to wait just a moment, to give me a chance to get further away, as I was afraid some gas had dripped on me as well. I had no intention of providing the camp with their entertainment for the rest of the evening.

Anyway, I threw the gasoline on the firewood and took off running, careful to run away from the direction I had come from, just in case the fire ran back down the spilled gasoline. I heard the shot and saw the flames leap up out of one corner of my eye. Suddenly my feet were running over empty space. As I plummeted down, I realized what I had done. The embankment we were standing on was about thirty feet of high mud bank down to the river. I had run off the bank and fallen down and down — and, with a splash, landed in the dark water. I froze, not wanting to make more of a splash, for fear of attracting something that was lurking there, just waiting for its meal to drop in. What I really wanted to find out was whether I was bleeding. The piranha fish love the smell of blood.

Now, I like piranha well enough, but not when it's pitch black and I'm up to my neck in even *blacker* water, and I'm not sure I can get out; then I hope not to encounter them. But, thank the Lord, all my extremities answered roll call in the affirmative, and I breathed a sigh of relief. It was bad enough to be stranded on the river, cold and hungry, without having to be in pain, too.

I could just hear the others saying things like, "Boy, it's hard enough having to be hungry and cold, but to stay here stranded and have to listen to you groan all night, that is just too much." I groped all around myself in the darkness, being careful not to make any more noise than I had to. Suddenly I felt a large log beside me. Carefully I climbed out on it and stood there shaking, testing each limb to see if all were present and accounted for and still obeying orders from central command.

I was all right. No pain yet. Now, if they would only shine a light and help me back up the bank. . . . I could actually hear the others quite well, but for some reason my answers to their yells could not be heard. *This is ridiculous,* I thought. While they're up there yelling their fool heads off looking for me, something is probably sneaking up on me right now. I decided to inch my way higher up the huge log. When you are in this kind of predicament, your mind does you such a world of evil. I could have climbed on up the log and made it back to camp, but suddenly I wondered if there might not be some ferocious snake or man-eating jaguar lying on that log, just waiting to catch any poor thing trying to climb the bank. So there I sat, shivering with cold, waiting for someone to walk close enough to the drop-off that I could attract their attention. Finally, someone came close enough and heard my shouts. In the beam of the flashlight, the log lay bare and white and my panic subsided without a trace. I slowly clambered on up the log, standing on the riverbank, shivering in my wet clothes.

Another time, we were stranded on that same bank because the motor shaft running down the foot of our 100-horsepower outboard broke completely in two. We were desperate, because we had the only functioning motor from the mission station on our boat. The other motor we owned was in a cardboard box with us. We had taken it down to get it worked on in TamaTama. We had run out of time to fix it, so we'd decided to wait until we returned to Cosh to address the task. Gary had been able to find the necessary used parts to fix it, however, so we knew we could get it fixed when we got home. But we weren't home, and with the motor broken like it was, there was no way to get home, and no way to let the folks know we were broken down. Besides, there was no way for them to do anything even if we could let them know, so there we were.

Thankfully, it was not raining yet, but true to form we had nothing to eat in the boat. Gary kept looking at the box of parts, wishing he had his tools, but all he could find in the boat was a hammer, a screwdriver, and a pair of pliers. The work he had to do was major; as I said, the whole motor was in a box. All of a sudden, he made up his mind.

"Bring that box up here," he told us. We carried it up and he went to work. The sun disappeared but, thankfully, we had a full moon that night. Slowly the motor took shape as Gary transferred part after part from the box to the slowly emerging motor.

As it got late, my two youngest brothers grew sleepy and fell asleep there on the bank where we were working. The Indians who lived on the island had a bunch of pigs that ran more or less wild there. During the night we heard them rooting around the area. They were attracted to the fire, and since most humans they were acquainted with had food when they had a fire, they came in looking for scraps. We were so hungry at that point that Gary and I both eyed the pigs, wishing we didn't have a higher authority to answer to. *Would the Indians miss one pig? Does it get dark when the sun goes down?* We both knew that whatever pig we ate would all of a sudden become the most prized pig in old Fortunato's whole herd, and Dad would never quit paying for it. Gary turned back to his motor.

At that time I was getting pretty sleepy myself, so I kept myself awake watching first Gary, then the pigs. Suddenly I heard a pig snort next to where Joey was sleeping. It was rooting around right next to his face. Gary and I both jumped up, afraid the pig might bite him, but before we could get there, the pig nuzzled Joe in the face. I'm not sure what kind of a dream Joe was having, but he reached up and kissed the pig right on its dirty snout!

Thankfully, by the time the sun came back up, Gary had the motor all back together and ready to try. We put it on the boat and shoved out. The motor caught on the third or fourth pull, and away we went. I would like to say we went roaring up the river. Well, we roared all right, but not very fast. The boat really moved fast with the hundred-horsepower motor on it; as a matter of fact, it was the fastest boat in Amazonas. We could do the trip to TamaTama in one hour and fifteen minutes. Now, though, instead of the 100-hp running, we had an old, tired 18-hp slowly pushing us up the river—but at least we were moving. After sitting there all afternoon and night, it was a huge relief finally to be moving again.

Another time, Gary, Joe, and Jerald were traveling on the river when their motor broke down. Again, right at Chiquiri. They tied up, waiting for someone up in our village to realize that they were not going to make it and come down looking for them. This time Gary didn't have a box of motor parts to work his magic on, so they decided to just try to get some sleep. They walked up to the house the Yécuana women made their cassava bread in. At least it would provide some shelter from the ever-present rain that had blown in as soon as their motor broke down.

Wishing he had his hammock, Gary spotted the large pan the Yécuana ladies baked their cassava bread in. It was a huge pan, about five feet across. *Boy, that is large enough to use as a bed*, he thought. He walked over and touched it. It was still warm, even. Quickly he crawled up on it and stretched out. Jerald climbed up with him and they made themselves comfortable. Joey and Julio tried to get comfortable as well, but they had nowhere to lie down. They were cold. Julio got down and built up a fire under the big pan. Boy, that woke Gary and Jerald up quick! They jumped down and put out the fire. After scolding Julio and Joey, and after the pan cooled down, they climbed back up and went back to sleep. Some sixth sense must have awakened Gary, because at about 5:30 a.m. he suddenly woke up.

Remembering that the Yécuana women always got up early to make their bread, he jumped out of the pan. Jerald lay there, still sleeping. I never clearly understood why Gary decided to let Jerald sleep. When Jerald finally woke up, at about 6:30, he looked up to find a circle of Indian ladies standing all around their baking pan, looking down at him as if he was something from outer space.

Still, the best story for sheer, unadulterated terror and suffering belonged to Joey. He had loaded up the dugout canoe one day. (When I say dugout canoe, please don't get the picture of a little hollowed-out pole that can barely stay afloat. The Indians in our neck of the woods are master craftsmen of the dugout canoe, and some of their craft are huge and will actually haul tons of stuff.) This one was about forty-five feet long and normally rode high in the water. Still, the load he was putting in it was already causing it to sit deep. He looked at the bank, and then back at the boat, trying to judge how much more he could put in it. Already there were ten barrels of gasoline, four cases of oil, two large bottled gas cylinders for the stove, and other miscellaneous items he was taking up to our mission station. He looked back at the stuff still on the bank, then back at the sides of the boat, which were still out of the water. Quickly making up his mind, he called to Yacuwä.

"Come on, let's finish loading up the rest of these barrels so we can leave before it gets too much later," he called.

If any of his helpers had any doubts, they kept them to themselves and the last of the barrels was quickly loaded, then the boat pushed out. The heavily loaded boat made its sluggish way into the current. For a moment, a small doubt worried its way to the forefront of his mind. From his position in the back by the outboard engine, Joey could see the waves rushing by, bare inches from coming in over the sides. But the boat righted itself and bravely began making its slow way up the mighty Orinoco River.

Nightfall found them still many hours from the village, but they decided to push on and try to make it on home. The river was shallow, but not so shallow that they could not continue. Joe kept his eyes on a line of dark clouds.

"Oh, Lord," he prayed, "I sure don't want to get wet."

Well, I guess he should have saved his breath, because the next thing he knew he was treading water! He shook his head to clear it! *What in the heck happened?* The black of the night was only a backdrop for the inky blackness of the water in which he was swimming. Suddenly he became aware of the others swimming in the night with him. His hand brushed against something hard—the dugout canoe. It had rolled over and was upside down. But since it was made out of wood that floated he pulled himself up on it. From this vantage point he called the rest of the guys to him. They joined up with him and then, with all of them working together, they were able to roll the canoe back over and begin to bail. They worked it over to a close sandbar and finished bailing it out.

"What happened?" everyone kept asking.

"I have no idea," said Joey. "The only thing I remember is that I was looking at the clouds, hoping it would not rain, and the next minute I looked behind me and there was a huge wave bearing down on us. Before I could even call out it had overtaken and totally swamped us! The next thing I knew I was swimming in the river looking for you all," Joe told them.

A look of panic crossed Joe's face.

"Hey, what about the cargo? We have to get the fuel barrels back!" he urged. "My family is depending on me." Quickly they jumped back into the black water and began to swim around frantically, feeling in the dark for the barrels. The area they had swamped in was a backwash with very little current, and Joey's searching hand quickly found one of the barrels. Pushing it in front of him, he worked it over to the beach. Julio, Däduwä, Yacuwä, and the others were also working barrels onto the beach. Thankfully, the barrels of gasoline and the cans of oil floated, but it was a time-consuming job trying to locate each item in the dead of the night with not even the light of the stars to help with the job. They *had* had a flashlight with a battery, but it had perversely sunk to the river bottom, and they never did locate it. After what seemed like hours, they stopped to take stock. Counting with his hands in the darkness, Joey realized they had retrieved all fifteen of the barrels of gasoline, the two cylinders of bottled gas, and most of the oil. By that time, they were too cold to continue looking. All of a sudden, one of the guys, with a sound of panic in his voice, spoke up.

"Has anyone seen Leo?" he said.

Joe's heart sank. He had totally forgotten the old man. As a matter of fact, he had not even wanted to bring the old guy. He had showed up on the bank while they were loading the last of the barrels in TamaTama and had asked for a ride upriver.

83

"We are way too crowded, old grandfather," Joe had told him, but the old man insisted.

"There is no one else going up there; I won't take up much room," he had begged. Finally, Joe had given in. Now Leo was gone! Frantically Joe began to yell the old man's name. No answer. He began to run in the darkness down the beach, continuing to call the old man's name at the top of his lungs.

"Leo!" "Leo!" "Leo!" His frantic calls only echoed across the water. By this time, the other Yanomamö boys had joined him in his panic. Still no answer. Picturing the worst, they made their way back to where they had piled the barrels and tried to decide what they could do. They could not even get the motor started to head downriver and see if the old man had only floated off. It was pitch black and the little box of tools that they would need to get the water out of the motor was somewhere down on the bottom of the river. It was one thing to swim for a floating barrel, but it would be something else entirely to go under-water to try and feel along the bottom to find the toolbox.

"Let's just wait for morning," Joe said. "Then we can look for poor Leo."

In desperation, Joe called one more time: "*LEO!*" From not twenty feet up the beach they heard an angry retort.

"What do you want?"

Joe thought he must be hearing things. Surely the old man could not be that close! They had been looking for him for almost an hour. He called out again.

"*LEO!*"

"I am right here; stop calling me."

"Why did you not answer?" Joe demanded. The old man sat quietly without answering.

"He is pouting because we made him scared and cold in the dark," Yacuwä whispered to Joe.

Well, that was fine with Joe, in any case. He felt as if a huge weight had been lifted off his back. He had dreaded having to go back to the village and try to explain that they had accidentally drowned the old man. So now, if the old guy wanted to pout, that was fine.

"What we need is a fire. What do we have to start a fire?" Joe asked. Everyone began going through their bags, but all the matches they had brought were too wet to ever hope to start a fire. They found enough driftwood to make a good start, but by this time the rain that had been threatening to fall had started in earnest. Yes, this had all the makings of a long, long night.

The rain finally settled down to a cold drizzle, and while Däduwä poured a can of gasoline over the wet driftwood, Joe busied himself taking the pellets and wadding out of one of his three shotgun shells. Holding it steady, he pulled the trigger. A long blast of fire came flashing out of the barrel, throwing their expectant faces into marked relief. But that was all it did. No fire. Joe took out his second shell and had Däduwä throw on another can of gasoline, further soaking the wood. *This should do it,* he thought as he pulled the trigger again. No fire! He was down to his last shell, and while he hated not to have anything to load the gun with in case they needed it for defense in the night, he was just too cold to save it. He took the pellets out of his last shell.

"This time I am going to shoot the wood right as you are throwing the gas, so be careful!" Joe told them. Again he pulled the trigger. Again their faces were briefly exposed from the flash. *No fire!*

"Well, that is it," Joe told them. "That was all the shells I had." He put the gun down and dejectedly sat down on a barrel. He wished then that he knew what time it was, but guessed that even knowing this would only further discourage him.

Yacuwä came and sat on the barrel beside him. "Pepito" (this is what they called my brother), "Pepito, ask Leo if he has matches. You know old men always come prepared. I'll bet he has matches," he whispered.

Joe looked over in the direction where old Leo was still sulking. He could not see even a shape in the darkness, but he knew Leo was over there.

"Of course he does not have matches," Joe snorted. "He has to be colder than we are since he has not been moving around. He would want a fire worse than we do."

"Go on, ask him," Yacuwä insisted.

"Leo, do you have any matches?" Joe asked.

"Yes, I have some right here in my *tola* [his bamboo point-carrying case]. Here, come get them," the old man said.

"If I hadn't been so happy he was not drowned, I would have drowned him on the spot," Joe told me later. "Imagine him sitting there on the sand making me waste not just one but *three* shells! How he must have been laughing to himself watching us! I should have left him on the sandbar the next day."

A Question Answered

When we were out on *jeniomou* (an extended hunt) with the Yanomamö, we would always talk way into the night. I was fascinated then by the technologies I read about in the *World Book Encyclopedia*. Man had gone to the moon, fighter planes could fly faster than sound, and huge aircraft carriers sailed the oceans like moving islands. Submarines lurked in the deep, and there were missiles aimed at different points of the globe that could destroy entire cities with just the push of a button. All this, as I said, was incredibly fascinating to me, but to my warrior Yanomamö friends it seemed too fantastic to be true. How they would have loved to have some buttons to push in their own village! I tried to explain everything as best I could to them, and they never tired of hearing the latest thing I had just read about.

One night, after I described some aspect of modern jet planes and how they now could rise straight up like a helicopter and could actually hover in midair, Agusto asked me a question.

"Maikiwä, how come your people can just make anything they want? They want clothes, they make themselves clothes to wear. They want to fly, they make an airplane. They want to cross the great water, they make these huge canoes you are telling us of . . . whereas my people do not have anything. We cannot even clothe ourselves to get protection from the bugs. Our children have huge sores all the time because they have to live naked and get bit all day long. If I need a machete to clear a garden, I have to beg it from you all. We do not know how to make anything. Why is that? How come you all can make anything you want and we live naked in the jungle? Why are we different?"

His question stumped me. I didn't know what to tell him. "I do not know," I said. It really bothered me, and I could tell it bothered every one of us lying around the fire in our hammocks, because all talk died down, each of us pondering the question of what made the difference between us. I listened to the night sounds . . . sounds I had grown up to love. The shrill chirping of who-knows-how-many crickets . . . and then the deep, incessant *bloe, bloe* of the jungle tree frog, fittingly called a *bloebloemö* in Yanomamö. Soft rustlings in the underbrush told of the passing in the night of some small rodent.

Normally our laughter and talking drowned out the small, close sounds, but now, with our silent introspection, everything sounded loud in the silence. My mind kept returning to the question of *what made the difference* between us. I knew they were basically the same as me. When they were cut, they bled the same color blood as I did. They felt pain and joy; they laughed and cried the same as I did. *Why were we so different?*

Suddenly Agusto broke the silence. "I know," he said. "You have told us of how your ancestors came across the great waters to serve *Yai Bada* like His Word says to do. They followed *Yai Bada*, and obeyed Him. *Yai Bada's* Word says that He is the Source of all wisdom. It has to be true, as your people have gotten so wise. My ancestors followed and served Satan and his *jecula* (demons). They have taught us nothing! They have kept us blinded here in the jungle. That has to be the difference."

"What you say is so true," I told him.

I felt relieved that he had come up with an answer that satisfied us . . . me, also. I knew that as human beings we were all cut from the same piece of clay and that any difference between us had to come from our knowledge of and response to the Creator God of the Universe. He had indeed taught us many things and given us His wisdom.

9

JAGUAR!

"**W**hat is that swimming downriver?" my brother Joey yelled above the roar of our 150-horsepower outboard motor. He jumped up to see better and waved his right arm in the direction of the swimming animal. By this time I too was standing up in the boat, and my eyes followed his pointing arm until I could make out, far in the distance, the head of *some* large animal swimming across the Orinoco River.

We were on one of our many trips down to TamaTama and had just passed the island of Chiquiri. I steered an interception course and coaxed a few more rpms out of the motor. I didn't have to worry about the animal, whatever it was, making shore before we got to it, because at this point the Orinoco is very wide.

As we got closer, it became obvious what the creature was. From the way his ears were laid back toward his wide, snarling mouth, it was clear we had ourselves a very angry jaguar. *But what to do with him?* Joey wanted to kill him and take him with us. A *tigre* (Spanish word for jaguar) hide would make a very attractive wall hanging, after all.

89

Frankly, I didn't want to bother with skinning a cat, any cat, as I was on my way down to visit my girlfriend at the time. I tried to talk Joey out of killing it.

"Listen," I said, "we are going to be in TamaTama for two days. What will we do with the meat? We don't want to just throw it away. Now if we were coming home and saw it, we could take it, and we could keep the skin and the Yanomamö in Cosh could eat the meat. It just seems wrong to kill something just for the skin. Hey, I've got an idea! Why don't you count coup on it?" We both were avid Louis L'Amour fans and well knew the American Indian tradition of counting coup.

"OK, get closer," my brother said. Joey looked around for something to use to count coup with. Not having a coup stick, the only thing left for him to use was an old machete. He eyed it, wondering if maybe a coup stick shouldn't be longer. I knew it should be, but I was driving the boat, and besides, what could the cat do? It was in the water. Very deep water, I might add. I swung the boat closer. Leaning far out, Joey brought the machete down gently, flat side down, on the *tigre's* head.

"I count coup on you," he said, not knowing what the real words should be. The *tigre* snarled fiercely, but before it could do more than that the boat carried us away from it.

"Slow down," Joey said. "In good faith I could not say I really counted coup on him; you went by him so fast."

"OK," I said. I turned the boat back toward the now utterly infuriated cat. Slowing down even more, we moved up toward him. The way I had the boat angled, he was swimming right toward us broadside. Joey leaned out again. Before we got close enough for him to even reach out to touch his machete to the cat's head, the jaguar left the water. The next minutes are kind of blurred in my memory. I found myself looking into the eyes of a very mad cat. Worse yet, I was looking into some very large paws, with claws extended! The cat had somehow managed to jump from deep water. Honestly, all I saw were teeth and claws extended!

Time seemed to stand still as the cat hung suspended in space. I remember thinking, *Boy, I wonder who's going to count coup now?* With a loud jar, the cat's paws hit the side of the boat, just a little short of the edge. I think if it had waited another foot before jumping, we for sure would have had the cat in the boat with us!

I unfroze at the loud thump of the jaguar's claws and jammed the throttle home. This was a speedboat that was rated for an 85-horsepower motor. Thankfully, we were running a 150-horsepower motor on it. That boat could scoot! It lunged forward with the motor *screaming.* By this time Joe and I had added our own screams to the banshee wail of the outboard. We came up out of the water with the big cat still trying to hang on. For what seemed like an eternity he gamely kept trying to get into the boat, but the boat was going too fast by then and he had to let go. After our hearts started beating normally again (which took longer than you might think), we turned back to see what had happened to the cat. By now it was closer to shore.

We made lazy circles around it just watching (from far away), both of us glad we were still in our boat and that the cat was still where he should be . . . on the shoreline. For a couple of minutes we tried to imagine both of us in the water and the cat running off downriver in our speedboat. *How far would it have gone before running into the bank somewhere?* On the section of river we were on, that would have been hard to say. The river was long and straight, and I didn't enjoy even thinking about it. By this time the cat had climbed out onto the bank. Now that he had firm ground under him, he became even angrier. He stood on the far bank, just daring us to come in and count coup. But there were now two much smarter boys in the boat than before.

We headed on down the river, figuring that was the last of the encounter—but we hadn't figured on the cat's desire for revenge. We had humiliated him, and he was going to do anything he could to get back at someone. Two days later, as we made our way back home, we smiled and pointed to the spot where we had just about given our boat to the *tigre*.

Rounding the bend, we saw old man Fortunato from the island of Chiquiri standing on the bank. He motioned for us to come over. We pulled up to the bank beside him.

"Do you all think your folks would like to buy some pig meat?" he asked. I was astounded. Not too long ago those pigs had been kissing Joey. At various different times we had tried to buy one, but Fortunato would never sell.

"Why are you selling pig meat?" I asked. I couldn't believe my ears when he told us the reason.

"You guys will not believe what happened," he told us grimly. We looked at him, waiting for him to go on. With obvious effort he continued. "Last night about midnight I heard a commotion down with my pigs. I got my gun and ran down there as fast as I could. The screams of my pigs were terrible to hear. As I got closer the squeals were less and less. *What is going on?* I asked myself. Finally arriving at the place, I shined the light around. I could no longer hear anything. Suddenly I noticed a dead pig, then another, and another. What had happened? The pigs were just killed and tossed aside. I looked closer at one. The claw and bite marks could have only been from a very large *tigre*."

I looked at Joey. He was suddenly fiddling with something on the motor. "What kind of *tigre*?" I asked him.

"I do not know, but I think it was a spirit *tigre*. I never saw it, and it killed every one of my pigs. Every one! And you know what? It made no attempt to even eat one. This was a revenge killing." He shook his head, glancing over his shoulder as he said this.

I could tell he was spooked enough. *No sense in telling our little tigre story,* I thought. *No way it could have been the same cat, anyway. Besides, why would that cat have swum back across the river just to kill Fortunato's pigs?* Fortunato hadn't been the one counting coup on the cat . . . and they weren't our pigs. I forget whether we bought some meat from the old guy or not. I hope we did. Seems like the least we could have done for him, after all.

10

FIRST CONTACT
AND A
CRASH ON THE TRAIL

RUBEN
PINTOR

paused and straightened up from pulling the heavy boat.
I was tired, but since I was the youngest one along I didn't
want to be the first to admit it. I looked over at Paul. He was
the field chairman, but he was always out doing grunt work
with us, so he just seemed like a normal guy.

Before becoming field chairman, Paul had worked upriver
from where we worked on the Upper Padamo River. I'd known
him practically all my life. I knew he'd come to Venezuela as
a teenager and that his missionary father had been killed in

Bolivia while trying to make a friendly contact with the Ayore Indians there.

Because I spoke Yanomamö and had grown up with the tribe, I had been included on contacts to them quite a bit. I'd helped on the Panare and Pume contacts, with two tribes that live in Estado Bolivar and Estado Apure, farther north. Still, the contacts where we had the most fun were with Paul. He believed in giving teenagers responsibility and then standing back and letting them do it. So, with Paul, we were included in the planning and given real jobs instead of just being dishwashers or something. Not that we didn't help with the dishes, too, but you get what I mean.

I don't think Paul knew what *tired* meant. He had told us he wanted to be above the falls before noon so we could have a chance of making it to Ijilubäteli before dark. We were on an initial contact to try and set up a base for working with the Yanomamö in this area. It was a large area, yet had no missionaries. Paul and Danny Shaylor had flown over the area with a Missionary Aviation Fellowship (MAF) pilot, so they had some idea of where we were going.

This was our third or fourth day out. We had started up the Orinoco from TamaTama. Late on the second day we'd come to the Majecoto River. The Orinoco is broad and wide downstream, but where the Majecoto River diverges it is barely a river, winding between rocks and snags. It was low water, so already we had had to do more portaging than anticipated. We were way up in the middle of nowhere on the Majecoto, and that river didn't waste any time. It just stood up and climbed the mountain.

The first rapids we came to took us considerably longer to get around than Paul had planned. The main boat was just too big. We lugged it over the first one, and then over the second one. Finally a decision was made to leave it there. We would take it back home on our way back out.

Glancing back downstream, I was surprised to see, way downriver, a line of naked Yanomamö crossing the stream below us. From the arrows they carried and the packs on their backs, it looked like a hunting party. I didn't see any women or children with them. Catching Paul's eye, I spoke to him in Yanomamö.

"There are some Yanomamö below us . . . crossing the river," I said.

He looked down, but they had all disappeared into the trees on the far shore.

"Are you sure?" he asked me.

"*Awei*. Yes," I told him. "I saw about twelve or fifteen guys."

While speaking in Yanomamö, we had become accustomed to resorting to Spanish when using numbers. "One," "two," and "many" were the only numbers the Yanomamö language had, so it left a lot to be desired when trying to be precise. Calling us all together, Paul explained the problem. With Yanomamö below us, it was a given they would find the boat we had hidden down there. In that boat were all our supplies to make the long trip home.

"Mike, I want you to run back down to the boat and keep your eye on it," Paul said, looking at me intently. "If they show up, you'll know what to do. Then, as soon as we get the other two boats above this last major portage, I'll bring Wilfred and Phil back down to the boat. I'll get what supplies I need, and you guys go ahead and take the boat home."

I looked at him in confusion.

Home? There were some major whitewater rapids between our present location and home. It had taken all of us pulling for all we were worth to get the boat up through there. Of course, as Paul pointed out, it would be much easier going downstream . . .

"Let me run up to the far end and get my rifle and clothes," I asked him. He nodded his assent and I took off running up the trail. I wore only a ragged pair of cutoffs and a white bandana around my hair to keep it out of my eyes. I was running full bore, trying to get up there as quickly as possible—and also to make a more difficult target in case the Yanomamö I had seen crossing below us were unfriendly, as some could be.

I rounded a bend in the trail. The bend was formed by a huge tree growing there, which blocked the view of the trail regardless of which direction you were coming from. Unbeknownst to me, coming from the other direction around the tree, was a young Yanomamö warrior, running as hard as he could in my direction. We crashed into each other on the trail, throwing both of us off our feet. We both jumped back up. By the look in his eyes, he was even more terrified than I was (which was hard to believe at the time).

Grabbing up his arrows and bow, he clasped them to his body at the chest and began to back away. The youth was shaking violently and his arrows made little clacking noises as they vibrated together. At last I got my senses back.

"*Sholi noji, noji cä ya! Kili dijä!* [Brother in law, I am a friend; don't be frightened]," I said.

He kept backing away, still trembling.

At least he has something to clasp in his hands, I thought. *I stand here empty-handed.*

I was afraid to let him get far enough away to put an arrow in play; I followed after him, repeating myself again and again. "*Nojicä ya!* [I'm a friend]," I said excitedly.

Since I was the one with empty hands, I sure wanted him to believe me, but he refused to say a word. His eyes were about the size of saucers, and he kept backing away. He must have decided I was somebody's *boleana* (ghost), because suddenly he turned and dove into the jungle beside the trail and was gone. I stood there staring after him. Right then I began to feel all kinds of eyes staring intently at me from the jungle depths. In my mind, each pair of eyes was looking down a six-foot arrow. I ran as hard as I could to get my stuff. When I got there, I didn't even stop to put my clothes on; I just grabbed them and my rifle and ran back down the trail.

As he was taking me down to the big boat, I recounted my trail crash to Paul. He smiled at the image of what had happened in an instant there on the trail: two young men from different worlds colliding in the middle of the jungle. One white, one brown—and both scared to death! He laughed out loud, trying to imagine what the Yanomamö would be telling his family right now. Little did we know at the time.

I waited while Paul went on back upriver to get the other two guys who were going to be taking the big boat home with me. I wondered again how my friend from the "crash" was doing. *I sure would love to be in the village and eavesdrop on him while he is telling that story,* I mused to myself. But the roar of Paul's outboard motor shattered my musings as he skillfully guided his boat between the large submerged rocks and brought it to a complete stop beside the large dugout I was sitting in. We loaded him up with what supplies he thought they would need and he shoved off, heading back upriver.

We continued downriver the next day and arrived at the largest of the whitewater patches early the next afternoon. It was obvious there was no way three guys could hold this huge dugout canoe steady in that current. The place through which the boat would have passed was a relatively straight stretch, but it was wild! Wilfred's father had thrown in a couple of hundred feet of nylon rope for some reason, thinking it could be helpful. It lay there coiled in the bottom of the boat.

"Why don't we just tie the boat with that, and let it go?" I suggested. 'We can try and keep it off the rocks with the rope." It seemed like that was the best idea we had, so we tied the rope on and shoved her off. Down it went, with us whooping and yelling in our excitement. I'm not sure whose eyes were the biggest: mine (with me wondering how we would get home if the boat got away, or was smashed) or Wilfred's (wondering what his dad would say if he could see his boat heading down the river).

Paul told me later that when they finally arrived in the village of Ijilubäteli there was already a story going around about how this ugly, white spirit with a band around its shaggy hair and blazing eyes had grappled with and wrestled a young man to the ground . . . how he had jumped up, and how only by the most heroic and frantic struggling, he had managed to escape. Paul grinned as he heard the story, because I had already told him about the incident. I don't recall whether Paul ever told them that this *white spirit* with shaggy hair was himself just about scared to death by the encounter!

Thinking back, I've personally always wondered if our "crash" was really the same incident referred to in the Ijilubäteli stories Paul heard. I've never thought my hair was *that* shaggy, and at the time I certainly didn't have blazing eyes. Wide-open, scared-to-death eyes, maybe, but not *blazing*. Kinda makes you wonder just who the guy ran into on the trail, doesn't it? I know for a fact that a lot of unexplained things take place out in that jungle, and this may just have to remain one of them.

11

DUGOUT CANOES AND TRANSLATION

B *oy, sitting in this doggone dugout canoe is getting old,* I thought to myself, as we turned yet another bend in what seemed to be a river of endless bends. The scenery was beautiful, with orchids and every other type of jungle flower you could think of lining its shores. Macaws flew back and forth across the river, creating an even more colorful scene. In one stretch we counted well over a hundred birds before we finally quit counting. There were also toucans, gray and white herons, and many more waterfowl. Some of these were rare birds I only knew by their Yanomamö names, and all were beautiful.

We had been traveling for two days now, though, and the soreness of my bottom was bothering me—enough that even the colors and beauty couldn't distract me from it. *One day I am going to have a boat that has more than just a little pole across it for a seat,* I thought to myself. *Where in the world is that crazy village?* I knew we should be getting close to the village of Yoblobäteli, where we planned on spending the night. The day was getting late and the hot afternoon sun was turning pleasantly cooler. Even riding up the middle of the river in our dugout canoe, I could smell the hot humidity of the thick jungle. Some people find the smell disagreeable, as it smells of rotting leaves and dampness, but I liked it. I breathed in deeply. *What a place to be alive in and traveling with friends!* I thought to myself.

Finally, rounding another bend, I saw ahead of us the round roof of the village. *There's the* shabono *of Yoblobäteli. Wow! That sure is a big village,* I remember thinking to myself. *It looks bigger every time I see it! I hope they are friendlier this time.*

We had been up here about three months earlier and, while not exuberantly friendly, they had at least not been hostile. This time we had portions of the translated New Testament that Mom and Dad were working on. We were trying to get an idea of how far up this river this dialect was spoken, and whether it would be similar enough that the same translation would be usable. So far, in every village we had read it we felt very confident that they understood 100 percent of what we were reading.

I felt awed to have a small part in working on the translation. Dad and Mom were really feeling pressured to get it finished and into the hands of the people. Translation work with a monolingual people is not easy, however. Too often, you learn and start to use words that you find out later don't mean what you thought they did, so you have to go back and start over. Take, for instance, John 3:16. At first, the word we used for "love" in that verse was *nojimaö*. Later on, a stronger word for love was found (the folks thought). One of their fellow missionaries had heard a man telling his son how much he loved him. "I really *buji yäblao* you," he told his son. The missionary thought this would be the perfect word to describe the love that God feels for us. The translation was changed, from *nojimaö* to *buji yäblao*. Later on, as Dad and Mom were going over some verses with their informant, he seemed unhappy with their choice of words.

"What is wrong?" they asked him. They could not believe his response.

"You all tell me that God loves everyone."

"That is right," they assured him.

"Well, when did God start loving us?" he asked.

"God has always loved you," they assured him.

"But *this* word. . . ." He groped for the best way to explain it. "*Buji yäblao* is a word that is used when a man marries a woman and she already has a child. The man just tolerates the child, but it is not his. Slowly, as he is around the child, he begins to notice it and in spite of himself begins to feel some affection for this child that is not his. As time goes on, he begins to forget that the child is not his and begins to treat the child as his own. He *buji yäblaos* the child. In other words, he learns to love it because it is always around. You all tell me God loves me. That He has always loved me. Why do you then use a word that means God learned to love me?"

Dad and Mom were shocked. "We were told that this was the strongest word we could use for love," my parents said. "We wanted you Yanomamö to know how much God *truly* loves you. But He has always loved you. God did not have to *learn* to love you. We are sad that we caused you to misunderstand this."

Bautista flashed them his cheerful smile. "Well, you all always told us that God loved us. I believed you. Later on, when I heard this verse, I thought that maybe we were so far back in this jungle that even God did not know we existed. After you all arrived, God became aware that we were here. As He got to know us, he began to love us in spite of Himself. After all, we are such a lovable people. Who could help from loving us?"

"Well, we do not know about how *lovable* you are," quipped my dad, "but one thing we do know is that God has always loved you. So, this other is not the word we will use. We will go back to *nojimaö.*"

"Yes, that is a much better word," Bautista agreed.

That conversation had taken place almost three years ago. Dad and Mom had been working on their translation of the New Testament nonstop to try and get it into the hands of the people. They had originally thought they could do the version in one or two years, but they were still nowhere near finished. *They had not even wanted the job,* as I recalled. But there was no one else to do it, and it needed doing.

I remembered the day it was decided that they would tackle the translation project. Paul helped us take our houseboat up the river to Cosh. During the two-day trip, the Yanomamö translation was discussed. I had heard a lot about it, but really had never paid that much attention to it, as we weren't personally involved in the translation project.

We arrived in Cosh on Saturday evening, and the next day in church I really paid attention to see if I could understand the reading of the Crucifixion story as Mom read it in Yanomamö. As I mentioned earlier, I grew up speaking Yanomamö as a baby and can hold my own pretty well. Still, I couldn't follow the story. I kept getting lost in words and suffixes that I didn't know.

Later on, as the dinner-table talk turned again to the translation, I remember being a little nervous when Paul turned to me and asked me about it. "Mike, did you understand the Scripture reading this morning?" he asked me.

I looked around, not sure what to say. "Well, I knew she was reading about the Crucifixion," I told him. "But, you know what,

I think if I hadn't known the story already, I wouldn't have understood much of it."

Paul looked over at Mom and Dad. "You know, it's the same way for me. I just always assumed that it was because I don't speak Yanomamö like a native that I couldn't understand it, but I always assumed that the Yanomamö could. But if Mike can't understand it either, something needs to be done. We are going to have to do some kind of a revision on it."

Now, here we were, taking copies of the rough draft around to these far-off villages to see if the Yanomamö on the Ocamo and the Buta Rivers could use the same translation. Thankfully, we found that what we had told everyone was true. There was just not that big a difference between dialects on these rivers. I could understand everything that was said to me, and I knew they could understand everything I said to them. So, there would be no problem using the translation as far up the Ocamo and Buta Rivers as you could go.

As I said, we had been up here earlier. Though not unfriendly, the people had displayed a certain reservation around us. This made us tense. The pressure you feel when the people around you are being reserved gets really heavy after a while. The Yanomamö people can get violent in an incredibly short time, so we were always on our guard, but some villages are harder to read than others. The problem is, they sometimes harbor feelings of resentment that can go back for generations. While I'd heard many stories of what caused the hard feelings, I often only got one side of the story.

This is an area where our cultures were far too similar. The one telling the story would always make himself look as good as he could, and the blame always belonged to the other party. With them, everything said might have two meanings. They were always fishing for some bit of information or other, so you had to be extra-careful what you said. I knew that there was quite a bit of bad blood between our two villages, most of it going back longer then the majority of the people in either village could remember. The elder of our church, Bautista, now known as Shoefoot, had made numerous trips up here to try to make peace. The villages were both related, so it made a lot of sense to have peace with them.

This was Frannie Cochran's and my second trip up here. We had graduated from high school and had decided to stay and help out in the field before heading back and going to Bible school. Being given a job like taking the translation around was just about the most perfect job I could think of. I was sitting in front, with Frannie driving. Behind me sat one of my best friends, Joaquin, and beside him was Ramon, his cousin. Octavio sat behind them. He was the oldest in the party, the eldest son of the head man of our village, and he had many relatives in this village. Frannie cut the motor and we drifted into shore.

The Indians, having heard the sound of the motor coming up the river for the past fifteen minutes, were standing there waiting for us—but there wasn't the usual number of people standing on the bank. *Where are the rest of them?* I wondered. Something felt wrong, but I couldn't put my finger on it. I could feel the hair on the back of my neck stand up, trying to get my attention.

"Go on, get out," Octavio said from his place behind us. I remained seated. He climbed over me and went up the bank into the village.

There were men standing there, but I thought that their smiles seemed a bit hard, as if they were working at producing them. "Come on, why sit there and let the *bädö* [large gnats] eat you?" they said. "Come on up to the village and we will feed you all."

"No," I answered. "There is still enough daylight left, and we are going to head upriver a ways and see if we can catch a fish. We need to have some meat to eat. We are very *naiki* [meat-

106

hungry]! We have drunk so many bananas we want to eat some fish tonight," I told them.

"Oh, forget it," they insisted. "Come on up!" I shook my head *no*.

The rest of the guys in the boat looked at me as if I had lost my mind. We had all been complaining of wanting to get out of the boat, and here I was telling these guys we were going to stay in the boat and go fishing. A guy came up to where I was sitting in the prow of the dugout.

"Let me see your gun," he demanded.

Now, normally I never made an issue of my rifle. I was always quick to show it off. The Yanomamö are fascinated by any weapon, and were always amused that something with as small a bore hole as the .22 caliber I used could actually kill anything. Normally I would make a big show of taking the bullets out and passing them around. Listening to all their comments and tongue clicks was always good for a lot of laughs. It was also a good way of breaking the ice, as we began to swap hunting stories. We had killed quite a few tapir and even a couple of jaguars with this gun, so, like I said, stories of this were always good to break the ice with them.

Today, though, I felt really uncomfortable. The guys there looked like they were trying to hide something. They just didn't seem the same. I kept seeing them glance at each other, as if they were waiting for something to happen. Also, I was bothered by how quiet it was up in the village. A Yanomamö village is just not that quiet! *What is wrong here?* I asked myself again. *Am I just being paranoid?*

Anyway, I told the man, who was still standing with his hand outstretched to take my rifle: "The gun is loaded, and I do not want to take the bullets out. We are going after some fish . . . or a turkey. We will be back."

Pushing off, I didn't give my companions any opportunity to argue. Frannie started the motor. Gunning it, we went on around the bend. When we got far enough away, he stopped the motor.

"What is wrong with you?" everyone asked me.

"I don't know," I answered. "Something felt wrong in there. Did any of you feel anything? No? Well, something was very wrong. I don't know what it was, but it sure bothered me. Where were all the women and children? Oh well, I don't know . . . " I finished lamely.

Now that we were away from the village I felt foolish. *Why had I done that?*

"Well," I told them, "we've got to catch a fish now or the people will think I've flipped." We found a good place and managed to catch a couple of piranhas. They are good eating, so at least I wouldn't have to go back humiliated.

An hour or so later, we coasted back downriver. As we approached the bank I saw Octavio coming down the trail. Although he wasn't running, he was making good time. He grabbed the prow of the boat with both hands and gave it a violent shove back out into the current before we had even come to a stop.

"Let's go!" he said urgently. Again, Frannie gunned the motor, and we roared away around the bend, heading upriver.

As soon as we were far enough away, Octavio held up his hand, signaling Fran to stop the motor. As we coasted to a stop, he turned and asked me, "Why did you not get out of the boat? What was wrong?"

"I do not know," I told him. "I just felt like something was going to happen. Something really bothered me. I know I was probably just acting stupidly, but I could not shake the feeling that something was very wrong."

"Well, it sure was a good thing you did not get out," Octavio said with a tight grin. "You will never guess what I found when I walked into the village. They were ready to ambush Joaquin! Most of the men in the village were lined up on both sides of the opening to the village. The plan was for the warriors down at the landing to somehow get your gun and then, when you all walked into the village, they were going to hold you and Frannie down and beat Joaquin to death with their war clubs. They were ready! I thought we were all goners for sure. I was only sorry I had run up and left my arrows in the boat. I asked a kid to go back down and get them, but the men said no. By you refusing to get out of the boat, you made them think you knew what was going on. Then when you would not give the guy your rifle, they were *sure* you knew. They decided to wait for another opportunity."

I looked at him blankly, hardly believing his words. Actually I was just waiting for him to start laughing and making fun of what must have been my obvious fright.

"No, no . . . it is *true*," he told me. "As soon as I walked in, they would not let me leave and told me not to say a word. I do not think they would really do anything to me, as I have so many uncles and cousins in there, but I will tell you what— I was ready to give one good yell as you walked in to warn you. If they would have killed me, so be it."

We bowed our heads right there, floating down the Ocamo River, and praised the Lord God of heaven and earth that He had seen fit to warn us that something was wrong. Later Frannie and I had a long talk about what our response should be in that type of a situation. We just didn't know *what* to do. What would you do if your group were being attacked while on a missionary trip? We just did not know.

We began to tell the guys we were traveling with stories of men who had been martyred for Christ. Our first efforts fell on deaf ears. Now, the Yanomamö have nothing against having to die for something, but it sure grated on them that they shouldn't try and take as many with them as they could.

When traveling, you feel a close rapport with other members of your group. An attack on one member would be an attack on all. We were missionaries, however; what should our response be to such an attack? We wanted to protect our own, but also to be proper representatives of Christ and the message He had sent us to share.

"Oh God," I prayed later. "Help us to know how to respond. I want to be a good witness for you, but how could I stand by and watch someone club one of my best friends to death, a guy who trusts me and would stand up for me in any situation? Please keep us from ever having to make this kind of a decision," I prayed, and I'm sure that He heard my request.

12
MEDICAL CALL

RUBEN PINTOR

The two years Fran and I worked with the Yanomamö before returning to the United States for Bible school were some of the most enjoyable I have ever spent. We worked up the Ocamo, Buta, and Padamo Rivers. It seemed like every time we turned around we had some mighty fine adventure, followed almost immediately by a full-fledged crisis!

We started out by going to bases where there were already missionaries and holding the base down for them until they could get back from wherever it was they were going. Later, we were allowed to go out and work on our own. Personally, I don't think our ruining a boat had anything to do with our going in alone . . . but you never can tell. Anyway, this is what happened.

We would be flown into a village and the pilot would wait on the ground while the family that was leaving took time to show us all the do's and don'ts that always exist on a base. One time, right before getting on the plane to leave, the resident missionary told Fran and me one last thing: "Oh, my little boat is down at the port. You all are free to use it, but be careful; the water is rough."

We thanked him. I'm not sure what Cochran was thinking, but after working on the Padamo River for a year, I doubted there was any little old stream here that I would consider rough.

"We'll be careful," said Frannie, ever the diplomat.

The next day we decided to head down to the river and try out the boat. We were used to dugout canoes, and we knew that this missionary had one of those newfangled aluminum jobs, which were really light compared to the boats we were used to. After we were done with this trip, however, we wished we had stuck with the type of boat we knew best, instead of getting cute with someone's possibly priceless heirloom. But I'm getting ahead of myself . . .

The missionary had mentioned in passing that if we were to go downriver we would need to portage the boat across land to skip some rapids and get to a spot farther downriver. There we could put the boat in and proceed on down more easily. Well, we got to where the boat was and looked around. The little boat looked really nice. It was obviously well maintained. We scouted the river to see how conditions on it looked and right where the boat was stored there was a waterfall. Glancing downriver , I thought it looked quite passable, even though it was flowing pretty strongly. I sure didn't see any reason to go lugging the boat way across land somewhere if this was all the challenge the river had to offer. As far as I could see, we could navigate it easily.

"What do you think, Cochran, should we just put in here?"

He turned from looking at the river with a slight grin. "I'm just wondering where all that whitewater is," he said.

"We must be looking almost as far as we would drag the boat down. I say we go for it."

Did I mention that Fran had a friend visiting from the United States at the time? I'm not sure if that had anything to do with our decision here or not. I do know that when we visited back in the States, the guys we hung out with always had things to show off: cars, knowing how to order stuff at a McDonald's, going to stores, and such. Well, now we had a chance to show off a bit to this visiting friend, and what better way to show off than to head down this river through strong rapids and maybe scare him a bit?

That decided, we put the little boat in the water and got our fishing stuff ready. Fran paddled the front, his friend sat in the middle, and I paddled the stern. I nudged the prow into the current, which immediately caught us and thrust us downstream. Boy, she was lighter than a feather and paddled like a dream!

"Wow, I sure wish we had one of these," we both said. Everything was great. In the distance I listened to a toucan calling and, closer in, there was a family of scarlet macaws in a tree above us. What a life! We lazily floated down, paddling just enough to maintain steerage. I watched a giant blue butterfly float across the river, its reflection in the water mirroring its every beautiful detail.

"Isn't this living?" I asked them. Both nodded in agreement.

The current began to pick up and we straightened to our paddles. We were experienced whitewater people, after all, and knew what to do. We rounded the bend and laughed. So, this was the whitewater we had been told to watch out for? Why, it was nothing! Just two rocks with the current funneling between them. All we had to do was not hit either rock. No problem! We had most of the river to use to get around them.

How we managed what follows is still actually a mystery to me. I remember Cochran blaming me for most of it, I guess because I was steering. How in the world we managed to hit the first rock, I don't know, but it was more than I am willing to take *all* the blame for—I don't care who was steering. But anyway, we hit the first rock. I was accustomed to the dugout canoes we normally use just bumping and scraping off rocks. Then you'd go on, none the worse for wear. But this aluminum boat was no Yanomamö-style dugout! The prow lodged on the rock and, to make matters worse, the surging current caught the stern—and nothing I could do could stop it. We swiveled around till the back of the boat hit the second rock about three-fourths of the way down the length of the boat.

Picture this: There are only two rocks, and we have managed to hit both of them. And now the crazy canoe seems to be stuck!

We had not as yet capsized, so I grabbed my fishing stuff and gun, and walked over to the rock, which Fran and Lynn were already perched on, and stepped out onto it. We stood there for a moment savoring the fact that we were so free. We were about as far from anywhere as you could be and we were having a fine adventure. We were still dry. Life was good.

Life can change in a hurry, though. When we bent down to nudge our boat off, it wouldn't budge! It seemed to have gotten wedged between the rocks by the current. We still were not too concerned, figuring all we had to do was get a bit better leverage on it, and it would break free. Suddenly I noticed that the canoe was listing more into the current. The more it listed, the more the water flowed into it, and the more it listed. Then I saw something else that chilled the blood in my veins. I stared in disbelief at a definite bulge on the bottom of the canoe. The powerful, surging current was actually bending the back of the boat around the second rock!

This piece of news excited Frannie to no end. And, by the way, his pal Lynn was not looking too impressed with us. By this time, he had figured out that something was very wrong.

We began working to free the prow with a will and vigor matched only by the relentless fury of the current crashing against the boat. Working vigorously, we finally freed the prow and pushed it away from the rock. Now, if we'd done that same thing with a dugout canoe, the current would have pushed the prow down, and the stern would have swiveled right on up and off the second rock. Imagine our horror when, instead of doing that, the prow floated down off the rock and the canoe turned *inside out* right before our eyes. The force of the current pushing the prow down caused the stern to curl right around the rock. We now had a large piece of aluminum shaped like a boulder. For any of you canoe people out there, you can appreciate how worthless this was!

With the boat turned inside out like it was, there was nothing for the current to hold onto, and so it let go . . . and our piece of aluminum began to drift off the rock. We jumped into the current and towed it to shore, still hoping in our own minds that it wasn't as bad as it appeared. *Surely we couldn't have ruined a canoe that easily?*

Somehow we got it to shore, then pulled it up onto dry land. Well, as I'd feared, our first impression was right. You *can* ruin a canoe that easily. In fact, it was utterly demolished. It vaguely resembled a child's first attempt at making a floating device, but no longer looked anything like the sleek, beautiful little boat the owner had left in our care.

We spent the remainder of the two weeks the owners were gone trying to beat the aluminum boat back into some kind of presentable shape. Sad to say, it seemed like the more we did, the worse we made it. Aluminum can only be bent so much, you see, and then it breaks. We'd now passed that breaking point, so not only was the canoe sadly misshapen, it also had large, jagged cracks that ran almost the width of the canoe. If it had been insured, it would have been appraised as totaled. Actually, it *was* totaled; he just did not get paid for it.

By the time the missionary flew back in, we had exhausted our best efforts to redeem a bad situation. We even discussed just weighting the boat with rocks, drowning it, and telling him we'd lost it in the current. That seemed better than trying to tell him how we had ruined his boat. Finally, though, we decided that since we *had* ruined it, we had to face the music.

On the day of return, bad weather delayed the plane, so instead of our having about two hours with the missionary family once they got back in, we were cut short when the pilot said he had to leave immediately. We asked for ten minutes to discuss a private matter with them. We took the owner outside, away from everyone else, and tried to break it to him gently.

"We are very sorry . . . ," we started out, "but we have to tell you that we destroyed your boat."

"*Destroyed?* Oh, well, boys, these things happen."

"No, sir, we really did destroy your boat. We would like you to come down and look at it, so you can see it for yourself while we're still here. We feel responsible and all. . . ." I'm sure our voices trailed off before we could muster the courage to describe what a mess we'd made.

He laughed good-naturedly. "Well, boys, the pilot's in a hurry. I have seen dinged boats before, and doubtless will again. You all take off, and don't worry about it."

Fran and I looked at each other. Boy, he was taking this well. "Are you sure you don't want to go down and look at it?" we asked again.

"No, no, you all run along, I'll look at it later."

Relieved, we walked back to the plane and climbed in. I breathed a sigh of relief when we actually lifted off.

A couple of weeks later the plane went back in there. When it returned, Fran and I received a letter from this missionary.

"Well, boys, when you said 'destroyed,' I'm not sure what I was expecting, but I really thought there would be a bit more left of my boat than there was. What in the world happened?"

By then it was even harder for either of us to get all the details right, as our conveniently selective memories had tried hard to wipe out the most embarrassing details.

Time has likewise dulled many of the more mundane details of some of our escapades, but one I will never forget is the day we decided to go waterskiing one last time before heading in to hold down the base at Parima. Now, normally, we always skied with a good friend, Luis. We had a good arrangement with him on this. He had a government job that provided him with a speedboat and motor. I had the skis. We all helped with the gas.

Our whole lives, while going to high school in TamaTama, we went to school all week; then, as soon as Friday classes rolled to a finish, we took off on a hunting trip to get meat to sell to the dorms. (Cochran's parents were now dorm parents, and were not quite so bent on slave labor; besides, they really did need the meat.) Anyway, we would go hunting on Friday, and then return late on Saturday. We would sell whatever meat we had gotten on the hunt, and with that money we purchased gas to go skiing with Luis. I have to say, he was awfully good about it: many times we didn't get enough meat to pay for the gas that it took for us to go out, but Luis always kicked in the amount needed to make up the difference. We had an awful lot of fun waterskiing on the Orinoco River there in front of TamaTama with Luis. I'm sure the government wondered why so many motors broke down at their station in TamaTama, but it was a good arrangement.

When the girls were down swimming at the river, it gave us a nice crowd to show off to, which was even better. We really got pretty good at waterskiing. As a matter of fact, that was about the only sport I knew (though it turned out to be about worthless when all the other guys in Bible school were playing volleyball, football, or soccer).

As I said, the day before we were to head in to Parima to go hold down the base, a missionary came upriver with a beautiful boat. It was a real speedboat with front steering and everything. He offered to pull us and we jumped at the chance. To make it better, everyone was down at the swimming hole watching. When it was my turn, I decided to really put on a show! I was overjoyed at the response of my slalom ski with the higher horsepower engine on that boat. Boy, could I make that ski turn—but on one really wild maneuver I somehow kicked the back of the ski out of the water. The way it threw me, it twisted me sideways, and I landed smack on my left ear. Thankfully, I was wearing a life belt, because the force knocked me out for a bit. I came back to with my head ringing like a brass drum. Blood trickled out of my ear. Now, that was not good for two immediate reasons: (1) I was in the Orinoco River, and there were also blood-seeking piranha swimming in this same river; and (2) it hurt like heck. The boat came back over and I was helped aboard. Needless to say, that ended my skiing for the day.

The next day Cochran and I got in the plane and flew on up to Parima. My ear hurt, but not as badly as I had thought it would. It was just perversely allowing me to get as far away from medical help as possible before *really* sounding off.

About the second day, my head felt hollow and light. The pain in my ear was something to feel, I'll tell you. That morning my pillow was a mess where my ear had drained all night. Because of my own sensitive stomach, I won't go into detail about what it looked and smelled like, but it was very obvious that something was wrong. Cochran called out by radio and explained the situation to everyone. He was told to try penicillin shots for ten days, as I recall. Boy, I wasn't sure I liked that option any better than I liked my draining ear. I had seen Cochran give shots to the Yanomamö, and while he seemed to know what he was doing, as far as I was concerned he was still a novice—and I didn't think I wanted him practicing on me. But by that time my ear hurt so badly, I quit arguing. Ol' Cochran didn't do that badly, and though it isn't something I would do just for fun, I came away from the full treatment none the worse for wear. My ear finally got better, and he quit giving me the shots. I'm not sure who was the most relieved, him or me.

Another thing I remember about this particular trip was this lady and her daughter who passed by the house where we were staying, every morning about 5:30 a.m., and called out to us. We could hear the lady whisper to her daughter to call us. We would answer and we could hear the lady say, "Tell them we are going to the garden." The daughter would faithfully repeat every word. This went on day after day. Finally, we wondered how long the girl would call us if we did not answer. We lay there in the darkness and grinned to ourselves as she kept calling: first Fran, then me. She called and called. I know she called us, just monotone, for at least half an hour.

"Francisco, Maikiwä! Francisco, Maikiwä!" she cried, on and on. I don't remember who broke first, Fran or me, but it was probably me, as I have less patience than Fran does. But, finally, one of us answered.

"Tell them we are going to our garden," we could hear the mother say.

The funny thing was, neither Fran nor I realized *why* the lady was letting us know she was going to her garden. One day, though, while commenting on this to some friends, they looked at me funny, and asked, "Why do you think she was letting you know where she was going to be?" It was like a light went on, but thankfully we had been just too naïve to understand her patience back then.

The worse crises, by far, that we got into occurred when we were trying to help the Yanomamö with medical needs. I don't know if I've mentioned it, but working with them you had to be willing to handle medicine, whether you wanted to or not—or find someone who would. They were always sick. If they were *not* sick, they would pretend to be so that we would give them some medicine. I guess they thought that if they took the medicine when they were not sick it would keep them from getting ill. Nothing we told them could convince them otherwise.

Personally, since that time I've hated anything to do with medicine. I guess maybe I was traumatized by my experiences with Frannie during those early years. Frannie says I never helped with medicine at all, so why should I be traumatized?—but this is my story, and I remember *trauma!* Who knows what might have happened to ol' Cochran if I hadn't been able to hold the dogs at bay?

Let me tell you what happened. We had gone in to hold down a base so that the real missionaries who were stationed there could go out for their annual missionary conference. We were just teenagers, and so didn't need to go to the conference; besides, I'm sure the powers-that-be figured: what would *we* need a break from? Plus, I was dating the daughter of one of the field committee members. Now that I have my own daughters, I think I would send anyone they started dating as far away as I could get them, which must have been what this girl's father was thinking about me. Anyway, we were always shuffled out of the way during these get-togethers. So, we got to the base and the missionary showed us everything we would be doing to cover for them. Along with everything else was the usual list of sick people we would be treating. Now, normally the sick come to the dispensary building where, among other things, the missionary hands out or administers medicine.

I had nothing against that. Fran and I had worked out a good arrangement. He dispensed medicine and I stood around and swapped stories with all the people who showed up for medicine call. It was kind of a social hour for them. Anyway, I would be there just shooting the breeze and Fran would be attending to all the complaints and requests for help that are so typical of the Yanomamö. One of the best stories I had to tell the people was about the first time I introduced Franny to the world of medicine.

We were both about fourteen years old then, and our family was stationed in the village of Mavaca at the time. I tell you, those people were rough. It seemed like every time we turned around someone was being brought in either with an arrow wound, or a machete chop, or a gash on the head that had to be sewn shut. Now, I didn't do any sewing and, to be honest, most times didn't even go in for that close a look. Remember, I don't do medicine. On the day I remember, Frannie was up visiting from the school base in TamaTama, where his parents were the dorm parents for the mission school. Someone came running in saying this guy had beaten his wife up really badly. We ran over, some to help and others, like myself, just to see what had happened. When we got there, the woman was lying in a pool of her own blood, a huge crowd all around her. Half of the crowd was on her side of the quarrel, and the other half was on her husband's side. It looked like any minute there was going to be a half-dozen others needing treatment as well. With the Yanomamö, everyone takes sides, and there's no such thing as a private argument between a husband and wife, especially if he has taken a piece of firewood and beaten her over the head with it a couple of times. Dad and my older brothers, Steve and Gary, were able to successfully defuse the situation. They carried the lady off to the dispensary to tend to her wounds.

Gary loved medical work and would have made a fine surgeon. He and others started cleaning her off, then started sewing. I had seen about as much as I cared to see, so I turned to Cochran and asked him, "Well, Cochran, have you seen enough blood yet?"

About that time, without a word ol' Cochran turned as white as a sheet and keeled over on his back.

"Help!" I shouted. I hadn't had much experience with someone fainting, so I thought he had had a heart attack and died. Gary ran over, and between the two of us we revived him to consciousness and walked him out between us. We sat out under a tree until he had a bit of his color back.

Anyway, when I told this story I would really ham it up, until I had the people waiting to be tended to wondering if maybe they wouldn't be better off just sticking to the old witch doctor across the hut. But ol' Cochran was good . . . and patient, which was the prime attribute one had to have when working medicine with the Yanomamö. If you were the least bit gullible, they would go to any length to convince you how near to death they were so that you would give abundantly of whatever medicine they were trying to talk you out of.

In this village was a girl, about fourteen years old, who had been unfaithful to her husband. The Yanomamö girls are sold

RUBEN PINTOR

in marriage at a very early age. I have heard different folks defend the practice, saying it keeps the girls in line and assures their impoverished families a good supply of a high-protein diet, and so on. But, in reality, the poor little girls are subjected to the most obscene forms of child molestation that have ever been condoned by a society. Every night the old guy drags this little child to his hammock and entertains himself. The rest of the village has to put up with her screams of fright and pain. He officially doesn't take her as his wife until she reaches puberty— bear in mind, that's "officially." Most of the time, a young girl is given to an older, established man in the village, to be one of many wives. This leads to a lot of promiscuity, because the young girls don't want or care for the old man to whom their fathers or brothers have given her.

Well, this particular girl's husband was jealous and had followed her to where she was meeting her lover. Infuriated after catching them, he then quietly went on back to the village. His young wife came home, supposedly from being out killing crabs with her friends. She even had a small bundle of crabs tied up in leaves to prove it. She quickly built up her fire, letting it burn down to a nice, red bed of coals. She then placed her bundle of crabmeat on the coals to cook. Her husband lay in his hammock in an obvious foul mood, hands clasped together covering his mouth (like they do when they are really angry). Sullenly, he watched her work, expertly turning the bundle of leaves to keep them from catching fire and burning up. The trick was to get it hot enough to cook your food, but turning it often enough to keep from catching on fire and ruining your meal.

She finally decided it was cooked. Removing it from the fire, she split the leaves open, revealing the succulent pieces of crab-meat. She took a clean, broad *kediba* leaf and placed his portion on it. Handing it over to him, she said, "Here is your crabmeat."

"And here is yours," he shouted. Jumping up, he reached over and grabbed a burning brand out of the fire and thrust it between her legs, grinding it in. She screamed in pain and fell down, writhing on the ground. He was not finished. He took the still-burning brand and thrust it against her breast. The village was now in an uproar. As was typical, half the village sided with him and the other half sided with the girl, who was burned very badly. Someone ran to get the missionaries. They came and gave the poor girl first aid with what they had available.

Into this situation, two days later, arrived two seventeen-year-old boys. I listened in silence as the departing missionaries filled us in on what would have to be done to take care of the girl's burns.

Are they crazy? was my first thought when they told us about the girl. *I'm glad Fran's here,* I thought to myself.

That evening we made our first trip over to the village to treat our patient. What a sight! I will never forget the misery I saw in that poor girl's eyes. Poor Frannie had to change the dressings and doctor her. We were both at the age where we felt embarrassment acutely—and easily, and often. I tried to divert everyone's attention away from what Fran was doing by telling stories. I'm sure he probably appreciates my efforts now.

One job that I had, and that I tried to take as seriously as I could, was to protect Fran, the great dispenser of medicine, from all the Indian dogs. That might sound like a small thing, but until you have experienced walking into a Yanomamö village and being attacked by their pack of half-wild dogs, you can't begin to appreciate the constant danger we were in. In this village the dogs were particularly ferocious. Led by a wily, large, black dog, they were getting harder and harder to beat back every morning (and evening) when we went to treat the girl.

"Tie your dogs!" I'd call out from outside the village. "Tie your dogs!"

"OK, come on in," they would yell back. It became obvious that we were now a real show, with their dogs playing a leading role. Daily we would fight them off, only to be met by peals of laughter from around the whole village. I threatened them with everything I could think of, even saying we would stop coming over if they didn't help us control the dogs, but to no avail.

"You can't stop coming over here; that's why you are here," they told us with unarguable Yanomamö logic.

There was a large bush outside the village loaded with *nijilomö* fruit. These were not very good to eat, but they sure made good missiles to hurl at the dogs, and these volleys normally gave us time to get over to the safety of the hearth of the girl's family. These people at least kept the dogs away from us once we got there. But, *oh,* just getting there!

The dogs were progressively getting braver, and we were getting more desperate. I knew, I just knew, I was going to be bitten or, worse yet, that Frannie would. Then I would have to doctor the girl. I threw harder and yelled louder in my attempts at protecting him. One evening we were running a bit late. Wanting to make it back home before dark, we hurriedly grabbed our protection against the dogs and went on into the village with a bit less than the normal stock of missiles. *I hope this gives us enough ammunition to get to the other side of the village,* I remember thinking.

The dogs, possibly aware that we were less prepared than usual, were extra-brave. Making many false runs at us, they caused us to use our limited hoard up quickly. Halfway across the *shabono,* we stood there empty-handed.

"Call off your dogs!" I screamed. The leader of the pack, the old, black dog, came in low for the attack. Frantically, I looked around. My hands were empty. I wondered briefly if I might not be able to outrun Frannie, but that would still leave me having to doctor the girl if he didn't make it. Looking around desperately, I spied a used Yanomamö war club lying on the ground, almost at my feet. The dog was scant feet away from us, coming in hard. Bending down, I grabbed up the club. Swinging it hard, I clubbed the dog down. With a feeble yelp, the dog dropped where he was and lay still. The rest of the dogs, seeing their hero fall, quickly ran away. The silence echoed for a brief moment through the village. People stared, first at me, then at the owners of the dog. All bedlam broke loose! The owners of the dog began to scream and wail.

To kill a Yanomamö dog is to invite sure and terrible retribution. I was petrified. My fright made me angry. I began to yell insults at them. "Yes," I shouted, "you have made me kill your prized hunter! I begged daily for you to tie it, now you have made me kill this beautiful animal." In my fright I waxed eloquent! I went on and on. The owners tried to shout me down, but I refused to be silenced. Taking the pose of a dignified warrior, I stood out in the center of the village and kept up my monologue. "See what you have made me do?" I repeated.

Finally, sentiment in the village shifted to my side. Woman after woman in the village began to blame the owners of the dog for not tying him up. Seeing the way it was going, Fran and I made our way out of the limelight and over to where he had to treat the injured girl. She was beginning to improve, for which we were very grateful. The owner went over to his dog as his family cried out for their animal.

It is an interesting fact that a Yanomamö dog may be a mangy, worthless old cur . . . until someone kills it. It then becomes the best dog anyone has ever owned. Its worth as a hunting companion is beyond value. Suffice it to say these dog owners were now beside themselves with grief and rage. Bending down, the guy touched his dog—which suddenly quivered. It was alive! It got to its feet and ran crookedly across the *shabono*. Staggering, it ran into one of the posts that held up the roof. Everyone laughed in relief. No one laughed louder than Fran and I did, however.

After that, the dogs were always tied up before we got to the village. My gratitude was endless, yet I had to think of important things that I was doing to keep Fran from realizing that

I wasn't helping him in the least. Finally, as time passed, the girl got better. After that, we could just dispense medicine from the little hut that had been made for that purpose; that was, until they came running and told us someone had fallen out of a tree, was all broken up, and could not walk. Would we come and help get them to the village? Of course we went . . . but that's a different story.

Way up the Ocamo River, there was this old witch doctor who always had a runny nose and a bad cough; he probably had an allergy from his *ebena,* the drug he was always snorting. He had already drunk almost the entire stock of cough medicine Fran and I had with us. Then I heard him start.

"Give me some of that red liquid for my cough," he demanded, shifting his big cud of tobacco to a more comfortable position between his bottom lip and teeth. Fran had not spent that much time with the Yanomamö yet, so he was still having a hard time with the language, but he knew enough to say, "No, we are almost out, and it is not helping you, anyway."

"Yes, it does help me. Without it, I am in desperate pain." He coughed once to demonstrate how badly he needed the medicine.

"Hey, Dawson, tell him we can't give him any more because it's not helping him." Fran looked over at me for assistance.

"No, he says he can't give you anymore. We are almost out. Besides, if you drink too much of this stuff, it will hurt you," I told the old guy.

He then went into a fit of coughing that threatened to tear his lungs out. (He was a consummate actor; I could tell because I'd grown up with people like him, but Fran was forever falling for their lines.) *Only the most hardened person could withstand him now,* I thought to myself. Sure enough, Fran gave in.

"OK, stop coughing. I will give you some," he said. He took the bottle and poured the required amount out into the spoon he was using. Bending down over the old guy, he held the spoon out. Remember, this was an old witch doctor. A couple of hours earlier, he had been way off somewhere, under the influence of his drugs, which he had had blown up his nose by his assistant. The aftereffects were never pretty. Mucus would run down and out of his nose for hours. As this is a family-type book, I won't go into greater detail. Suffice it to say that a thick, green-colored slime was now running out of this guy's nose. To further enhance his looks, he had that huge wad of green-colored tobacco I told you about earlier between his lower teeth and his bottom lip.

Now, picture Fran bending down to give him the medicine. You know how, when you are trying to get someone to do something, you subconsciously do the same thing? Well, Fran was trying to get the old guy to open his mouth wide for the medicine. I looked at Fran; his own mouth was wide open as

he tried to maneuver the spoon past the old guy's tobacco without spilling the cough medicine. I don't know if the old guy really had to cough for real this time, or if he still felt he had to convince Fran how really sick he was, but he coughed once more. By this time Fran was eye-level with him. The ol' guy coughed and hacked. Out of his mouth and directly down Frannie's throat went this great big ball of yellow-green tobacco slime. Frannie's mouth popped shut. Too late! The big green ball of slime had shot right down his throat! He gagged. His face turned white and I saw his Adam's apple bulge. He hacked and spit. He then ran and got his toothbrush and spent the next fifteen minutes brushing his teeth. He continued to spit and hack for the rest of the day. Bless his heart, I don't think he ate a thing for the next couple of days. He just *knew* he was going to die, for sure.

One of the hardest things I did on that trip was to convince ol' Cochran to continue to be the medicine dispenser. But Fran did get the old guy back. A couple of days later he came around complaining with the classic symptoms of malaria. Back then we used Aralen to treat it. While I don't know the ingredients in them, let me tell you, those pills are bitter. They were *so* bitter that, even now, fifteen years since I have taken one of them, just writing about them gives me a bitter taste in my mouth. Anyway, the old man came complaining to Frannie. I thought it was admirable how Fran could forget what the man had done and sit there and listen carefully as he recounted his symptoms.

"Yes, you have malaria," said Fran. "I have pills here for that. But they have to be chewed up slowly, one at a time, without water," Fran told him with a straight face. He mimed what he was telling him to make sure the old guy understood him, in spite of his lack of fluency in the language. The old guy nodded his head and took the pills. The first dose was, I believe, four big pills. He studied them intently for a minute, then turned to me.

"I have to chew them up without water?" he asked, just to make sure he had heard right.

I looked over at Fran. "Yes, my friend says these are new pills, and they must be chewed," I told our patient solemnly.

The old guy nodded his head. Taking his large cud of tobacco out of his mouth, he placed it carefully on the top of his foot. Tilting his head back as far as he could, he threw a pill in his mouth and slowly began to chew. His face screwed up, but he methodically, slowly, kept chewing, making sure he had the whole pill ground up. By this time his whole face was all contorted from the effects of the pill. A small crowd had gathered, as they always do during medicine call. Another old guy with the same symptoms watched his friend chewing on the second pill.

"Is it bitter? Is it bitter?" he kept asking. By this time the old guy's mouth was all pulled in, I can't imagine how it must have felt with no water to wash the taste out. He started on his third, then his fourth, and last pill. I could not believe it.

Boy, the Yanomamö sure are waiteli (*fierce),* I remember thinking. I couldn't imagine chewing up one pill, let alone four. Meanwhile his friend continued staring at his screwed-up face.

"Is it bitter? Is it sweet?" he kept asking. Finally the guy finished his last pill. Frannie handed him the gourd we used to give water to people.

"Now you can drink water," he told him. The old guy gratefully took the water gourd and finished it with one big gulp.

"Is it sweet? Is it sweet?" his friend kept asking.

"*Ma! Ma! Ma!* [No! No! No!] Now take your own pills," he yelled at his friend.

I never did figure out if the old man realized that Fran had skillfully gotten revenge on him for hacking and spitting down Fran's throat, but Fran felt a bit better, in any case.

13

THE AIRSTRIP AND
THE ALLIGATOR

RUBEN PINTOR

Fran and I were once more heading up the Ocamo River. On our second trip, we had spent most of our time in the village of Wabutawäteli. The residents there were much friendlier than the people of Yoblobä, perhaps because we had with us a young boy by the name of Shiocolewä. He had gone with his father to visit Cosh, and since he had relatives there he just stayed when his father went back home.

When we went downriver to TamaTama to build a houseboat, Shiocolewä went with us, staying there with us for about

131

six months. When he heard we were going to do a survey up the Ocamo River, he asked if he could go with us. Knowing the value of having someone along from the area, we readily agreed.

While in Wabutawäteli, the men of the village asked Fran and me if someone would come live with them full time and teach them about this new *Way* we were telling them about. "We like the sound of what you say," Shiocolewä's father told us, "but we do not know the trail. We need someone who has been down the trail to show us the way. We are willing to build a house for someone to live with us. We could even build you a landing path for your bird," he told us.

He had seen the plane when he was visiting in our village and been impressed with how fast it could go. I knew he would love to be the first village up here to have the noisy bird come down, carrying its load of foreigners.

"Well, we cannot make that decision," we told them. "We will have to go and ask our *Bada cabä* [leaders]."

"OK, go and ask them, but come right back. We want to get started right away," they urged us.

Now we were on our way back upriver. The leadership of the mission had told us to go up and help them build an airstrip. This would allow someone to fly in and do itinerant teaching in that entire area. *It would be exciting to get back there,* I thought.

We had had a good time with them and formed some close friendships. Still, there was always a bit of trepidation as well, because with the Yanomamö you never knew how you would be received. *What has happened in our absence? Who will be there this time, I wonder?*

But the biggest question was always: *I wonder who has died in our absence?* The hard thing was, it might take days to find out for sure. It is offensive to ask where so-and-so is if he *has* died—and if someone has died, his name is taboo. So, what to do? Generally, you pay attention. You observe carefully and notice how the people are acting. You watch for signs of recent grief.

This would include seeing someone's wife, mother, grown daughter, or some other close female relative with black on her face.

If someone was missing, I would wait around until none of his relatives was present. Then, quietly, I would try and ask. Even then, I had to be careful how I phrased my question. If the man had had a young son or daughter, it was easier.

"I have not seen [name-the-little-boy-or-girl's] father," I'd start out. "Have you all been with grief in my absence?" My voice is kept respectfully low and I make a point of making sure no one can overhear me. If the person has, in fact, passed away, the one I asked will nod his head in the affirmative. Then he might add a phrase or two.

"The arrow has in fact broken; don't mention it anymore." When speaking of the dead, the Yanomamö never refer directly to the person who has died. They begin speaking in a very formal style of Yanomamö, where they make vague references to the loss, and refer to the dead by such common objects as arrows, in the case of a man, or a clay pot or a water gourd in the case of a woman. The little-boy arrows, the *lujumasi,* are referred to in connection with the death of a little boy, and a little gourd in the case of a girl child.

"We had much sadness; we are still with much sadness." He will go on and on, with his hands clasped over his mouth, showing his displeasure. He will then go into the details of what happened, with the perceived, appropriate blame placed on the responsible village. To the Yanomamö, no death is accidental, so it must be avenged. Your informant will then fill you in on what has been done. Even their *attempts* at vengeance will be recounted. If a raid was unsuccessful, the village would be in a foul mood, ready to strike out at anyone. With all these reasons to expect possible violence, tension always mounted before arriving at a village.

And here we were, just a short way below the village of Wabutawä. I glanced back at my friends in the boat. Frannie was driving again. Ramon and Tito sat in the middle. Shiocolewä sat right behind me. He had insisted that he wanted to stay with Fran and me until we came back the second time.

The last time we had been in his village, I'd overheard his mother complain to him, "You let him still call you by your baby name, *Shiocolewä*?" she said with a frown. "You need to get you a man's name. You are a man now. I am unwilling to have people mocking you with a child's name."

"He is my friend," he had responded. "He is not mocking me. I will tell him when I get a new name. But when I want a new name, I am going to get me a real foreigner's name. I will use this one until I tire of it."

I grinned to myself. We had figured him to be about fourteen, and he didn't even look *that* old. *I guess his mother should know about how old he is,* I thought. He was a hard worker . . . and such a prankster! He was the life of our party. I sure didn't want to be offending him, so as we rode back downriver we tried to think of Spanish names he might like. Yanomamö hate a name someone else already has, so after a while we had used up the names of all our aunts and uncles, cousins, and any other names we could think of. I could come up with no new name, so he let it drop.

Later on, after we returned to TamaTama, I heard him asking my brother Gary to help him with a new name. Just as with every name I'd come up with, Shiocolewä knew someone else with the same name. Gary had just returned from the United States with his bride. They were going to be working here for a year before continuing in their missionary training.

"Marie, give Shiocolewä a new name," Gary said.

"I have a brother named Fernando," she answered. "How about that name?"

Shiocolewä thought for a moment. "Yes, I like it. That is my new name. Anyone who calls me *Shiocolewä* again will have to answer to me." It didn't take us long to shorten his name to Nando. So, he was proud to get home to his village and show off his new name. I knew I would have to be careful. The last thing I wanted to do was embarrass him by calling him *Shiocolewä* in front of his family.

When we arrived, the people of the village were all out on trek. Their gardens were not producing, so they were out hunting and gathering in the jungle until their gardens could support them again. Nando knew the areas his villagers trekked in, so we went out to see if we could find them. We finally did manage to locate them, and we told them the leaders of the mission had given permission for us to help them build an airstrip.

There was immediate enthusiasm for the project. With the Yanomamö, as long as you can make something a big game, you can hold their attention indefinitely, but let them just for a moment think that something is *work,* or a bore, and you will lose them. Now, having an airplane come to their village was about as exciting as you could get, so enthusiasm was high the next day as our group, along with about twenty-five of the men of the village, went to the spot where we planned to build the strip. It was about an hour-and-a-half walk from the village. That was considered too far away to walk back and forth every day, so we built temporary houses out near where we were building. Our one problem was water. The only water near our location was a small, landlocked swamp. The water was green and scummy. To get to water, you first had to scrape a thick scum out of the way. I dreaded even bathing in it. I felt much dirtier *after* bathing with that water than I did before getting into it, even after working in the hot sun all day long. (I mention this just so you can get an idea of the condition of the water.) The second day we were there Fran and I decided to quit at about 3:00 p.m. and walk out to the main river to get a decent drink. I was so thirsty I didn't even mind the three-hour walk (out and back) to the river. While out there, we bathed and washed our clothes. The water felt so cool and clean after the scum we had been drinking and bathing in!

None of the Yanomamö from Wabutawä walked out with us. They didn't understand what the fuss was all about, anyway. So you had to strain the water between your teeth? Just get used to it. One drank what was there. They thought it was enormously funny that we would go that far to get a drink of water. But we went—Fran, Ramon, Nando, and myself. We carried a one-gallon thermos with us to bring water back so we could have some decent water, at least for a bit, after we got back. I had even hoped to have enough to make a real pot of coffee. That swamp water was so strong it even ruined coffee. Sad to say, all those who'd had no desire to walk that far for a good drink had no qualms whatsoever about drinking whatever we brought back, so as soon as we got back, and after they passed our jug around, our fresh water supply was gone.

Did I mention that conditions up on the Upper Ocamo were in a near-crisis state? The area was, at that time, in the grip of a severe drought. This was the reason our water supply was so desperate. It also created other hazards.

One day, while walking back from the river, before arriving back at our camp, we smelled smoke. "Boy, I hope one of those guys didn't start a fire," Fran said. He was right. The Yanomamö are great pyromaniacs. We feared for our campsite, which was located right on the edge of the small grassland where we were building the airstrip. We hurried back the rest of the way. Sure enough, one of the guys had started a fire that had gotten out of hand. Turning with the wind that sprang up (just to overrun us, of course), the fire swept through our camp. Thankfully, Fran, Nando, and I had been camped a bit apart so as to keep away from the smoke of the fires the Yanomamö used to keep warm at night, and our stuff was unscathed. Most of the others were not so lucky. The fire destroyed many hammocks. This was the first of many setbacks we were to experience as we created the airstrip.

After our camp was destroyed by fire, we moved right out to where we had already cleared land for the airstrip. This way, we figured, we wouldn't have to worry anymore about fires getting out of control. It was gorgeous up there. We were in a valley that was completely surrounded by mountains. There were *edeweshi* palms all along the creeks, crisscrossing the grassland, the savanna—which, just because *we* were there, had all perversely dried up. Parrots of every size and shape and color came in every evening to roost. The noise was deafening, but the birds were so beautiful, especially the macaws! They were bright red and blue and gold. Some were just blue and gold, but as they wheeled in flight overhead, then came in low, most of them paired up, flying in perfect formation. What a sight! Every evening we were treated to the most beautiful aerial ballet you can imagine. It was just gorgeous and awe-inspiring! Gazing at them in the evening, it was easy to forget that tensions in camp were getting a bit high.

The biggest reason we were having problems was that it was becoming too much like work out in the hot sun day after day for our Yanomamö brethren. The excitement had worn off, and they either wanted the plane to land *now,* or just forget the whole thing. Different men, while not willing to call us outright liars, outwardly doubted our knowledge of how to construct an airstrip, especially when it came to the great length we were saying it had to be. Finally, everything came to a head.

"We quit!" they all announced one evening. "That plane is never going to land. You all just want us to grow old clearing land. And for what? This trail [pointing to the partially cleared airstrip] is much longer than that little *balimi* [eternal, their word for "metal"] thing we have seen fly over. What are you trying to do to us, anyway? I have seen your bird fly over, and it is no bigger than a large buzzard. Buzzards come in and land, *ktak,* on a branch! This is way longer than a buzzard would need. We are just doomed to work the rest of our lives hoping to catch a glimpse of this mythical *duudömö."*

"We also have ones that can land on branches," I said, crossing my fingers (and guessing that if the branch were big enough, some of the lighter helicopters could possibly land on a *couple* of them). "But the ones we have up here in the jungle have to run a long ways. If I call the plane in now, it will run off the end and crash and burn. Is that what you all want to happen? Come on, you guys; you have only been working about one moon. We told you when you started it would take a long time."

The head guy stood tall. "We have labored here many, many days." He held up the fingers on both hands to emphasize the large number of days that had indeed passed. "The sun has come and gone, with us away from our families. Moons have passed. We are tired. Call the airplane in now. We are tired of working while so many of us are saying there is no airplane to come in, anyway. If we could only see the plane, then maybe we would believe it is going to come in, and maybe I could talk the guys into working more."

Fran and I looked at each other. What could we do? How could we convince them that the one-hundred-plus meters we had carved out was only a third of the minimum space the pilots had told us they needed to land? The fact that the Yanomamö numbering system consisted only of one, two (a few), or many made it difficult for us to even tell them accurately how much longer it would take to finish. I tried everything I could think of, but still at least a third of the men went home in disappointment. The rest were dejected and long faced. We had to do something or we would lose them all.

That night our group got together and talked about what we could do. I forget who suggested it, but someone came up with the idea of us leaving early the next day and walking out to the river, where we had left our boat. We could head upriver while there was still light and get as far as we could before dark. After dark, we could begin to float downriver and try and hunt a tapir or some alligators. We could come back the next day with a lot of meat. This would encourage the guys who were working, and we could tell the women and children of the men working and they could come in and have a feast with their men. This would make everyone happy.

That sounded like a good idea! To be perfectly honest, I was getting a bit tired of all this pick-and-machete work myself. It would be great to get away for a while, even for one day.

We left bright and early the next morning. When we got to where we had left our boat, we found that the rest of the village was back in their permanent home. They had returned from being out on trek.

"Make sure you kill us a lot of meat," one of the guys who had left the work area told us.

"Listen," I said with a grin, "if you want meat, you had better get back out there and work, because there is no way we can try to kill meat for this whole village. If you want some of this meat, you have to be out there. Right there is where we are going to eat whatever we kill."

"You just kill something; I'll worry about where I eat it," I was told by one man with a smug grin. The guy talking had been one of the biggest troublemakers out on the work site. He was forever stirring up trouble. Looking back with the benefit of a few years, I see where I should have left it alone. But I was young and a bit hotheaded.

"You do not work; you do not eat," I told him, solemnly.

The next afternoon we came back into port with a lot of meat in our boat. Wouldn't you know it, the guy who had insisted that he would eat some, wherever he was, was right there waiting for us. As soon as we landed, and before we could even get out of the boat, he marched up to us. Reaching in, he grabbed up an alligator.

"Foreigners, I am eating this one," he challenged. I was tired, and, as I said, young and hotheaded.

"No, you are not. Put it down," I commanded. He tightened his grip on the gator's tail.

"This one is mine. There are plenty more in the boat to feed those poor miserable ones out at your folly. Leave it alone. I am eating this one."

I glanced into his eyes. He was very determined. The bad thing was that I had already crossed a line. I had *said* he would not eat it. Now, unless I was prepared to be known as someone who could be walked on, from then on, I had to back up what I'd said.

Staring him in the face, I told him, "Drop the alligator. It is mine. I say who is going to eat it. Who do you think I am? Do I look like a young child that you can just take meat away from?" I was getting a little hot about his attitude.

"You are worse than a child," he said. "You are a foreigner! Just a *nabä!*" He made the word sound like the worst insult he could think of. The crowd that had by now gathered laughed. The situation was quickly getting out of hand.

"Just give him the alligator, but cut off the tail," Ramon told me. "He is very mad right now, and it is not worth fighting over one alligator."

Ramon had been in many fights and probably figured he would have to jump in and take some blows for me, so he wanted to start giving me a way of compromising and saving face. But I was too far gone to listen to reason. "No, I told him when we left. I was only hunting for the men who are working. If he wants to eat alligator, let him go and start working—or go and kill his own alligator."

The man started yelling insults and threats at me. By then I'd realized I should have tried to compromise when Ramon suggested it. Now it looked like it was too late. I didn't know what was going to happen next.

Nando's father, the head man of the village, came down to the port. "What is going on?" he inquired. The crowd quickly filled him in.

"Give the alligator back," he told the man, who was still clutching the tail of the largest one. The rest of the villagers quickly sided with Nando's father and began yelling at the man for being a lazy good-for-nothing and worse.

Dropping the tail of the alligator, the man glared at me. "I will kill you for this," he told me. He was so angry he was literally shaking with rage. Like I said, I was young and hadn't learned to keep my mouth shut yet.

"You had better shoot straight," I told him, "because if you just wound me, I will be the last one you ever shoot."

His eyes bugged out. "I will shoot you," he repeated. "I will pretend I am not angry anymore, then I will go hunting with you. I will show you something to shoot, and when you shoot it, and your gun is empty, I will shoot you in the gut with a poison point."

"Well, now that you have told me that, do you think I am stupid enough to go anywhere with you?" I asked him, my voice full of contempt. By now I realized I was in way over my head, but I just didn't know how to get out. I felt it was important that we have the respect of the villagers we were working with, but how to get that respect without getting killed in the process, I still didn't know. I took a shell out of my rifle.

"This is what I would shoot the bird with," I told him. I jacked another shell out. "This is what I would shoot you with when you tried to kill me." Purposely, I jacked shell after shell out to show him how quickly I could shoot bullet after bullet. His experience with guns had been only with old, single-shot shotguns. He was impressed. By that time I had all twelve bullets in my hand.

"And there are this many more bullets still in the gun," I lied to him. "Do not mess with me. My skin says foreigner, but

I was born and raised with the Yanomamö of Coshilowäteli, and you know how *waiteli* [fierce] they are!"

Turning on his heel, he stalked away from the crowd. *That is one guy I hope never to have to confront again,* I thought to myself as we watched him go. *Boy, what a missionary I am! Not only am I not doing a good job demonstrating God's love, I am threatening to shoot the natives over a stinking alligator!* I felt terrible the whole way back out to the work site. I wondered how it would all end. I felt the man would be an enemy for life. Imagine my surprise when, as the meat was cooking, I looked up to see the guy join the other workers, his machete in hand.

"Well, if I have to humor you to get a piece of meat, I will pretend to work," he told me with a grin. I grinned in relief.

"Thank you, God," I prayed, "for protecting even stupid missionary wannabes." If there was one lesson I learned on those early trips, it was to be careful what you say. Don't make a big issue out of something that might not be that important.

The water situation continued to get worse. Thank goodness, though, on one of Ramon's hunting excursions he stumbled across a little stream that still had a good flow of water. This was only about half-an-hour's walk away from us. Now, every day we quit a bit early and rushed off to our stream. We took our thermos and as soon as we got back dumped it into the pot we used to boil coffee, so we even had a decent cup of coffee every day!

Something about the walk bothered Ramon, however, and he insisted every day that we walk down to the stream heavily armed. Nando had his arrows, Fran had an old shotgun, Ramon had his shotgun, and I carried my little .22 rifle. One day as we lay basking in the coolness of the water we heard something (or many *someones*) walking up on the high bank above us. Motioning us to silence, Ramon edged his way to shore, where he had placed his gun within arm's reach of the water. The rest of us had not taken his attitude of watchfulness to heart.

I looked for my gun. There it was, about twenty yards away, leaning against a tree. Boy, if I needed that in a hurry, I was a goner. Anyway, we listened to this whole troop of whoever they were walking through the dry leaves in the jungle above us. Normally you would never hear a Yanomamö war party like that, but the drought had made the leaves so dry that it was impossible to walk quietly. Ramon kept his gun ready. We heard them finally disappear in the distance.

Ramon worked his way carefully up the bank. Sticking his head up so he could see over the top of the bank, he watched carefully. Finally he slid back down.

"That was Yanomamö," he said. "I am not sure who they are after, but anyone coming this way and walking like that has to be on a raid to somewhere. We need to be very careful and quiet going home. And we need to warn the guys we are with about this. Their enemies may have heard that we have them out here working, and they might figure this would be a good time to avenge themselves. They know that while the guys are working it is hard to be constantly on guard."

I nodded grimly. That was the last thing we needed—for one of the guys we had out here working with us to get shot. We began to take Ramon's watchfulness much more seriously and also began to pray diligently for the Lord's protection over our entire group as we worked.

What a day it was when the strip was finally long enough for an airplane to land! We had a shortwave radio with us, and Fran used it to call Walt Mood, the Missionary Aviation Fellowship pilot.

"We have 330 meters of good, hard ground here, with a good approach," we told him.

"Where have you all been?" He demanded. "Everyone has been trying to call you for the last two weeks. But you all hold on tight, I'll be in next week," he told us.

They say time passes quickly when you're having fun, but it also just *passes.* Day had passed into day, and before we knew it, it had been three or four weeks since we had turned the radio on. We had been trying to conserve our battery, and so had not bothered with it—but try and tell *that* to your upset mom! We honestly had not realized that our families had been trying for a number of days to call us. They had just about decided to send someone up to find out what had happened to us when we called out. Quickly getting on the air, Dad asked us if we were OK.

"Yes, everything is fine," we told him.

"Have you all been attacked by anyone?" was his next question. I looked at the microphone in disbelief.

"Did he say 'attacked'?" I asked Fran. "We're fine," I repeated. "What's going on?"

He told us.

It seems our old friends in Yoblobä were at it again. Two months earlier, after we had passed their village, someone in the village had been bitten by a snake. Upon his return to the village, the witch doctor decided this was too powerful a spirit for him to deal with. Remember, nothing like this is ever an accident, or just an act of nature. A snake bite is always the result of some witchcraft. Quickly, the bitten man was rubbed down with leaves. Runners were sent with the leaves to the village of Seducudawä, where the most powerful shaman on the Padamo lived.

"He is not home," the runners were told, "He is down in Coshilowäteli." The runners headed there as fast as their feet could travel.

Getting there, they had no trouble locating their man.

"Yes, I will do what you ask," they were told. Coshishiwä placed the leaves they had brought with them just so and got the rest of his stuff ready. Quickly getting his dope stick and his little bundle of dope powder, he prepared to have someone blow it up his nose. The Yanomamö use *ebena* (*yopo* in Spanish) as the medium to help them get in contact with their spirits.

Meanwhile, a crowd had gathered. This was a Christian village now, and no one in the village did that anymore. Someone called the church leaders.

Bautista, the man better known as Shoefoot, confronted Freddie, the witch doctor. "No, we do not want our children seeing this. I do not want them hearing you chant and sing to the *jecula* here. If you want to do this, go home to your village. We do not want that here anymore."

Freddie the witch doctor was furious. "Just let him die," he told his new friends. "You see, I was willing to help, but they will not let me. I cannot do anything. Just let him die. The fault will be theirs." He packed up his *ebena* and his dope stick and tied up his hammock. Then, grabbing his stuff, he marched out of the village in a rage.

The men from Yoblobä left angry, as well. By the time they returned to their village, the man had in fact died. I'm sure he would have died anyway; from all accounts, the snake had been very large. That did not, however, stop the village from blaming Shoefoot and the entire village of Cosh. And guess who was only three hours above their village and didn't know a thing about it (and thus would not be on their guard)? Two young foreigners and Shoefoot's brother and brother-in-law. They made their plans.

When we heard everything that was going on, we began to put two and two together. Those raiders we had heard had been after us! Now Ramon was convinced he knew why he always felt so funny going to the small stream. "I know there have been eyes watching us," he told us solemnly. We agreed. Hindsight is always such that once suggested, everyone quickly recalls having had a similar experience.

Dad came back on the radio. "They've told everyone they're going to ambush you all as you come downriver by their village. We want you guys to fly out when the plane gets there," he said.

I looked at the rest of the guys. The boat and motor were mine, and I hated to lose them—but I also had quite an aversion to being shot. I left the choice up to them. "You all can fly," I told them, "but I don't have another boat and motor. I will take it out at night."

They all looked at each other.

"I'm sure I would get sick flying," Ramon said. "Besides, if they hear we flew out in fright, I would never be able to come up here again. I will go with you."

Everyone agreed. We then discussed how and when we should go. We had to wait for the plane, as someone had to be on the ground when the pilots went into an area for the first time. Still, we felt it was too dangerous to be out on the grassland so close to Yoblobä. And besides, with the airstrip done there was no reason to stay out here away from a good water source.

"Let's move out to the island," Nando suggested. "We only have to kill a week, so there is no reason to stay out here where there is no water."

What a beautiful idea! We could go and rest and swim on a beautiful island out in the middle of the Ocamo River. That had the added benefit of being hard for raiders to approach. We would be safe out there. So, we packed up, telling the guys who had been helping work on the airstrip that we would be coming back in seven days. I held up one hand: this day; I lowered one finger: this day; then another finger, until I'd used up the five fingers on one hand. Raising two on the other hand, I showed them when we would be back.

"You make sure you all come back on this day," I said. I slowly dropped and wiggled my last finger. "We will come back when the sun is about there." I pointed in the general direction of where 9:00 a.m. would be. "We have asked the pilot to bring in a machete for each of you." They were happy, and assured us that they would all be back. Naturally, they were!

We had some fine adventures out on that island, but what I remember the most is we about starved to death. I don't know where the game was, but we couldn't find a thing. Finally, on the third day of our hunt we saw a group of river otters. Normally the Yanomamö don't eat them, but we were all so hungry we made an exception. After cooking one up, we found out why they don't eat otter. The meat is tough and stringy. It reeks of fish and has none of the redeeming qualities of fish. But it was *food*.

Because we were having such a hard time finding anything to eat, we went back over to the airstrip two days early. We *borrowed* (and I use the term as they would) some bananas from the Yanomamö garden and went on out to wait for them to come back. Ramon immediately went on a scouting tour around our camp. He came back excited.

"They have been here," he said, "a large party. But they left about two days ago. Give me some shells."

I looked at him. He had not been saved too long, and I was hoping he wasn't starting to take this personally. "Ramon, remember what I said about people dying for God?" I looked at him intently.

"What are you talking about?" he asked. "I found a fruit tree, and there are a lot of turkeys in it. I can kill one for supper," he smiled. "I have buckshot anyway for those guys if they want to start something with me; I just need some birdshot."

I decided I needed to do some real teaching on what it might mean to suffer for the Lord, and possibly to be martyred. But I also figured it was too late to start that lesson on this trip. I just prayed that Ramon wouldn't stumble on someone lying in wait for us. He was an incredible warrior and a fantastic shot with either a bow and arrows or a shotgun.

He came back with two fat turkeys. Boy, we ate well that night! Ol' Cochran was a mighty fine cook if he had a little bit to work with. So, as I said, we ate well. We looked up at all the stars overhead. The nights were so clear it seemed you could reach up and touch them. We had watched those stars for so many nights it was like watching family. We both agreed that the constellation Orion wore black pants and a green shirt. It just seemed like something a hunter would wear.

Later that night I got up to use the restroom, and I use the term *restroom* loosely, too. Actually, I just walked a ways away from our hut, but I felt something touch my left arm. By the time I got back to my hammock my arm felt a little funny. Not really painful, just kind of funny. I fell asleep, but woke up about 4:00 a.m. with my whole arm throbbing. *What is going on?* I wondered. I woke the rest of the guys up and they looked at my arm. It was swollen to about two times its normal size. The pain and pressure were really uncomfortable. I took some pain medicine that Fran gave me and dozed back off again. We woke up at first light and began to break camp. We would be leaving for home as soon as the plane landed and we'd given out the machetes we had promised our helpers.

I should say everyone else broke camp. My arm hurt so badly it was all I could do just to sit quietly and keep it still. Every move jarred it to where I thought it was going to burst open. It was also now so swollen it had started to discolor.

At about nine in the morning the Yanomamö arrived, just as they'd said they would. It was amazing that even with such a poor counting system, as long as you gave them enough fingers or toes to count off every day, and pointed them to where the sun should be, they could keep any appointment.

We had the radio on and were gratified to hear that we had not been forgotten. The plane was coming. After dropping off a load of supplies at some other base, pilot Walt Mood told us he was on his way. "I'll be there in about half an hour," he told us. I translated this for the Yanomamö.

"He is on his way," I told them. Their excitement mounted. This was for real! The plane was really coming. What magic these *nabäs* had that they could throw their voices so far with that little black box. Some of them still eyed the radio transmission skeptically. They had to take on faith that I'd told them what the box had really said; they preferred to wait and see.

One of them noticed my arm because of how I sat holding it. By then, the pain was hard to hide. Looking at my arm intently, they talked among themselves. "Yes," they said. "He will die shortly." They talked about me in the third person, as if I were not there.

"He will die," they kept repeating. My arm hurt so much at that point I could believe them. I cleared my throat to make them aware that I was listening.

"What happened?" they asked me.

"I do not really know. I never really felt anything bite me. Something just touched me in the dark."

They looked at each other again. "Yes," they told me solemnly, "you are going to die. We saw this happen before. Someone goes out, and something touches them. Then they swell up until their arm or leg, whatever has been touched, just pops. Then they die. It is probably the bite of a spirit snake," they told me. "You are going to die."

Boy, what comforters, I thought. A few of the women who had come in with their husbands, hearing the commotion, came over to take a closer look.

"Yes," they said. They began to wail, further helping to encourage me.

I was grateful to finally hear someone yell that he could hear the sound of a motor off in the distance. That took everyone's attention off my arm. "Whew! Talk about encouraging," I told Frannie.

We waited for the plane. What a sight it was as we watched it swoop in, getting a closer look at the strip. Walt made three or four low passes over the strip. The Yanomamö were beside themselves with excitement. I couldn't help but rub it in.

"Now does it look like a buzzard?" I asked them. They all grinned sheepishly. A Cessna 185 might look pretty small flying over at about 6,000 feet, but it looks pretty big swooping in for a landing right in front of you.

Walt made his customary beautiful landing and rolled to a stop. The Yanomamö crowded around. Imagine their fascination. I liken their fascination and amazement to what we might feel if we suddenly came face to face with an alien spacecraft. They laughed in their exuberance. They yelled and hollered their appreciation when we unloaded not just machetes but axes and files for all the men, as well. Walt looked at Fran and me.

"I was told to bring you guys out if you want to come," he told me. Fran looked at me.

"Dawson, you go ahead and go so you can get your arm looked at," he told me.

Walt looked at me. "What happened to your arm?" he asked. I showed it to him.

"Yes, you'd better come with me," he told me.

"No, I can't. I talked all the rest of you guys into staying because of my boat and motor. It wouldn't look right for me to be the only one to leave," I told them. We talked a bit longer and Walt told us he had to go. We watched him taxi to the far end, then turn around. What a beautiful sight it was to watch that plane woosh up and away. We stood there watching it until it was out of sight behind the mountains. "OK," I finally said, "let's go home!"

Boy, my arm sure hurt! By the time we got out to our boat I was walking in a blur. The pain was making me hazy. It was a huge relief when we got out of the village and got into our boat and I could sit down.

"What should we do, Ramon?" I asked him. He had already told us he would not go down the river at night like a dog with its tail stuck between his legs. This had been my first thought. I've seen what their *lajacas* will do. I didn't even want to think about their poison points. But Ramon was firm, and I was hurting too much to argue.

"They will have a lookout posted on the bank where the river cuts in close above the village. Remember, then the river goes way back a ways. It will take us a while to go around, so they will know right when we are coming. We just need to be holding every weapon we own so that whoever is sitting there knows we are ready. He will know they cannot surprise us. He will go back and tell everyone that we are expecting trouble. To save face, once they know we know, they will all be gone from their village so they can say they never saw us go by."

It sounded good to us, so that is what we did—and Ramon was right. We never saw man, woman, or child as we came around the bend and went by the village. Two days later we pulled into TamaTama. My arm still hurt like the dickens and I was still young enough that it felt awfully nice to have my mom and sisters worry over me. We never found out what had caused my arm to swell, but it looked terrible when we arrived in TamaTama. They checked it for infection but couldn't get anything out. Dad fell back on his standard procedure.

"Let's pray," he told us, bowing his head. By the next day my arm was almost back to normal and, best of all, I was back home and still alive. Praise the Lord!

14

THE ANACONDA AND THE SWAMP

We started slowly across the swamp. Now, I think I am about as brave as most guys—at least, I've always tried to act that way. But something about swamps brings out the goosebumps in me. By the time we were halfway across, even my goosebumps had goosebumps. This swamp just looked like prime real estate for the giant anacondas the Indians liked telling so many stories about. These snakes *are* huge, and it's easy to believe even the most outlandish story about them, especially when you find yourself chin-deep in water so murky you can't see two inches below the surface.

At our campsite the night before, Ramon had told of a snake that had spent hours trying to eat Waica, a man we all knew from the village of Seducudawä. The only reason it didn't kill him was that this man had gotten between a bunch of vines, and the snake couldn't throw its coils over him. It had bitten the man high up on his leg, and had its jaws locked. Waica was losing strength fast and knew he couldn't hold out much longer. Suddenly he heard his little dog coming. It bravely began to

153

harass the snake. Finally the snake released its hold on the man's upper thigh and struck violently at the dog.

Waica figured this might be his only opportunity. He jumped out from the middle of the vines. Grabbing up his machete from the spot where he had dropped it, he lifted it high and brought it down with all his strength on the snake's sinewy body. His machete was razor-sharp and sliced right through the giant's mighty backbone. It writhed and thrashed violently, but now it was basically harmless and would soon be dead. Waica looked down at his leg. Blood was gushing out of the multiple puncture wounds in his thigh. He sat down, shaking. His dog came up to him, shaking its tail and whining. He clasped the dog's head to his chest.

"What a brave little dog you are," he groaned. He was in a bad way and desperately needed help.

He whistled the whistle the Yanomamö use when they need help in the jungle and was grateful to hear someone answer from not too far away. Together they got him back to his village, and the women went out to bring in the snake. There is a lot of meat on a snake that size, and they would not let it go to waste.

That afternoon, people from his village came to get medical help. I drove Gary and Sharon upriver by boat to treat him. (Remember, I don't do medicine.) I watched, though, as they cleaned his leg up. It looked like someone had taken a meat grinder to his thigh. We took Waica back to our village, where they spent weeks doctoring him as he fought infection. He finally did get better, but it took a long time. So that was one story they told that I knew to be true. My youngest brother, Jerald, chimed in with his own story.

"I remember it well," he started out. He paused to make sure he had everyone's attention. "One does not easily forget such a brush with death. Well, maybe not *death*. Maybe just plain idiocy would be a better word."

"It all started out innocently enough," Jerald continued. "My older brother, Joe, and I were on our way to TamaTama, the mission school base, to visit some friends before Joe left for college. Actually, I think there was a woman involved in the whole thing somehow, but for me it was just an excuse to spend some time traveling the river and to spend time with my friends.

"It was the beginning of summer vacation and the water had started its rise up the banks, but it was still low enough to make it necessary to navigate around sandbars. The trip to TT was uneventful"—which is to say the motor didn't break down, something that happened with alarming frequency for us.

"We enjoyed time with the friends in TT and started on the three-hour trip back up to Cosh. Our 20-horsepower Mercury outboard buzzed monotonously on the back of the fourteen-foot aluminum speedboat as we cruised up the river. As we were passing the island of Tigre (near Tigre Mountain), I looked over at the bank of the river and saw a huge anaconda snake curled up, sunning itself there. I yelled at Joe from the back of the boat and motioned over to the snake. Joe's eyes widened with excitement.

"'Holy cow!' he yelled. 'Let's stop and see if we can kill it. I heard they offer a lot of money for snake skins in the States!'"

"'Are you crazy?' I yelled back. Even so, I'd already slowed the boat and turned it in towards shore. We crawled out of the boat to get a better look at the leviathan, hoping that something would come to mind about how to kill it. Looking back years later, I wonder why we didn't have a shotgun with us, as we had always been taught that the only time you ever see anything worth shooting is when you've forgotten your gun. Sadly, not only had we forgotten our gun, but we also seemed to have forgotten any other lethal weapon, all the way down to a knife. I secretly wondered if Joe was going to try his hand at snake wrestling, like we'd heard about on TV.

"He was in love, though, and we all know what *that* does to our better judgment.

"Then Joe said, 'Hey, we can run over to Tigre Island and pick up some big rocks. Then we'll climb up on the log he's lying under and drop them on him. If we get one big enough, I bet it will kill him.'

"By this time I was beginning to get into the spirit of it. After all, this was a big snake, probably about twenty-eight to thirty feet long. Killing something like this without the use of modern tools would really be a feather in my cap, and certainly a story I could tell.

"We hopped in the boat and ran over to the island. After a bit of looking, we found some large rocks that weighed between fifty to seventy-five pounds each. We were able to carry them, but just barely. We hoisted three of them into the boat and made our way back over to the snake. As we wrestled the rocks out of the boat I kept throwing glances at the snake, hoping he wasn't going to get tired of the clanking and slither away.

"After we unloaded the rocks, Joe handed me one of the small wooden paddles we had for paddling the boat. 'Here, once I hit him with a rock he might try to make a run for it. If he does, finish him off with this paddle,' he said.

"I looked at the paddle, then at the snake. Had I been thinking clearly, I would have pointed out to Joe that if a seventy-five-pound rock didn't kill that snake, what made him think that a five-pound paddle would? But now was not the time for thinking! Now was the time for doing! I could almost hear the girls oooohing and aaahhing over me as I told the story of how I single-handedly killed a thirty-foot snake. I dutifully took my spot between the snake and the river as Joe picked up one of the rocks and scooted up the log to a place above the snake. I watched as Joe let go of the rock, expecting to see blood spurt or the snake jerk, or something. Instead I heard a 'plop' as the rock landed on the snake's back and then sank into the soft mud. Nothing, not even a quiver. *Was it dead?* Joe and I looked at each other.

"'Go check it out,' he said to me.

"'Um, let's throw one more rock at it to make sure,' was my reply. Joe grunted another rock up the log. *Plop.* This time the rock landed right on the snake's head. We grinned at each other. *This time for sure!* But wait, the snake had moved. I guess the large rock resting on his head was making him a bit uncomfortable, because he moved his head out from under the rock, but otherwise stayed just as he had been.

"'Boy, I'm glad I didn't go down there when you wanted me to,' I said to Joe.

"'I think he's injured, though,' Joe said. 'He's not running for the river and you'd think he would if he could by this time.'

"Right away my mind kicked into overdrive. *If I was the one who'd finished him off* . . . 'Here, you take the paddle and let me hit him with the last rock,' I told Joe. Since it was obvious that the snake was on his last leg, I guess Joe thought it was safe to man the paddle. I took the rock, the smallest of the three, and gingerly slid up the log. No sense in tempting fate by falling on top of a thirty-foot snake, I figured. I looked back at Joe and he nodded his readiness. As I lifted the rock above my head, I could almost feel myself counting all the money that this snakeskin was going to bring in. Not to mention the glory I would be basking in.

Whack! The rock landed on the snake's head. Whether he'd finally gotten tired of people throwing rocks at him or we finally managed to wake him up, we'll never know. Whatever it was, the snake had had enough. Slowly, he started to unwind himself. Slowly, he slithered his huge bulk toward the river.

"'Hit him with the paddle, Joe; don't let him get away!' I screamed. I looked back, expecting to see Joe bravely flailing the paddle in a desperate attempt to stop the snake. Instead, I heard the chain clanking in the boat as Joe untied the chain as fast as his shaking chicken hands could do it. Instead of trying to stop the snake, he was leaving me and hightailing it out of there.

"'Wait for me!' I screamed. Joe looked back at me, and then looked at the snake, which was still slowly disappearing into the water.

"'I'll come back when it's gone,' he shouted, shoving the boat out into the water. We both stared at the snake: he from the relative safety of the boat and about twenty meters of distance, and I from a more precarious position, perched over the snake on the deadfall. However, with every foot of snake that disappeared I felt better, since that was putting the head, or better yet, the *mouth* of the snake farther from me and closer to Joe. He must have realized this also, because as soon as the tail disappeared into the muddy water of the Orinoco, Chicken Joe came paddling back over to pick me up.

"After Joe brought the boat back I stepped into it and sat down. We both sat there for a couple of minutes in complete silence. Finally, I looked at Joe and said, 'You know, you've heard of the Hardy Boys; well, we're the *foolhardy* boys!' With that, I stepped to the back of the boat, started the motor, and headed the boat back up the river. So ended one of my many brushes with large anacondas. Yeah, there were others, though you'd think I'd have learned better after just one."

All of us nodded as my brother ended his story. We also had been guilty of carelessness when it came to huge snakes. One forgets how quickly they can move, getting carried away by the spirit of the fine and high adventure you are having with this creature. I, for one, always started rehearsing how I would tell the story once I got home as soon as we found the snake.

Joaquin and I had a story that was about on a par with Jerald's as far as acting like idiots. We had been paddling up this long swamp and, all of a sudden, I looked over to the bank and just about had a heart attack. There was one of the biggest snakes

I had ever seen. The only one bigger was possibly the one that Dad had speared so many years ago. It was coil on top of coil, sleeping in the hot, lazy afternoon. Joaquin immediately started dreaming about what it would be like to paddle back into the village with that much meat in our boat.

I started rehearsing the story I would tell to my girlfriend in TamaTama next week. We pulled into shore and very quietly got out of the boat. Creeping up to within about twenty yards of him, we began looking for his head. I had my gun ready, cocked, and aimed. I was ready for action. We walked around and around but simply could *not* locate the crazy head. As time went on and the sleeping giant showed no signs of waking up, we became careless. Before I knew it, I had leaned my rifle against a tree, and there we were . . . leaning right over this huge mountain of snake, peering in between the coils, trying to find his head. Evidently because of the ever-present bumblebees getting in his nostrils and eyes, the anaconda had hidden his head so that the bugs couldn't find it, which meant neither could we.

I was getting frustrated. Looking around, I spotted a large stick lying on the beach. It was about the size of a long baseball bat. "Here, Joaquin, take that stick, and hit him," I commanded. "Then when he wakes up to see what is bothering him, I will shoot him between the eyes."

Joaquin was about as big an idiot as I was, because without a moment's hesitation he picked up the stick and gave the snake a whack! I was so ready. One twitch and I was going to let the snake have it. It didn't move!

"Come on, you have to hit him harder than that. You did not even wake him up." Joaquin's jungle survival instincts were probably a bit sharper than my own, he being a Yanomamö. I never noticed him move over, so he was not between the snake and the water. Not only had I not noticed Joaquin move, but I had edged right into the place he had vacated, which is to say that I was standing between the snake and the river.

Joaquin reared back and let go with a *whap* that is still vibrating inside my head. Just then it occurred to me, for the first time, that standing between a water snake and the water, especially a frightened, giant water snake, is not too smart. The snake's coils disappeared like a stick of margarine placed in a microwave. *Shoot him in the eye?* Why, I never even saw its head, let alone its eye; it whipped by me in such a blur. Thankfully, the snake was more interested in getting to safety than in avenging himself. With barely a ripple, so great was his speed, he was gone.

Luckily, the swamp was shallow, so we jumped in our boat and furiously paddled after him. We could see his wake in the water, and so knew exactly where he was. As soon as he surfaced to breathe I was able to get him with a well-placed shot. These large snakes do not instantly stop moving, but continue to coil and turn for what seems like hours. It took us a long while to finally get him in our boat; every time we dragged one coil in, more of the snake climbed back out. We were two hot, tired, and muddy boys when we paddled back down to the village, but also, oh, so proud! This was a lot of meat and represented a feast for the entire village.

What stories I had with this one! He measured out at just a bit more than . . . wait, I can't put that in print. It would stunt his growth! Because, as any hunter can tell you, with a bit of coaxing, a fertile mind, and time to haze it out, any large game animal will continue to grow indefinitely.

I have to say here that, looking back, it was a whole lot more fun when we were young telling these stories to our girlfriends. They appreciated bravery. Our wives, in stark contrast, just flat-out told us we were fools, and to *grow up* already! Kinda took the fun out of a lot of it . . . but maybe they were right.

Back to the swamp. Chin-deep in the middle of it, it was easy to see that they were *so* right, but for some reason it was awfully hard to remember that.

Of course, while wading through the swamp it's easy to remember not to be stupid. Unfortunately, at that point all your mind wants to do is turn traitor. You remember all the snakes that you made angry and that got away. "No, no," my mind screams, "not that one; that snake is still out there, possibly wanting revenge." Once my brain got started on a memory, though, trying to shut it off was like trying to staunch Niagara Falls with a Band-Aid. It was like this.

We had portaged our boat up the falls at Shokeke. Ramon found this snake asleep in a deep hole in the rocks. It was obvious that the snake had eaten something large the previous week, so his meat would be inedible. We decided to leave him alone. Maybe another day we could find him and get him when his meat would be good to eat.

However, we were traveling with two friends from the United States, and they wanted to see the snake and get some pictures. We decided to pull him out. Well, you have never seen such a fight between man and reptile. We wanted him out, but he, with equal if not greater force of mind, had no intention of coming out of that hole. We managed to get a loop around his neck, and with the brute strength of about ten guys finally hauled him out. But that snake was mad!

That brings me to another thing. I've watched numerous shows on TV where someone jumps into the water and wrestles around for a bit, then comes climbing back out with this huge snake slung over his neck. I'm not sure where they get those snakes, but I'd be willing to wager money, they wouldn't do that to one of our *Amazonas* snakes. These snakes have never been told the house rules. They just *fight.*

But I digress: Back to the snake we'd encountered. We got him out, and our friends got their pictures. Then, of course, we had to let the snake go. Now, for those of you wondering, that was about as difficult as catching him. As I said, this snake was mad and couldn't care less what we wanted to do. How were we going to release him?

We probably should have just taken care of him in a more permanent manner, but they had gotten their pictures, so we let him go. Still, not a time went by, when we portaged through that spot, that I didn't think about that old snake, hoping he had forgotten the incident and had since moved on. Like I said, he was one *mad* snake.

So there I was with a group of guys halfway across this crazy swamp, and my mind was busy reviewing, cataloging, and refiling all the various snake stories I'd heard. My eyes desperately tried to pierce the water's murky depths, but to no avail. If something *was* in there, it would have me in a death grip before I was even aware that it was close. I knew that, but my eyes refused to accept defeat, and about wore themselves out darting hither and yon, trying to see. To be honest, chin-deep as we were, I don't know what I could have done to defend myself anyway—possibly just shoot myself to keep myself from suffering so much at the hands, or coils, or whatever part you want, of the snake.

Finally the water started to get shallower. Now, instead of chin-deep, it was chest-deep, then knee-deep. My goosebumps, feeling themselves safe again, began to relax and fade away. Suddenly Yacuwä stopped right in front of me so abruptly that I stumbled in my attempt to stop. He pointed. There in the knee-deep water was my worst nightmare: a giant anaconda. It was obviously hunting, as it was lying right on top of the tracks we had left in the swamp that morning as we started after the monkeys. Thankfully, it had chosen to wait in water shallow enough that we could see it.

We backed away, making a wide detour around it, then regrouping on the shore. The snake was easily visible in the shallow water.

"I want that snake," said Yacuwä. He pointed to a tree that had fallen out into the swamp. "We could crawl out on that, and that would put us right above the snake," he suggested.

"True," we all agreed, but then what? With its head under water, it was impossible to shoot him with my rifle. Yacuwä pointed at the bow and arrows Nando had. We could spear him with Nando's bow, he suggested. Nando took the bowstring off his six-foot-plus bow. The wood used for these bows is incredibly dense, so they do make good spears.

Yacuwä took the bow and climbed out onto the log. He peered intently into the water, making sure he could see the snake's head in the middle of the coils. Satisfied, he held the spear high and plunged it into the snake with as much power as he could. The water boiled and became so muddy we could no longer see anything.

"I know I killed it," he said. "Let's wait for the water to clear up so we can pull him out."

We enjoyed our brief rest, talking and laughing over the day's hunt. We were coming back loaded with spider monkeys, a Yanomamö delicacy, so everyone was happy.

Finally, the water started to clear. Nando climbed out onto the log to look. Quickly he backed off of it. "Give me your rifle," he said. "The snake's head is out of the water. You missed him," he told Yacuwä. We all trooped after him to look. Nando took careful aim, shot, and missed!

This was one insult too many for this snake. He wasn't sure what was going on, but it was enough! With a violent lunge he struck at Nando. All I saw before I was run over by someone was mouth! Snake's mouth! I'm not sure how it happened. Nando was farthest out on the log, but he beat us all back to shore. I looked around; Yacuwä was up a tree. I looked back around to see where the snake was. Thankfully, even though Yacuwä had missed the snake's head, he had pierced through its tail, effectively nailing it to the ground with the bow. The snake had come to the end of its body's length and had then had to stop because, as I said, he was nailed to the ground. Well, Yacuwä sheepishly climbed out of his tree, and Nando tried to explain how he had gotten over us to reach safe ground first.

He was mad. That snake had scared him! This had now become a personal fight. Putting his bowstring back on, Nando took up one of his arrows. "You can keep your silly little gun," he told me. "These arrows are a man's weapon."

He then shot and killed the snake with a well-placed arrow between the eyes.

15

DAD AND THE WIZARD OF OZ

Thinking back on yesterday when we were young and free,
The jungle was our kingdom and the river was our sea,
We played that we were mermaids and we did only good,
We even knew some golden elves who lived out in the woods.
Our laughter rang from tree to tree; we climbed their every limb.
Yes, we were young and happy when we lived way back then.

Now we are no longer mermaids; the elves were only in our minds.
We find that things are different; our dreams changed with the times.
But now, although we're older, when there's still a chance to be,
The jungle's still our kingdom; the river's still our sea!

—SANDY DAWSON JANK

No book about my life would be complete without a chapter devoted to my sisters. Did I mention I have five? As a matter of fact, I don't think I have even mentioned the fact that I have *nine* brothers and sisters. Yes, I have four brothers and five sisters. We are, from oldest to youngest: Steve, Gary, Faith, Velma, myself, Susan, Sandy, Sharon, Joseph, and Jerald. As a family, we were quite a crowd! I remember that when we were traveling back and forth between Venezuela and the United

States in the early days, it was cheaper to return by freighter. These tramp freighters stopped at most ports coming south, so it took a little over a week to get to Venezuela, but they had room for twelve passengers. Well, our family was in itself twelve persons, so it meant we had the whole boat to ourselves. It must have been quite a scene, because the return trips are all I remember of those early furloughs.

Back to my sisters . . . I guess with five brothers they *had* to become a feisty bunch, because they sure were. I remember we were always trying to keep them from getting so involved in fights among the Indians. The really difficult ones for them to stay out of were when some Yanomamö was beating up or abusing one of their little girlfriends.

One day the village of Seducudawäteli came down to try and get Mamodishoma. She was a skinny little girl, maybe eleven or twelve years old. Several men ran in and grabbed her by the arm and began to drag her to the river, where they had tied their canoe. She was, of course, screaming bloody murder! A crowd quickly formed. Her mother was hanging onto her other arm for dear life. Her brother Jacobo ran to help. Before too long she was the rope in a violent game of tug-of-war. Mamodishoma was not happy!

The commotion quickly drew us out, as well. By this time the tug-of-war had become just a snarled mass of humanity, with people screaming and yelling. Seducudawä still wanted to get her to the river, but the sheer mass of the weight they were now trying to pull made this a difficult task. They tried pulling people off the girl, but for every person they pulled off, someone else attached themselves to her.

My sisters became concerned that the crush of people on their friend was going to cause the girl to suffocate, or her arms to be pulled right off her little body. They stepped in. It was hard to tell in the mass of swirling brown bodies which ones were ours and which ones were invaders from the enemy village.

Sandy grabbed the first body she could get a good hold on. Jerking him up and off the pile, she held him up and looked at him.

"Oh, you are one of ours!" she apologized to Jacobo. Without even thinking about what she was doing, she casually threw him back onto the pile of people.

Fearing that with the girls getting involved their chances were getting worse, the Seducudawä men told the girls to go home. They were quite insistent, and one of them even pushed Sandy. That was too much for my hotheaded little sister. It was bad enough that they still had not been able to get Mamodishoma out from under the crowd, but now Sandy was being pushed. She rolled up her sleeves and gave them a piece of her mind.

"Come on!" she told her assailant. "Let's fight it out right here." I don't remember what or who stopped her, but she didn't get her fight. Our village *did* finally get Mamodishoma loose, and while the warriors kept the men of Seducudawä occupied my sister spirited her away to the sanctuary of our house.

By the way, Jacobo is a really small, short, little guy. Even though my sister is not that big, she somehow managed to hold him up in such a way that his feet were running briskly in midair. For years this story was always good for a few laughs. Someone would say, "How did his feet go?" They would then mimic someone trying to run in the air, and then they would say, "Oh, you are one of ours," and make the motion for throwing him back. How we howled . . . Sandy and Jacobo loudest of all.

Did I mention that we started a cattle program for the Yanomamö? We wanted to assure the Yanomamö of a supply of meat when their hunting got poor, and also figured it would be a good source of income for them. My sisters, of course, started naming every one of them (the cows, not the Indians).

"Only name the cows," we told them. "We will keep *them* a lot longer. The bulls will be killed, and then you all will feel bad."

Before we knew it, though, even the steers had names. My sisters are the most creative people you ever want to see when it comes to naming something. Well, they named the big bull Jabba the Hutt, after the *Star Wars* movie character. Jabba had one big flaw: we didn't have a fence that could even begin to hold him. Why, if we could have entered him in fence-jumping competitions we could all have retired as rich men by now! But there was no competition in the village, just peoples' gardens that he would not stay out of. Plus, we had an airstrip running right through the village. We figured the pilots would frown on running into a 1,500-pound head of beef, so we decided to rectify the situation in the only way possible. We were careful to keep the impending slaughter from my sisters, my wife (Reneé), and my boys, but the day of slaughter soon came and went, and things like this are hard to keep secret. So, there we were, enjoying a delicious steak luncheon, when Joshua looked at me with eyes as big as saucers.

"Dad, I heard we are eating Jabba. Are we eating Jabba, Dad?"

What could I say? The meat tasted so good, and I sure didn't want to spoil the meal for him. "We are eating beef, Josh, *beef!*"

He nodded. After a couple of more good chews, he piped up again. "Was Jabba's last name *Beef,* Dad?" I couldn't help but laugh. What could I say?

We grew up on Southern gospel music. Dad and Mom knew a preacher out of Washington, D.C. On one of our furloughs he gave them a whole bunch of records: *The Blackwood Brothers, The Stamps, The Happy Goodmans, The Statesmen Quartet,* and so many more. We all loved music, but no one more than my sisters. The whole time we were outside working or doing anything in or around the house you could hear them singing along with whoever was singing on our old record player. They would have it turned up so loud you could hear it from all around. And you know what? It is just about impossible to be in or get into a bad mood with such good music being played. The louder, the better. Well, that's what I thought, anyway. Many times I remember, as kids, we would be listening to one of the great old songs with the record player turned up as loud as it would go, and would finally realize that the loud thumping was coming not from the music, but from someone pounding on our door. We would open it and there would be three or four of the village shamans.

"Pepe! [That's what they called my dad.] Pepe, tell your daughters to turn that noise off," they would yell over the sound of the record player. "Tell them to turn it off, because when that noise is coming from your house, our spirits won't come to us. We chant and chant, but they won't come. They just stand far away, but won't come close. Tell them to turn off the noise!" (It's funny, even back then my sisters always got the blame for everything.)

My dad, ever the peacemaker, would try and soothe them by telling them that we were singing songs to the Supreme Spirit—and this Supreme Being loved them! They would mumble and move on back to their village. Dad would turn to us and speak, with a little smile.

"Turn it up, if it will go any higher!"

During my teenage years I had an on-again, off-again relationship with a cute little MK girl down at the dorm in TamaTama. One day I came home from visiting her, and it had not been one of our better visits, which meant it was off again. I wanted to play some country-and-western love music and feel sorry for myself while swinging in our hammock, but the girls were already using the record player and nothing I could say could talk them out of it. They were listening to the sound track of *The Wizard of Oz,* and in my brokenhearted condition it was the last thing in this world I wanted to hear. Finally, I stomped downstairs in a huff. Flopping into a chair, I must have muttered something because Dad and Mom asked me what was wrong. Without even thinking I told them.

"I want to listen to the record player, but the girls are listening to that stupid wizard record again."

Well! Dad was so against anything to do with witchcraft and whatnot that he stormed up the stairs. "I've allowed wild man Diamond, and rock-and-roll Elvis in this house," he roared, "but I am not about to allow any wizards." The girls' attempts to tell him it was a comedy fell on deaf ears. I ran up behind to lend him moral support. I couldn't help but put in one more point.

"Yes, and playing those 45 r.p.m. records is going to ruin our only needle, too."

That was too much for Sharon. Picking the plastic record up in frustration, she threw it toward me on the table. "Look, it's not a 45; it is a full-size record," she insisted.

Dad only saw her toss the record, without hearing what she had said. "Well, I can do better than that," he told her. Picking up the record, he stepped to the door of our houseboat. Drawing back, he "frisbeed" it out into the middle of the river.

The funniest thing about this incident was that a few days later the argument was totally forgotten. Our family didn't know how to keep grudges. We were all singing one of the songs and laughing about the story of *The Wizard of Oz*. Dad was sitting there listening and really enjoying himself, laughing about the story. "Boy, I would love to hear that. Where is that record? Let me listen to the story."

We all stared at him. "Dad," Sharon said as gently as she could, "you threw it in the river a couple of days ago."

Dad stared, first at her, and then at the rest of us. Finally, he looked at me. Knowing he was just about ready to come down on me, I'm sure I tried to sidetrack him about something else. That story still is good for a chuckle in our house!

Back on the subject of our *Great Hymns* records. I'm sure there are many reasons for Dad's and Mom's success with the Yanomamö, but I've always wondered how much of their success was because of the music we played praising our Lord. The demons just could not stand to hang around so much, so the people were able to listen better. The church in Coshilowäteli, even today, is still one of the only functioning churches among the Yanomamö Indians, so I think there is something to this theory.

Years later, when Reneé and I moved into the village of Shimaraña, I had cause to remember those old shamans coming to our house with complaints about the gospel music, saying their spirits would not come to them. We had just arrived, and had spent the better part of the day trying to get settled in. As it started to get dark, I found the old kerosene lantern left by the former missionary family. Quickly making sure it had fuel and that the wick was trimmed down properly, I struck a match and lit it. Then I hung it up on a nail on one of the rafter poles spanning the room and grinned at Reneé.

"Just like a second honeymoon!" I told her. (We had only been married about six months, and honestly still were on our honeymoon, it seemed.) "What more could you ask for? There is a beautiful river, with beautiful mountains all around, and now a nice, cozy little honeymoon cottage."

Suddenly our stillness was shattered by a loud chanting noise coming from the next hut over. *What in the world is that noise?* Reneé wondered. She had never heard a witch doctor before. Suddenly there were two more shamans chanting full bore. *This is just too creepy,* she finally decided.

Suddenly it did not seem like that cozy a spot. The honeymoon atmosphere was gone. We became very aware that the Bible says we are engaged in spiritual warfare. The forces of darkness seemed to be arrayed against us. It was then that I remembered the response we had had from the shamans as kids when my sisters played gospel music.

"What we need is a good tape recorder," I told Reneé. "That will take care of them, and if it won't, at least we could drown out the noise a bit."

Night after night we lay there listening to the witch doctors chant to their spirits. During the day they would come around and I would hang out in their houses, talking with them. It was obvious that Satan had them blinded to their bondage and fate. It got so that it was hard to sleep. Have you heard of things going bump in the night, or had the experience of just waking up in terror for no reason? Well, that's the kind of thing that was happening to us on a nightly basis. We began to declaim verse after verse of protection and victory, trying to build up our defenses against this oppression.

"Greater is He that is in you than he that is in the world," we would repeat to each other. But honestly, nothing helped . . . at least that we could see. Finally, after three months, it was time to return to the city to buy some food. We were pretty poorly supported back then, and I think most months we averaged less than $300 per month income to live on. Still, the fact that we spent most of our time out in the jungle where there was nothing to spend our money on helped us, allowing our saved money to grow. Then, when we came out we could spend it all before heading back to the jungle.

This time I determined not to spend it all on food. I was going to surprise Reneé. I went down to the store that sold good stereos. They had one there that I really liked. It cost almost as much as we made in one month, but I felt it would be worth it. I bought that stereo and carried it back out to the house.

"Here, maybe now we will be able to sleep," I told her. Her family had sent her a bunch of cassette tapes. I remember there were some good Michael Card cassettes and, of course, many of the Southern gospel groups that I had grown up with.

We flew back in to Shimaraña. The first day we again spent getting everything ready. The first thing I unpacked was the new stereo.

"Give me that tape that has the song, 'Dragon Slayer,'" I told Reneé. Before the shamans could get started that evening, we began playing the music. We didn't try to blast them out, but always tried to have it loud enough that we could hear our music without being bothered by their chanting. They would chant louder, and we would turn up the volume. The louder they went, the louder we turned up the volume. I remember wondering what was going to wear out first: their throats or our volume control. This stereo even had a *repeat* feature, so it would play over and over. Boy, we slept well that night, and the next, and the next. On the third day, about four of the main witch doctors came over to our house. They beat around the bush by talking of this and that. Finally, one of them cleared his throat.

"Listen," he said, "that *täa* that you listen to over here . . . that noise is really bothering us."

"Oh, what noise?" I asked him.

"That noise that you *hushöö* [play] all night. We don't like it."

I played innocent. "Oh, you mean my wife's *musica*," I said, using the word for music in Spanish. They don't have a good word in Yanomamö for music. "She plays that because you all were keeping her awake with all your chanting. She is not used to it like I am, and she could not sleep. So she plays that to drown out your chanting. Chant quieter," I told them with a grin.

"It does us no good to even chant," they told me, very seriously. "The *jecula* will not come when you play that noise. They stay far away. We want you to quit!"

I was thrilled and even a bit surprised to hear them say the same thing those other shamans had said so long ago on the Mavaca. Taking a deep breath, I told them all the reasons I could not quit. I also told them the reason their *jecula* would not come. Using all the stories I had been told by other shamans describing heaven, I began telling them of the Supreme Being that they called *Yai Wanonabälewä,* and how their *jecula* used to live there. Since I was telling them things from their own culture, they listened quietly.

"This Supreme Being loves you!" I told them, "and sent His own Son to become a Yanomamö so He could show you the way to get to His beautiful land. But, you know what? Most of you will never get to know this Being of Love. You are going to see Him with His arm raised in anger, because you have rejected the Good News that has been preached to you for over twenty years by other missionaries. You have heard and with your mouths you agree, but in your hearts you are unwilling to change."

All of a sudden they were quiet. *What was I saying?* They enjoyed hearing about a God of love. They were, of course, convinced of how lovable each and every one of them was. *Why would God not love them?* Slowly each man returned to his own house. I wondered if I had gone too far with them. We were still relatively new here. Were they going to accept us, or would this day mark the beginning of the end for us here?

The next day one of the men, Ketoni, showed up bright and early.

"Tell me more," he told me. His face was troubled. "I could not sleep last night thinking about a God that would have His arm raised in anger at me."

I started at John 3:16 and read those precious words: "For God so loved the world that He gave His only begotten Son that whosoever believeth on Him should not perish but have everlasting life." The Yanomamö didn't have the entire New Testament in their language, but they had enough for the verses I wanted.

I kept reading how Jesus told them He had not come to judge the world, but that the world was judged already because they had rejected the Son of God.

Ketoni listened very quietly. When I was finished he stayed silent for a while, just thinking. "I don't want to see an angry God," he finally told me. "I want to reach out to His outstretched hand that He is reaching out to me with right now." I could not believe my ears. The night before I had been afraid we were going to be asked to leave, and now here was one of the witch doctors asking how he could reach out and grasp the hand that God was reaching out to him! We talked longer . . . long enough for me to be very convinced that he really understood the gospel story. The years that other missionaries had spent in there, when it seemed they had been wasting their time, were suddenly starting to bear fruit. I called Reneé and the three of us bowed our heads as Ketoni asked the King of the Universe to forgive his sins and to make him one of His children. When we opened our eyes, I looked over at Reneé. Tears glistened in her eyes and she smiled at me.

"This is what it is all about, isn't it?" she said.

After one of our furloughs, when I was about seventeen years old, the mission leadership decided everyone needed to learn Spanish. Their argument was that since we were in Venezuela, a Spanish-speaking country, regardless of what tribe you worked in you needed to come out to Puerto Ayacucho and take the Spanish course. So, we found ourselves in town for a year, with my mom and dad and about five other families who were trying to learn Spanish—with myself and the other teenagers trying to stay out of trouble and, also, not die of boredom.

One day my sister Susan; Lynn Jank; Lynn's brother, Bobby; Jakie Towes; and I were over visiting an older couple who had been our dorm parents. We loved this couple dearly and showed it by always teasing "Mr. Lee," as Lynn called him.

On this particular day he was telling us that someone had broken into their house and stolen his tape recorder, which they used for language study.

"Well, Mr. Lee, they must have come in right over that wall," we told him. We pointed to a wall that consisted of tin sheets nailed up to form a wall but stopped about three-quarters of the way up the wall.

"Oh, no!" said Mr. Lee immediately. "My ears were tuned to the sound of that tin. There is no way anyone could get over that tin wall without waking me. I think it is the owners of the house that took it, and they have a set of keys. I am going to have to change the locks," he replied.

Well, all I had to hear was someone tell me that something could *not* be done and immediately it made me want to try. I looked at Jakie, and I could tell by the look in his eyes that he, too, was wondering how difficult it could be. After we left the house, I asked him about it.

"Well, can we do it?" I said.

Without missing a beat he answered. "Let's go in and take his alarm clock," he said.

We waited a couple of days and then got Gary Conklin and Bobby Jank. The four of us snuck around Mr. Lee's house until we were crouched down right outside the tin wall. It was about 11:00 p.m.

"Jake and I will go over and pass it to you guys," I whispered to them.

They nodded. I went in first, passing over the tin wall, with Jakie right behind me. The Lees were asleep in a side room, but they had left a light on, and boy, did I ever feel exposed. The first room we came to was the kitchen.

"Let's at least take something, just in case we have to flee before we get the alarm clock," Jakie whispered. I nodded, looking around. Spying the coffee pot, I passed it over the wall. Jakie grabbed the toaster. The next thing I knew, we were handing over the kitchen table, chairs, and anything else that wasn't fastened down.

We moved over into the living room. What possessed us I will never know. Neither Jakie nor I have ever been that motivated when it came to work, and here we were passing out sofas, end tables, couches, and anything else we could lay hands on. We snuck into a side room and finally found the alarm clock.

Jakie, not content with that, went into every room . . . and even unscrewed every light bulb. The only light left was the one that was burning in the hallway. We looked around, checking our work, and saw that the house was bare. Quickly, we climbed back over the wall. What a mountain of stuff! We wondered what to do with it. Someone came up with the idea of taking it over to our mission complex right down the block and surprising Mr. Lee with it when they came over to tell of the "great robbery."

"What are you all doing?" a voice behind me said.

I jerked around. Recognizing Gonzales, a Yécuana friend from up in our area of the jungle, we laughed and explained the prank we were playing on Mr. Lee.

"Well, my friend the barman over there was just getting ready to call the cops when I recognized you all and told him to wait until I could check you out," he told us, smiling. We assured him we were not permanently robbing the Lees and that we would put the stuff back.

We then worked harder than I can even describe. Not only did we have to lug the stuff around the block and up the street, but we had to boost the stuff over a nine-foot wall and down some stairs before we got to the print shop where Mr. Lee worked. We then put everything away and turned to go home. It was now about 2:00 a.m. Agreeing to meet back at the Lee house at about 6:00 a.m., we went to our separate houses.

Jake and I met back at the Lee house a little before six, but Gary and Bobby were nowhere to be found. Something felt wrong. I noticed the door was padlocked from the outside.

The house was empty. I got a sick feeling in my stomach. It was only going to be funny if we were there when they discovered their empty house and we could run around and help them look for their stuff. *What to do?* Jake could think a bit better on his feet than I could and I could tell from the look on his face that he was visualizing about the same thing I was.

"Let's put it all back!" he told me, verbalizing my panic.

If anything, my panic was worse than his. His father was on the field committee and would at least be able to save him from the rope, so to speak, whereas there were too many in the field who would have been more than happy to pull on any rope that was around my neck! We rushed around like idiots. It was at least easier getting the stuff out of the mission, as the huge gate was open, but we still had to boost everything back over Mr. Lee's wall—and now we were doing everything with two fewer people! Finally, we were almost finished, and only had to replace the light bulbs. We ran back outside to retrieve the basket Jakie had hidden them in when who should we see but Mr. Lee and his wife walking dejectedly up the sidewalk to their front door. As I said, we really thought the world of them and would never have done anything to intentionally hurt them, but it was obvious that we had. Mrs. Lee started to cry.

"We know what you all have done, and we forgive you," she sobbed.

Boy, I felt terrible. As I said, though, Jakie can think a bit faster on his feet than I can, and he came up with a winner.

"What? What have we done?"

"What have you done?" Mr. Lee shouted. I thought he was going to bust a blood vessel or something. "What have you done?" He repeated. He flung open the door. "That is what you've done! You've robbed us blind!"

Slowly his eyes began to bug out as they took in the scene. His mouth dropped open. Because there, back in perfect place, from the end tables to the coffee pot, including all the sofas and couches, was everything the couple owned. Only the light bulbs were still missing (Jakie still had the basket full of them in his hand). But because the sun was up and the house was awash with light streaming in through the windows and open door, and especially over the half-wall that had caused all this work and trouble, Mr. Lee didn't notice their absence.

"What?" Jakie repeated.

We almost got away with it. But in trying to put everything back so carefully, we'd been caught red-handed, as it were. We were marched over to the mission. We were two very subdued boys as we listened to everyone talking about "the robbery." I wondered where Gary Conklin and Bobby Jank were. I was really beginning to feel alone. Suddenly I heard someone speak.

"Well, it was wrong what they did, and I don't care if Gary Conklin has skipped the country! He needs to be brought back and made to pay for his crime!"

Holy Toledo! I thought. *It is jail for sure!* Gary was the only other noncommittee son in on the deal with us. I remembered too late that he and his family were scheduled to head back to their jungle base that morning. I figured Jakie and Bobby were fine; their dads would see that it didn't go too rough on them, but now, if Gary was gone, that would leave me to face the music all by myself. I looked around, trying to judge the attitude of the rest of the crowd. From the looks on their faces, I knew we were in for a long haul.

Slowly the whole story came out. Mrs. Lee had gotten up in the night to use the restroom. She tried to turn on the light and it didn't work. She glanced down to see what time it was and couldn't see the clock. She walked out to the kitchen to get a drink of water. The hall light was on, but nothing else worked. She groped her way around to where the bottle of water sat on the table. *Where was the water bottle, anyway?* It was a bit dark, but since by this time her eyes had adjusted to the night, it was not that dark. *She ought to be able to see the confounded table! Where in the heck was the silly thing? Mercy! It was gone!* Frantically she looked around. She ran in and called Mr. Lee.

"We have been robbed! The house is empty!" she wailed.

He jumped up! "It has to be the landlords! Maybe if I run over there I can catch them unloading the stuff," he told her.

He looked at his watch. It was a bit after 2:30 a.m. He quickly got dressed and rushed out. When he got to his landlord's house it was quiet and dark. Thinking quickly, he decided to head on down to the police station and report the crime. By this time it was about 4:00 a.m. and his game leg was really starting to bother him. He got home at about 5:30, but they were both too agitated to sleep, so they decided to go on down to the head committee person's house and report to him what had happened.

My eyes darted around the room of solemn-looking men, trying to judge the mood. I tried to catch Don's eye, as he and I went a long ways back. Of all the missionaries in the field, I considered Don and his wife, Jean, to be some of my closest friends. The only reason his son Mark had not been in on it was because he'd been up at boarding school at the time. Mark and I were as close as brothers. I hoped Don would remember that. I'd stayed with them for a long time when I was recovering from a lung infection. I now tried to read the expression on his face. I knew it would not have made him happy to be awakened at that time of night to be told of a robbery.

"What would you boys have done if a policeman had come by when you were carrying someone else's furniture down the street at two in the morning?" Jakie Toews father asked us.

The questions went on and on. We were lectured about the dangers of playing practical jokes until I think it would have been more merciful to have just taken us out and hung us. Of course, there was nothing we could do but sit there and nod our heads at the proper times. Finally it was over, or at least I thought it was over . . .

Fast forward to 1985. Susan was now Susan Lee (no relative of Mr. Lee), and Lynn Jank was now Lynn Olmstead. Susan and her husband, Jerry; Lynn and her husband, Steve; and Bobby were over at Reneé's and my house drinking coffee and shooting the breeze. I had a friend down visiting from the States. He was a single guy, and somehow the stories we were all telling got around to tales of past practical jokes. Bobby had somehow escaped untraumatized by the episode I've just related, so he started telling Tom about our practical joke on Mr. Lee. I had never enjoyed the story much and, as a matter of fact, had all but given up on practical jokes, *period*. So he told the whole story. Tom laughed till we thought he was having some kind of a fit or something.

The next week Tom left to go visit my brother Gary up in the jungle. Passing through Puerto Ayacucho, he stayed overnight there with a missionary couple. Tom, trying to be friendly, I'm sure, started telling the latest gossip and funny stories he had heard recently. One story led to another, and before he knew it, he was telling this couple he didn't know from Adam this story about how Mike Dawson, Bobby Jank, Jakie Toews, and Gary Conklin had stolen this couple's things, and etc., etc., etc. . . .

Well, the couple sat there and listened without cracking a smile. Tom knew he was at least a *decent* storyteller, so why weren't these people laughing? He finally finished his story, telling it just as Bobby had told him. A silence echoed through the room.

"Now, let me tell you what really happened," said a solemn Mr. Lee.

16

CULTURE SHOCK U.S.A.

I have had people tell me how hard culture shock hits during their first years on the mission field, but for me—and I'm sure I speak for most missionary kids—our culture shock takes place in the good old U.S.A. Furloughs were bad enough, but when we left Venezuela to go to Bible school, our first days of adjustment were rough!

This time when I left Venezuela, my best friend, Fran Cochran, and I traveled back together. We went through Camdenton, Missouri, to pick up a car that my brother Gary was lending us. It was an old Dodge, and I'll tell you what: people think it is dangerous in the Amazon jungle, but the jungle can't hold a candle to the danger we and everyone else on the U.S. highways between Camdenton and Jackson, Michigan, were subjected to during that first couple of days as Fran and I made our way up to Bible school in Jackson. Remember, up to this time we had only driven a dugout canoe. How in the world we ever got driver's licenses is beyond me!

What a time we had learning to drive in traffic, as we made our way on up the road. I think we both had our eyes closed as we drove through rush-hour traffic around Chicago. But miracles still happen and, yes, we have guardian angels (though I'm sure mine has asked to be reassigned more than once). Between our driving and the hollering from the one who wasn't driving giving directions to the other, by the time we arrived at the Bible school we were so tense and nervous it was a wonder we ever got the car parked and found our way into the lobby.

Once we got there and I took a good look around, I sure wondered what we were doing. I am a jungle boy, and the Bible school was in downtown Jackson. Not the pretty part of downtown, either! The farthest thing from my mind was any story that could come of this experience: good, bad, or indifferent. I furtively glanced around the crowded lobby of the Bible school, wondering if everyone there felt as lost as I did. *What feelings did they have hidden under all those cheerful smiles?* I checked to be sure my own smile was still firmly attached to my face. It was, but I knew it was just a facade. I glanced over at Fran Cochran. We had gone through a lot together during the two years we had worked with the Yanomamö in the Amazon jungles of Venezuela, but we'd finally come to the time when we couldn't talk the mission leadership out of even an extra month of service. They were firm! We had to go back to the States and go through missionary training school if we wanted to be missionaries.

Back then, I never quite understood what they thought we would learn in the United States that would make us better missionaries, but there was nothing else we could do. The New Tribes Mission's Venezuelan Field Policy stated that after finishing high school, you could stay down and work for one year. I had already gotten some extra time added to that by dragging my heels on my high school correspondence courses, but I *had* finally graduated, proving wrong many people who had said I would never finish school. Then, somehow, we had managed to get an extra year of missionary service after our first year was up, so now, as I said, they were standing firm on the requirements for our continuation.

Bible school started in August or early September; I forget the exact date. Franny and I left Venezuela with just enough time to arrive the day before classes started. Talk about your country bumpkins! We didn't even know what a pumpkin looked like, let alone what that *frost* on it was. Back where we'd grown up, everybody substituted squash for pumpkin, which is maybe one reason I still can't stomach pumpkin pie . . . but I digress. There we were. The first day was spent getting settled in, figuring out classes, and whatnot. The second day, we got a note to go and see the Dean of Students.

His name was Vern Bartlett. When I walked into his office and looked into his cold eyes, I knew this was not a social call. He offered us chairs and we sat on the edges of them with our feet under us, possibly to get a better run at the door. I looked at Cochran, feeling confident that I could beat him to the door, but didn't know if it was right to run off and leave my fellow man in danger. I didn't know if the same laws of conduct we had learned in the jungle applied here. Besides, it wasn't as if he had to worry about mad dogs or anything.

Mr. Bartlett started out by perusing some sheets of paper on his desk. I figured out later that they were our applications to the school, which we had done and sent in at the last minute. I was surprised to see they had actually beaten us here, as the Venezuelan mail system is so slow.

He looked up. Staring at each of us in turn, he finally settled on me. "What are your plans?" he asked me.

His question shocked me. *What did he mean by that? Wasn't it obvious? We were here to go to Bible school, so we could return and continue working with the Yanomamö.*

I nervously cleared my throat. I have sat in enough meetings to know that sometimes the simplest questions can be trick

185

ones. He continued gazing at me intently, waiting for an answer. Finally I blurted something out. "Well, we want to go to Bible school, and then return to Venezuela so we can help reach the Yanomamö." Franny nodded eagerly, thereby hoping to be let off a bit easier. If I had expected this administrator's frown to disappear, I was quite mistaken. He looked back down at our applications.

"I see here that neither of you have paid a cent towards your tuition, nor the $120 registration fee," he stated. "What are we to do with that?" He drummed his fingers on his desk as he waited for our reply. I looked at Franny.

Go ahead, I told him with my eyes. *Answer him.*

Franny cleared his throat. "Well, we figured we could get jobs and work it off," my friend started. "We were hoping the school would have different programs we could participate in, whereby we could earn some of our way—or maybe that you all could help us find a job," he finished lamely.

Boy, this is really going great! I thought. Here we are, finally. *The mission insisted that we come, and now we are both going to get kicked out on the second day.* To be honest, we still really were not sure what the big problem was. For me, I wasn't sure I wanted to be here, but I sure hated to get kicked out on my second day.

For the next twenty minutes or so Mr. Bartlett filled us in. "I am so tired of you spoiled 'MKs' coming here thinking you are something special and expecting others to pay your way. You have been out of school for the past two years. Why have you not gotten jobs and saved your money so you don't have to be a burden to someone? You probably figure to just sponge off of your parents. There they are down on the field, barely making ends meet, and instead of you boys getting jobs and working and helping them, you want to sponge off them."

He went on and on. We never could get a word in edgewise. I kept looking over at Franny, hoping he would tell the man we had just arrived from Venezuela and had had no time to get jobs just yet.

"I'm placing the both of you on probation," he declared. "If your grades don't measure up, and if you don't pay something towards your tuition, I'm kicking you both out of here. This is not a home for spoiled boys. If you are serious about studying, you won't have any trouble. That is all."

He picked up some other papers and barely glanced our way as we shamefacedly slunk toward the door.

What in the world are we doing here? I wondered. We sat off in a corner licking our wounds, probably looking like something the dog dragged in. We had not had time yet to check out the clothes in the school's mission barrel, so were still wearing our jungle clothes. We were sure everyone in the school knew we were already on probation, and we kept our eyes down so as not to be recognized.

Two pretty girls walked by, glancing our way. They stopped and said something to each other. They smiled and walked back toward us. We glanced furtively around, trying to find an escape route—at least *I* did. Cochran says he knew the taller of the two girls was the only girl for him as soon as they started walking toward us. They stopped in front of us.

"Hi!" the taller one said. "Would you by any chance be MKs?" Not waiting for an answer, her next question was, "What field are you all from?"

What in the heck gave us away? I wondered. We would spend the next two years in Bible school hearing all the different things that had given us away, not a single one of them complimentary. The reasons ranged from the way we were dressed to our "old, beaten-dog look," as this young lady put it. Our clothes may have been a bit out of style, but I sure didn't agree that we looked like beaten dogs. Sure, ol' Mr. Bartlett had taken a few whacks at us, verbally of course, but we were a long way from being licked.

But right then the two girls were a godsend. "Would you all like to go to the donut shop and get some donuts?" they asked. We both looked at each other. We didn't know a lot, but we did know that if you went to a place of eating with a girl, the guys were supposed to pay, and brother, were we broke! Still, we were packing a sweet tooth that wouldn't quit.

"Uh, not now; maybe later," we said wistfully. Janet insisted.

"Oh, come on, you can buy some other time. This will be my treat." They would not take no for an answer, so we followed them, meekly, to the donut shop at the front of the building. They introduced themselves. Janet was a missionary kid from Bolivia and Ruth was her friend.

"I can spot you jungle MKs from clear across the cafeteria!" Janet boasted. "But you two . . . " she finished lamely, letting her eyes say the rest without going into detail. I would have tried to come back with a quick retort, but it didn't seem right back-talking her with my mouth full of donut that she'd paid for.

By the time we were through a couple of donuts and the same amount of free refills on the coffee, Janet and Ruth had the whole story about our run-in with Mr. Bartlett. "You mean you all didn't even send in the $120 registration fee?" they asked. We looked at each other.

"What registration fee?"

It seems we were to have included some money with our applications when we mailed them in. I honestly never knew that, and Franny maintained his innocence as well.

"No wonder you guys about got kicked out," they both told us. "You have to have that money just to have your application looked at. What did you all do? Wait until the last minute, and then try and beat the applications here so they would have to take you?"

We hadn't realized there would be any doubt or any problem. The way the mission leadership had talked, there was a great big job to do and not enough people to do it, and we wanted to help. *What did this mean—that we might not be accepted?*

We finally did get settled in and even found some decent clothes out of the mission barrel. We found ourselves getting into a nice routine of classes in the morning, studying for the next day's classes, and then meeting Ruth and Janet for donuts. They both had jobs with the U.S. Postal Service, so they always insisted on buying. It was a good routine. Fran and I finally were able to get jobs as custodians with the Jackson School Department, so we were able to start paying some money toward our school bill, thereby keeping the powers-that-be happy enough to let us stay.

I met and became good friends with Paul Bramson from California. He was also in our class. One evening he was showing our floor some home movies he had taken, so I showed him some film that Fran and I had taken on one of our last trips. I asked Paul if he could help us edit the film. He agreed, and he was truly an artist in his field. After we finished the job, he was so pleased with the results of the pictures of the Yanomamö we had brought that he told our floor supervisor about the movie. We were asked if we wanted to show it. *Did we?* He shouldn't have even had to ask!

They gave us a date for the viewing. Paul, Fran, and I got to the chapel early to get set up, and I was surprised to see Mr. Bartlett come in and sit down toward the back. This was mainly a student activity and the only teacher who had to be there was the one on duty. But here was Mr. Bartlett. *Hmmm . . .*

O, God, I prayed, *please don't let anything happen. I sure would not want to have another run-in with him.*

We lowered the lights and started the movie. It played flawlessly. I was so thrilled. We had somehow captured the spirit of traveling by dugout canoe up whitewater with waves that will scare you to death, but with such incredible beauty. The pictures we had of the Yanomamö were worked in really well. As I said, Paul was a real artist.

After the film ended, students stood around asking questions. Mr. Bartlett remained seated. I was beginning to get a bit nervous. Finally, most of the students left and we began to take our equipment down. Just then, I felt someone standing behind me and turned around.

"I really enjoyed your film," he said, holding out his hand. "Did you take that?"

"Fran and I took it," I told him. "And Paul here edited it for us."

"I really enjoyed your film," he said again. "It brought back a lot of memories." He stood there looking at me for a long time. Then, tears came to his eyes. "I am terribly sorry for jumping on you all without finding out more about you," he said. "Could you both forgive me?" I could not believe it! He went on.

"I jumped to conclusions about you because of some personal problems of my own. Please forgive me." He stood around talking for a bit longer and then left.

Later I found out that Mr. Bartlett had worked with the Yanomamö in Brazil. His heart was still there, but because of medical problems he had not been allowed to return to the mission field. Seeing our film reminded him of his time working with this fascinating tribe.

In all my time growing up as a MK and working around missionaries, I suppose I could count on one hand the ones who have ever apologized to me for anything, let alone with tears in their eyes. I have never forgotten Mr. Bartlett. Of all my teachers in Bible school—shoot, I'll get broader than that, I'll say any school from elementary school all the way past the final phase of missionary training—I never met a teacher that I respected more.

17

TROUBLE ON THE PADAMO

As mentioned, Fran and I had gotten into a very good routine at school, but about two months after our arrival I received a letter from my brother, Gary, with some bad news. As soon as possible I called him. He was in the final phase of the New Tribes Mission training, known as Language School.

"What happened?" I asked, and he proceeded to tell me. Yacuwä, my best Yanomamö friend, had been up at his father's village and had gone on a raid with the villagers and had killed a man. I stared at the phone, not believing what I was hearing. Gary went on. Yacuwä had gone with them on a chest-pounding duel that had gotten out of hand. Nine guys were dead, and Yacuwä had killed one of them. I felt an instant sense of terror. *How could this have happened?*

"What should we do?" I asked Gary.

Dad was down in Cosh by himself. With a war up on the Padamo, it could very easily engulf Cosh. Bautista would probably try and mediate peace with them. Neither Gary nor I wanted Dad to be going up the Padamo without us, as the river is very dangerous. Gary had only four more months before he was

191

finished with school for good. I was only in my second month, with a long stretch of studies ahead, so it made good sense to me that I should go back until the problem was resolved. Yacuwä and I went so far back together anyway; I felt I should be down there if he needed help.

The next day found me in Mr. Bartlett's office. I explained everything to him. He listened in silence.

"So, what do you want from me?" he asked when I was finished.

"I just want you to understand what I am doing and why," I answered. He nodded his head.

"Come back when you can," he told me.

Less then a week later, I was paddling down the river with Yacuwä. We both quit paddling and just let the canoe drift. The boat kept heading down the river with the current. It had been a long day. We'd left Cosh at about 5:00 p.m., heading down to TamaTama to get some fuel and mail. It was now about 6:00 p.m. of the following day, and we were very tired. Still, we were only about three hours outside of TT, so we were making good time.

The quiet on the river was calming after the hectic week I had just passed getting my tickets and catching airplanes from Chicago to Miami, then to Caracas, and on to Puerto Ayacucho. I had made prior arrangements with the Missionary Aviation Fellowship, and they flew me in the next day. *Boy, it was good to be home!*

We were paddling downriver now to get some gas for our motor; we'd run out of this crucial supply in the village. I wanted to make a trip upriver to find out what was going on, but I needed to get gasoline first. Also, I wanted to find out as much as I could from Yacuwä. *What had happened? Who was blaming whom? Hopefully they have some gasoline in TT so we can get home,* I thought.

I knew it would take us about thirty hours of hard paddling to get down there, but I didn't care, as we had plenty to eat and I was happy to be back with my friend Yacuwä. He had been gone for more than a year, up visiting his parents in their village. It had been a hard year for him, and I could tell from the look in his eyes that he was burdened and sad. I knew the reason, of course; there are few, if any, secrets in the jungle. As we floated down the river, though, I let him tell me his story.

"As you know . . . " he began. Slowly his story came out. He had gone home last year to show his new bride to his parents. On his way back downriver with his young bride, eight or nine guys from the village of Toloboteli ("Rat Village"—*tolobo* honestly does mean "rat") had seen them paddling by and had jumped into their own canoes and caught up with them. While holding him down, they "took turns" with his wife. Yacuwä was devastated. Although his village—our village—had gone up there and given those guys a sound thrashing, it was hard for him to face the humiliation of what had happened to his wife. He left her there with her parents and went home to his family.

While up there, tensions that had been growing between his parents' village and a village just downriver erupted. His dad and all his uncles went with the rest of the village to avenge their pride against this other village. Yacuwä went along to watch. The other men in the village taunted him for not taking a more active role. He was, after all, the oldest nephew of the head man of the village. He was his father's oldest son. It looked bad for him not to be at their side.

It had not been expected to get out of hand. They were going to have a chest-pounding duel, and maybe a fight with war clubs. As a matter of fact, Yacuwä's village had left their lethal weapons outside the village with their wives.

At first light the men got ready to enter the other village. They painted their faces and upper bodies black. Many of them made wavy lines in their war paint to further enhance their fierce look.

The early morning fog hung thickly over the trees. Birds called, and somewhere in the distance Yacuwä heard a group of howler monkeys. He looked around. Everyone was ready! They were going to go in and teach this upstart village what it meant to really *badiquiayou* (pound with fist)! *No, they did not need arrows to teach this bunch! They would pound them so hard they would never take a deep breath again.*

But the offending village had other plans. While the men were still filing in to take the traditional pose, someone from inside the village stuck the barrel of an old Brazilian shotgun out through the palms and fired off a shot at point-blank range. Screams filled the early morning air as a warrior dropped dead. Old Nakishima (Black Tooth), the head man of his village, stood proud.

"Quick, women, bring my arrows! They have killed me!" he called. (The head man is always known by the name of his village, and anything done to anyone in his village is considered done to him.) The women ran in with the arrows, each one with her own man's weapons.

Suddenly Yacuwä found himself with his own arrows ready. He was still not prepared to kill anyone. He had accepted the message of peace, and had enjoyed such contentment when he'd committed his life to Christ that he had no intention of getting back into a life of fear and killing. He would just watch . . . but his arrows were in his hands.

His father, two uncles, and the rest of the men of his village were at a tremendous disadvantage. They were right out in the middle of the village and they were totally surrounded. They dodged arrow after arrow from men shooting in all directions. Arrow after arrow found its mark.

Suddenly, *tak!* An arrow found its mark in his uncle's back. *Where did that arrow come from?* Looking in the direction of where the arrow came from, Yacuwä saw a man running back behind a wall of firewood. Before he knew it, his bow was drawn back, his arrow steady. The man had almost made it to safety. Leading the target as he had been taught to do during our many mock wars, Yacuwä let fly his arrow. The arrow flew true, and he watched in horror as the man pitched over on his face and lay still. He was dead. Yacuwä, the Yanomamö boy who wanted nothing but to tell his people about a God who loved them so much that He had sent His only Son to become a Yanomamö, had killed a man. God could never use him now. His life was over.

And still there were arrows flying everywhere. Yacuwä and his father managed to get the warriors who could still shoot to edge their way slowly toward the place that had been left unguarded by the man Yacuwä had shot. They made their way out of the village and took stock. Four of their number were missing. Yacuwä had seen his uncle fall, with at least four arrows in him. He had also seen his uncle kill three of the four guys who had been foolish enough to show themselves when they shot at him, and Yacuwä had killed the fourth. The fifth guy, who had really finished him off, had, to the Yanomamö way of thinking, been a coward. He was the guy who had started the whole thing by shooting from a point of ambush. He had stuck his gun back out and, while remaining hidden himself, had shot old Black Tooth in the neck, finishing him off.

The early morning fog still shrouded the trees. The birds no longer could be heard over the noise of grief and anger. The women were wailing, bemoaning their dead on both sides. The old ladies went inside the village to bring out their dead. Screaming insults as only a Yanomamö female can do, they gently gathered up each dead warrior and moved slowly out of the offending village. The women inside answered insult for insult, but there were no victors in this battle. Each village suffered many dead: four from one village and five from the other.

In Yanomamö terms, it was a horrible slaughter. Normally their fights consist of one or two deaths from ambush. This time they had four men dead, and the other village had five dead. The wailing now was almost louder than you could imagine.

Even the warriors joined in the loud weeping. Many still wanted to avenge themselves even more than they already had. There was talk of setting fire to the village to drive the people out, but the older and wiser ones prevailed.

Slowly they made their way back down the trail to their canoes. Inside the village, five men lay dead or dying, with three more wounded. One guy, Chivirito, had a long gash across his face where he had narrowly escaped death by jerking his head back at the last minute. He was going to survive this fight, but he would carry the scar from that *lajaca* (large bamboo point) for the rest of his life.

Yacuwä had other scars. He could not get the sight of the man running, and at the last minute throwing up his arms and falling down with Yacuwä's arrow standing tall in his back, out of his mind. Nightly he relived the whole sequence. To be honest, he had tried to talk his father out of going. But it had become a pride issue, and nothing he could say would dissuade his father from going and standing with his brothers. Now one of the brothers was dead, as were three other men from their village. The death wail sounded loud in the village, long into the night. He knew it was the same in the other village. *Why had he gone?* For all his reluctance, giving in and going had resulted in the obvious: unresolved resentment, fuel for another possible fight, and, for the Yanomamö, the most feared outcome of all, causing a death!

He went along with the other ones who had killed as they did the *unocai* ritual. This meant that there was very little food he could eat and that he could not touch himself with his hands. His hands were dirty. He had killed a man. According to Yanomamö tradition, if he touched himself his body would break out in large sores. If he touched anywhere near his eyes, he would slowly go blind. Why, everyone knew the stories about guys who forgot this and touched themselves; the results were too horrible even to want to think about. So now he had to be extremely careful. Not only were the sores painful, but they would slowly eat away at him until he died, a victim of his own touch, because he had not cleansed himself properly.

Yacuwä had two little sticks stuck in the holes through his earlobes. With these sticks he scratched himself. Also with these sticks, while in *unocai,* he would pick up what food he could still eat. This mainly consisted of the small plantain called *maicoshi.* These could be eaten only after being roasted in the fire. They had to be done perfectly; they could not be burned in any way. They could not be boiled, nor could one make a drink out of them. You had to be careful not to let the sticks fall, nor to touch anything else. When he was done with the sticks, he cleaned them with water and placed them back in the holes in his earlobes. They could touch him only. They were unclean. He listened carefully as an older man who had done the cleansing ritual many times told him what to expect.

"You will see as if in a dream the one you have killed coming towards you," he was told. "Do not show fear. He will have either a *lajaca,* or an arrow with this bamboo point in it. He will come at you to spear you with it. Lie there in your hammock with your hand covering your mouth so he will know you are unafraid. Do not attempt to get away. When he spears you, don't scream, just go *'herrrr.'* This will show him you were a worthy opponent. If you pass this test, this will assure that you have gotten what he had to make him *waiteli.* But if you try and get away, or if you scream like a woman, then he will have avenged himself against you even in death. You will get none of his good attributes, and will always be *quilishi,* or afraid.

"If the one you killed was a good shot with an arrow, a true *Sujilinawä* (a legendary figure in Yanomamö mythology who is said to have shot the moon so that blood dripped out), pay special attention. Once he spears you with his arrow and you have passed the bravery test by not trying to get away or screaming, he will give you his arrow. At that point he will stop being like one who is angry, and will greet you like a brother. The arrow he gives you will ensure that you become the very best possible shot. You will be able to hit the smallest bird up in the highest tree . . . or shoot the leaping *basho* [spider monkey], as he makes his flying leaps from the top of the tallest jungle tree. [Note: During the *unocai* ritual, much of what made a Yanomamö *waiteli* (fierce), or a good shot, was transferred to the person doing the ritual. Because of this, the Yanomamö only want to kill someone who is known as fierce or a good shot; in other words, they want to kill the best warrior. They almost never kill indiscriminately.]

"Finally, when your ritual is coming to an end, you will see the great *mojomö,* the harpy eagle. He will come flying down from the top of the *walimaji* [kapok tree] where he lives. He will fly down and land near you. He might even land right on your shoulder. Don't be afraid. Even when he pecks your chest or face, just stand there. This is the spirit of the one you killed. The *mojomö* is the spirit image of the man. The eagle will look at you and then will fly away. Then your ritual is over."

These rituals vary in length from group to group, but after about seven days, they all put together their little sticks that they ate and scratched themselves with. Making a bundle of their hammocks, they go out into the jungle. They stay there together as a group until they come to a place in the trail. There they each split off on their own, looking for a certain type of tree.

Yacuwä was careful. Finding the *tomolo* tree of the right size, he took out the little bag of feathers and *nana* (onoto) paint he had brought for just this purpose. He used these feathers and paint and decorated the tree. Up about where his head was he stuck the white, downy feathers of the hawk. Down lower, he tied the armband made of the head feathers of the curasao bird; then he stuck the tail feathers of the scarlet macaw between these and the trunk of the tree, with the macaw feathers sticking straight up. Then, hanging from the armband he placed all the feathers of the *moi* bird. (These are very small, colorful birds, and the Yanomamö use the feathers to make themselves colorful.) The deep blues, reds, and whites of the feathers contrast beautifully with the red nana-painted tree trunk.

When Yacuwä had the tree decorated to his satisfaction, he tied his hammock just so, letting the hammock hang down. Carefully he placed the small sticks he had used in his ritual. Beside them he placed the gourd he had used to drink out of. Standing beside them, tied up with a length of *mlacamö toto,* he left his bow and arrows. The act was now complete. The tree would take the guilt for the life he had claimed. His village would avoid this place for a long time. It was death! But he could now forget it. It was over.

I looked at Yacuwä. The sadness in his eyes was evidence to me that it was not over for him, either emotionally or spiritually.

"If it is over, why are you still so sad?" I asked him. He looked away, possibly so I would not see the tears welling up in his eyes.

"When I had God's Spirit living in me, I always felt so alive. Now my life is heavy. My spirit is always sad. When I finished *unocaimou,* I was supposed to forget everything. I should sing the songs of bravery. I avenged my uncle on the spot. Before his killer could even boast of his good shot, I wiped him out— as if he never was! No more will his name be heard. His bones are still hanging in a basket, so that when his young son gets old enough his people will tell him about a father he never got to know. Not so his son will know him, or miss him, but to infuriate him, so he will drink his bones, and come after us, and try to kill someone from my father's village to avenge the death of a father he barely knew. *I did that.* I caused this death. I caused this young child to have to grow up without a father. Where will it end? Why did I not just stay home? Now God's Spirit has left me, and I am alone with my grief. God says you should not kill, because He made man and breathed His own breath into him. I took that man's breath away. Now God has no purpose for me," he ended, with great, sad eyes staring out at me.

Looking intently at Yacuwä, I asked him, "What does God's Word say?"

"I do not know," he answered. "All I know is He says not to kill."

"Yes, but what does His Word say we are to do when we disobey?" I insisted.

We did not as yet have the entire New Testament in Yanomamö, but we did have most of it printed up in little booklet form. Yacuwä had some portion of this with him. I was always amazed that he carried it so faithfully. He had never learned to read well, but always had his copy of the Scriptures with him, and whenever in our travels it was convenient, he would pull it out and go over different verses. He had never learned to read to himself, so you could hear him going over the verse, first breaking it down in syllables, then haltingly saying a word, then repeating the word with more confidence. He repeated this process for every word in the sentence. Finally, when he was finished the sentence, he would start over from the beginning and read it right through. It was a long process, and by the time he had finished a verse he—and everyone within earshot—was exhausted.

We got out his copy, finding 1 John 1:9. Because I wanted him to *really* understand it, I read it to him. "If we confess our sins, He is faithful and just to forgive us our sins, and to cleanse us from all unrighteousness."

After reading this, I told him, "God desires to make your heart light again. He says that if you confess your sin to Him, He will clean your heart out. Not in the way that the tree couldn't do, because it was just a tree. God can cleanse your heart because His Son Jesus took that sin of you killing that man, and paid the full price for that sin. Jesus took the punishment for that mistake, as if He Himself had shot that arrow and killed that man."

Tears were running down Yacuwä's face for real now. "Could God really forgive me?" he whispered.

"God's Word says it, and God Himself has said He cannot lie," I told him. Together we bowed our heads.

"Father God," Yacuwä said. "I went somewhere where I knew I had no business going. I shot and killed a man . . . a man you breathed your own breath into. I took this man's breath away. This is bad. My spirit is really heavy over this, and I am suffering greatly. Your Word says that if I come to you, telling You what I have done, You will clean my heart out, so it will not be heavy anymore. I desire to live my life for You, if You still want me. Father, make my heart clean again! I desire to serve You, and live my life for You."

I looked up, surprised to see the lights of TamaTama ahead of us on the river. I honestly had not even noticed that it was getting dark, let alone that we were already there. We grabbed our paddles and fought the current, striving to bring the big dugout canoe onto the bank. Tying it up, we walked up the hill together, looking for someone to help us get the needed fuel to head back home. I wasn't sure, but it appeared to me that Yacuwä's step had a lightness to it that I had not noticed previously.

On future trips up to the area that Bautista and I made, we found that both villages were very sick of killing. Both villages were willing to stop the fighting, as there had been almost an equal number of deaths. Both sides told us that if the other village was willing to stop killing, they were willing to stop it as well. The fighting was over!

18

THE MOST
BEAUTIFUL GIRL

Between trips upriver with Bautista, I was able to help Mom and Dad out and to spend enough time there to encourage Yacuwä. Before I knew it, the year was gone and summer was almost over. Then Gary and his wife, Marie, returned to Venezuela, so I no longer had an excuse to stick around. The mission leadership was once again starting to ask what I had in mind, so I decided to return to Bible school and see if this time I couldn't finish.

Also, upon arriving back in Venezuela, my girlfriend, the one I'd maintained the on-again, off-again relationship with, broke up with me for good. *So . . .* let's just fast-forward through the next couple of years. After she broke up with me, I didn't think there was much to live for, let alone to write about. Still, time does keep going and life goes on, even when relationships don't work out. Now, at last, here I was still stateside and in the final phase of missionary training: Language School.

I hope the time goes fast, was all I could think. It seems we had studied so long that the joy of what we were studying had worn off. We studied till it seemed as if there was merit just in the fact that we were studying, not whether we ever did anything with what we'd learned. But anyway, I was here and, Lord willing, in another five months I would be finished!

About this time I had driven up from Florida, where I had done my missionary boot-camp training with a friend, Mark Archer. Bible school and boot camp all blurred together in my mind. My eyes were fixed on the finish line now, and all I had left to finish was Language School. I did not want any complications. As we were driving into the campus, though, looking for our cabin, we passed two girls walking toward us. As we passed them, one of the girls must have said something amusing because the taller, dark-haired girl smiled the most dazzling smile I had ever seen. I could not help but stare as my breath was caught up by her beauty.

"Who is that girl?" I wondered aloud to Mark.

We walked down to the lake that first day after we arrived in Camdenton, Missouri. We had decided it was just too hot to do anything but go swimming for a bit. We got down to the swimming area, ran out on the dock, and jumped into the lake. In the background I thought I heard someone blowing a whistle. When I came up, I could really hear the whistleblower! It was urgently sounding "buddy call," and would not be silent. Looking toward the offending sound, my heart stopped. The whistle-blower was the same olive-skinned girl with the beautiful smile I had seen on the pathway the day before. My heart started to pound. *Is this what Cochran meant?* I wondered? *Is this what he felt when he first met Janet?* By the way, ol' Cochran and Janet ended up getting married a year after she came and picked us off the bench and fed us all those donuts.

Back to the present, however. The whistleblower was not smiling now, and she seemed to be directing her whistleblowing at us. We waved in acknowledgment. She motioned for us to get out of the water. Trying to act nonchalant, we slowly swam over to the dock. Slower yet, I clambered up to stand beside Mark.

I tried to act cool, but deep down inside my heart was pounding. I could not take my eyes off the angry girl walking toward us. Her hair flowed in soft, black waves that framed her beautiful, oval face. Her piercing, dark eyes sparkled as she made some unheard comment to her friend, who was walking beside her. The look she directed at us was anything but friendly, however, and she wasted no time delivering her message.

"Look, if you all want to swim here, you have to take a swim test so that we know your limits. I am the lifeguard and I can give you the test in about fifteen minutes," she stated.

"Look, you saw us swimming. Can't you just let us swim?" I asked, trying to turn on my most winning smile. I was smiling, but inside my heart just hammered away in my chest. I had never seen a more beautiful woman.

"I really should kick you all out of the water for the rest of the day for just running and jumping in, but if you will just be patient I will give you the test. Rules are rules," she added, a little too smugly, I thought.

What a crock! Rules are rules! Boy, didn't I know that. How many times had I heard that?

"Oh, well," I told Mark, "we'll just have to wait because she sure doesn't look like she will change her mind."

The fifteen minutes passed and it was time for our test. Mark went first. The test consisted of having to swim out to a raft that was anchored out in deep water in a certain amount of time. The stopwatch was started when your feet left the dock and was stopped when you climbed out on the raft. I measured the distance in my mind. It really didn't look much farther than the big rocks that were out from TamaTama. There was a big rock on shore that we called the "four footer," and then farther upriver were other big rocks. On many occasions while playing tag there I had swum all that way underwater to tag an opponent. I decided to try it now. Besides, this girl was starting to bother me.

When it was my turn I dove off the dock. Instead of coming to the surface and swimming, I continued to swim strongly in the direction of the raft, but underwater. I had grown up swimming in fast current rivers, so this lake with no current was a piece of cake. Coming up beside the raft, I pulled myself up. I waved to make sure she would stop her watch and then dove back in and swam back to the dock. Getting there, I looked up at her and smiled.

"Well, did I pass?" I asked.

"Showoff," was the word I think she muttered as she nodded her head, turned, and walked away.

The next day we started classes and I found myself in the same Spanish class with her. In the meantime I had found out her name was Reneé Pintor. She looked Latin, so I was surprised to see she did not speak Spanish. I didn't speak Spanish that well, either, which was always an embarrassment, as I was from a Spanish-speaking country. Up where we lived, no one spoke Spanish, just Yanomamö.

After that first day at the waterfront we really hit it off. We found out we had a lot in common. I loved watching her smile. She had the most dazzling smile I had ever seen—but I think I said that, didn't I?

Talk about destiny! Reneé told me she had saved her money for a Florida vacation. She really hadn't wanted anything to do with going to Bible school or being a missionary. Her sister Debbie was a student at Waukesha, Wisconsin, at the New Tribes Bible Institute, and although she had repeatedly talked to Reneé about joining her, Reneé had held out. She had a successful job, and life was pretty good, so she didn't see any need for it.

Her vacation was planned for early summer. She and her friend had been planning it for months. But the day appointed dawned with dark clouds and became only blacker the closer her flight time came. Although it was late in the year for snow, it actually started to snow . . . great big, heavy globs of snow.

O'Hare Airport in Chicago is very seldom shut down, even in the wintertime—they have snow removal down to a science—but this was too much. The snow kept coming; the streets became impassable. Word went out over the airwaves that O'Hare Airport was closed. There was nothing to do but wait it out. Somewhere in the midst of all this the Lord began to work in a stubborn heart.

"I control the weather, and I desire to use you for my glory," a still, small Voice told her. Reneé could hear the Lord speaking to her about choosing His Will for her life over her own. She resisted for a time, but finally told God: "Here I am, Lord. Send me." She took the money she had saved for her vacation and enrolled in the fall semester of New Tribes Mission Bible School at Waukesha, Wisconsin.

This was the same semester that found Cochran and me enrolling in Bible school—but we were enrolled in the Bible school at Jackson, Michigan. Because I'd left only a couple of months after starting there and was out for an entire year, Reneé finished school an entire year before I did. If she had gone straight into boot camp after Bible school, as she had planned to do, we never would have met. However, her grandfather had gotten sick, so Reneé had offered to help with his care. After a year or so, her grandfather passed away, and Reneé then made plans to go on to boot camp. Meanwhile, I was in my junior year at Bible school. I was burdened by the many Yanomamö I knew to be passing on to a Christless eternity without ever having the opportunity to hear about a God who loved them so much that He had sent His only Son to become one of them and teach them His Way. One day while talking to the dean of students, I mentioned my burden. He pulled out my file and looked at it for a few minutes.

"Mike, why don't you put in a request to be considered to be allowed to graduate after this term? We can do that if you have shown that you know the material. And from the look of your grades, I would say that that would not be an issue."

I stared at him, hardly daring to believe what I was hearing. "You mean they would release me to go to boot camp a whole semester early?" I asked him.

"Well, it is the entire committee's decision, but I'm pretty sure your request would be granted, if you asked us to consider it," was his response.

The next two weeks stretched on forever as I waited to hear what the committee's decision was going to be. I was overjoyed to finally get word that I had been granted early graduation. I began to make plans to head on to boot camp as soon as the next missionary boot camp term started.

So again, our mismatched schedules found Reneé and me each starting the second phase of missionary training at the same time. But—and this was big—we were going to be starting in different parts of the United States. She was in Jersey Shore, Pennsylvania, and I was in Oviedo, Florida. It seemed as if our paths would never cross. I'm sure, had I known that she was out there, I would have been very frustrated by this time. Of course, I hadn't met her yet, so I had no idea of what I was missing and was relatively happy in my ignorance. *You know what?* Miracles do still happen; slowly God, in His time, was bringing us together.

Possibly the greatest miracle of all was that I was released from boot camp after only the required two semesters, so that I could go on to Language School. Reneé's release was a given: everyone loved and got along with her. She had one of those personalities that as soon as you met her, you felt like you had known her all your life. She was ever-quick with a smile or a word of encouragement. So, as I said, everyone loved her, from the head of the camp on down.

Somehow we ended up with the same class schedule at Language School, and before I knew it we were not only sitting together for most of our classes, but we began to do our homework together, as well. Life was good!

Sitting there one day, working on our homework, I looked across the table at the beautiful girl who was smiling at me. If anything, she looked more beautiful every day. Somehow I knew this was the only girl for me. Now, if only I could convince *her* of that fact.

19
"GREATER IS HE THAT IS IN US..."

I tried to get a bit more comfortable in the boat. "I can't believe it," I muttered. "With all the technological advances I've seen, I would think we could make a dugout canoe a bit more comfortable, or come up with something that could take its place. Oh well, maybe someday."

There I was sitting in the front of our dugout canoe. I looked back. We had quite a few people in the boat, and I was hoping we wouldn't have to do too much portaging. Seated right behind me was Reneé. It had taken a while, but I *had* finally been able to convince her that she was the only girl for me. It was now March of 1981. We married in September of 1980 and arrived in Venezuela in January of 1981. After a few weeks in town doing paperwork, we had finally arrived back in the jungle: this was the first extended river trip she had taken with me. She flashed me another of her dazzling smiles and my discomfort evaporated. I could not believe how fortunate I was to be back working with the people I loved and with such a girl. It felt so right to have her in the boat with me. Life was good.

I had to shake my head sometimes to make myself believe I was actually here. At the end of school, I had floundered a bit in my desire to work with the Yanomamö, when struck with an almost equal desire to fly. I tried rationalizing everything with the Lord.

"I'll still serve You," I promised, but I was trying to serve God on my own terms. I enrolled in a school of aviation, hoping to get my airframe and power-plant mechanic's license. This was one of the requirements needed for application to the Missionary Aviation Fellowship. Before being considered as a potential pilot, you had to have, at the least, your commercial pilot's license and your mechanic's license. These courses cost money, so I was working full time, while also trying to go to school. The harder I tried, the more elusive my goals seemed to be.

Finally, Reneé told me what I needed to hear: "You talk a good missionary, but unless you allow the Lord to change you, you will never make it to the field. I gave my life to the Lord to serve Him. I thought we could serve Him together, but here is your ring back. I am going to counsel at my church's summer camp, and then I am going to Mexico to help my sister. If you ever get your act together, look me up."

I looked deep into her dark, tear-filled eyes and knew I was losing the most precious thing I had ever *almost* had. Still, I was too stubborn to back down. I quietly accepted my ring back and slipped it into my pocket.

I know God can use anything at His disposal to get our attention. With me, he chose to use a dream. About a week after Reneé gave me back my ring, I came home tired from a long day of classes, and then a full eight hours at the local airport, where I was working as an aircraft mechanic's apprentice. I loved the work but, like I said, I was tired. I immediately fell into a deep sleep. Suddenly I was not asleep anymore, but standing by the throne of God.

I realized I was watching God judge the nations. From my vantage point beside the throne I watched the lines of people slowly pass by for judgment. Suddenly I saw a line of Yanomamö waiting their turn. They were dressed in their feathered finery, with the white eagle down in their hair making a striking contrast to the blood-red macaw feathers stuck in their armbands. They made their way to the front and stood before God's throne. Listening carefully, I heard the order given to make a diligent search for their names. Their names were not found. Their eyes widened in despair as they were told to depart; there was no place for them in heaven.

Because of where I stood, the Yanomamö had to file past me. The leader of the group noticed me standing there and stopped in front of me.

"Maikiwä," he said, using my Yanomamö name, "where were you? You knew my culture and my language, but why did you not bother to come and tell us?"

I groped for a way to try and explain that I was *going* to come, I just needed to learn some more things first. I wanted to fly. "I was going to come," I finished lamely. As I said the words, they sounded empty and selfish even to me.

"Why have I wasted my life?" I cried. Tears ran down my face as the Yanomamö filed past me forever. My tears were real and they woke me up. What a relief to find myself still in bed! I slipped out of bed and down to my knees. My own stubborn heart melted, as Reneé's had, at the Lord's gentle prodding.

God, if You can still use me, I will serve You wherever You want me, I told Him.

I gave notice that I was quitting to the school I was attending and turned in a two-week notice at the airport where I was working. I called Reneé and asked her if there would be a place I could help at the camp, as well. This was in early May of 1980. She called and told me they could use me on their waterfront. I had worked as a lifeguard at Disney World for a while, so I had my certificate. I knew she would be on the waterfront as well, so I was happy. I finally felt at peace.

The church camp where Reneé grew up was called Silver Birch Ranch and had been founded by Pastor Richard Wager. My summer up there went so fast. It is a beautiful camp and was just a wonderful place to relax and get back to a close walk with the Lord. I hadn't even realized I had wandered off that much, but the Lord used the quiet and solitude of the camp to peel away layer after layer of selfish pride. *Finally*, with all my heart I desired to give myself totally to serve Him. I had no idea of what the future held for me, but I was ready to step out totally trusting God. On our many walks, Reneé and I talked of what our future might hold working with the Yanomamö. I was so excited to finally be heading back, not on my terms, but on God's. *What peace I had!*

The summer quickly came to an end. I stayed there until camp ended the last week in August. Reneé had gone home a week earlier to prepare for our wedding. We had counseled with Pastor Wager about our future. He offered to send us out as missionaries sponsored by the Emmanuel Bible Church of Berwyn, Reneé's home church.

Now, here we were, just a few short months later, headed up the Iyowei River toward the village of Jalalusiteli. Two of my brothers were with us: my older brother Gary and my youngest brother, Jerald. Tagging along were Ramon; his sister, Vanessa; and her husband, Pedro. Pedro was from Jalalusiteli and kept insisting that the trail we were looking for was right around the next bend. I had traveled with the Yanomamö so much that I rarely paid attention when they estimated travel time or distances, because they always told me exactly what they thought I wanted to hear. If they thought you wanted the distance to be close, they would say, "It is close. Just listen, you can already hear the ladies fussing," they would assure you. Gary and I knew, though, that Pedro had never been up this river before, so he had no more idea than we did how far away the trail was.

Reneé wanted to get there quickly. Around every bend she strained her eyes to be the first to spot the trail.

"You won't recognize it anyway," I kept trying to tell her. "It won't be a port or anything—just a Yanomamö trail heading up into the jungle."

To most outsiders, a Yanomamö trail is almost indistinguishable from just normal jungle. It might have a broken branch or two to mark the way, but that will be all. Still, Reneé kept looking. We traveled and traveled. Our way became more and more labored, as we had to stop and hack our way through fallen trees that blocked the way ahead of us. The worst part about having to push your way through all the brush and trees that had fallen across the river was that there was always sure to be some crazy spider or a family of ants that had nothing better to do than to let go just as you were passing underneath, and then they would run like you-know-what to get to the deepest place inside your shirt or, better yet, your pants.

Nothing so vitalizes a person as to suddenly have a spider rushing around inside your clothing. This was bad enough, but every so often a snake would get thrown in just to keep the excitement up. Anyway, I suppose I could write an entire book on the comical antics the members of a boat perform as they chop their way through a tree-filled *caño*. After a bit, all this excitement makes you edgy and irritable, especially with the guy who keeps saying the trail is around the next bend. Gary and I, noticing the level of anxiety in Reneé's eyes, told Pedro he was not helping and asked if he could really just *shut up* on that for a while.

Pedro sat back with a pained look in his eyes, staring defiantly back at Gary and me. "I tell you, I sure do know where I am! You all think I don't know, but I do!" He glared around at the surrounding jungle and at the never-ending river heading around yet another bend. Suddenly he pointed. "Right there . . . see that tree? Just last dry season we were down here eating fruit. I recognize that tree!" he kept insisting.

I just wished we were there already. If agreeing with Pedro would help us get there faster, I was all for it. We knew, though, that the river went on way farther than Pedro could possibly have walked down with his friends. By the time that became obvious, it didn't even seem worth mentioning.

We continued, on and on and on. It got dark, and we knew we were going to have to spend another night in the jungle. It had been raining off and on all day and looked as if it would start pouring again any minute. We hurriedly put up our shelter and cooked a meal before it got too dark. Once again I could see I had not done too badly. Not only was Reneé much better looking than ol' Cochran, she was also a better cook!

The next day, at about noon (so much for Pedro recognizing that tree, which we continually pointed out to him!), we came to a huge tree that spanned the entire width of the river. Sometime during one of the frequent storms in the rainforest, the tree had given up and fallen. I sure would have appreciated it if it had had the decency to fall the other way, but no: perversely, I felt, it had had to fall right across the river, completely blocking it. There was no way we could chop our way through the trunk of this tree, as it was halfway in the water. It was too big to push the boat over it, so we decided to turn around and head home. Most people in the boat wanted to leave poor Pedro to run up the "just one more bend" and get help from his village, but Vanessa talked us out of it. We turned around and headed for home.

Going downstream, since the current was helping us and since we had already chopped our way through most of the stuff blocking the way, we made really good time. Reneé had had enough of sleeping in the jungle, so I told her that if we made it back out to the Ocamo before dark we would run all the way home. It is a large enough river, and we had run it enough that we knew where all the rocks were. I was confident that we could get home with no trouble. Well, we made it out to the big river just before nightfall, and Jerald really cranked the motor up as we sped downriver into the night.

Still, I had not figured on the storm. We were just about to the village of Iyoweiteli when it came down in a downpour that you would not have believed. Ramon suggested we stop and seek shelter with old Justo, an old friend who lived there. Gary and I agreed. Reneé did not wish to stop. In fact, she was totally unreasonable in her demand that we keep going.

"You promised we would keep going till we got home," she told me, her lip trembling as she fought for control. I couldn't believe she would even want to keep going in such weather. The pitch-black night was shattered again as another lightning bolt tore through the darkness over our heads. I instinctively ducked, waiting until the thunder subsided to only a roar.

Blinking my eyes to clear them from the water running down my face, I put my head next to hers. "I know I did, but it's dangerous in this storm," I told her quietly.

"Well, just go. I am going to stay in the boat," she told me.

Everyone else busied themselves getting their things out of the boat, acting like we weren't there. Ignoring the storm, I tried to keep my voice calm. "Honey, I can't let you stay in the boat; it's not safe down here," I said, peering into the blackness made even darker by the howling storm, trying to gauge how much to tell her about the true dangers of the nighttime jungle. "There are a lot of things that come out at night. I can't leave you here by yourself," I said, sitting down beside her. "But if you want to stay here, I will stay with you." She glared at me.

"Oh, no, you don't! You just want to play the martyr," she exclaimed, grabbing her hammock bag and starting up the bank. I grinned at Ramon and hurried after her. Passing her on the bank, I took her bag from her. She followed me up to the village.

After the usual ruckus of waking a sleeping Yanomamö village, and after we had said our greetings, I hung up our hammocks. The hearth we had been shown to hang our hammocks on was the hearth of old Justo himself. He always called me "son" and swore that I would have starved to death if he hadn't gotten to TT and taken food to my parents in the early days there. (Of course, Dad tells the story quite differently than Justo does. In Dad's version, old Justo was the one about to starve to death, until Mom and Dad took him in and fed him. I sure wasn't going to argue the point tonight! I wanted a place to sleep, and if calling this old witch doctor "father" would assure us of better hospitality . . . well, "when in Rome, do as the Romans do," I always say.)

By this time Reneé was not speaking to me. She felt I had lied to her and just didn't want to honor my promise. I helped her climb into her hammock, then hung my own up. Things started to quiet back down as the rest of us got in our hammocks and began to doze off. Reneé would not answer me, even with a "*Goodnight.*" I knew she was tired and would feel better in the morning. The storm still howled. Thunder crashed and lightning split the sky from horizon to horizon.

Suddenly, there in the hearth, right next to where we were trying to sleep, old Justo and a buddy started up in full voice. There was a sick baby, and the parents had come for their services. For those of you who have never heard a Yanomamö witch doctor, believe me when I tell you: it is unnerving. When you are lying there in the pitch blackness, with thunder and lightning all around you, the spookiness factor intensifies by a factor of ten.

As I said, these two old guys really began going at it, calling loudly to their demons to come and heal the boy. They began to make chopping sounds, as if with an axe, as they tried to chop the sickness. Then they began to suck and gag as they sucked the sickness into their own bodies to get rid of it. The noise was so loud that even the storm couldn't drown them out.

I tried to shut my ears against them. Suddenly I felt someone at my hammock. Reneé climbed in and covered her head with my blanket. She was shaking, partly from the cold but mostly because she was terrified. She was still not speaking to me, but at least we were getting closer. I belatedly realized that this was the first really primitive village she had slept in and she was scared to death. I hugged her, telling her to go to sleep.

"They are just two old men chanting in the night," I told her. Then, to further calm her, I told her: "Honey, the best verse I learned for this type of a situation is found in 1 John 4:4: 'Ye are of God, little children, and have overcome them, because greater is He that is in you than he that is in the world.'" She finally dozed off. At about 5:30 in the morning I woke up as I heard the village start to stir.

Shaking Reneé awake, I told her, "Get up; if they catch you in my hammock they will laugh at us, and I will be the brunt of all the jokes for the rest of the day." She looked at me, puzzled for a moment. Suddenly realizing what I was saying, she smiled a mischievous grin.

"Let them laugh," she said, nudging me, but she began moving to get up.

All of a sudden, with a loud snap the rope that was holding our hammock broke, dumping us both on the floor of the village. We were in a *shabono*, which is just one large circular roof and no inside walls, so everything is wide open. Everyone looked to see what the commotion was. You can imagine the laughter that rocked the village that morning! What could we do but join in?

After that incident Reneé never had any more trouble sleeping in Yanomamö villages. I guess she figured, *what could be worse than that night?* The Yanomamö love it when you can laugh at yourself and don't try and take yourself too seriously. And boy, did Reneé love to laugh!

We finally did make it to the village of Jalalusiteli, but we did not get there by river; we just walked in. The village of Jalalusiteli was situated right between the Metaconi, our river, and the Ocamo River. We traveled by canoe up past the first major rapids on the Metaconi, then got out and started walking east. Late on the second day we arrived at the village. It was a brutal trip. The village had already started talking about moving out to the Iyowei River. We really encouraged them to do so, as it would cut off an entire day's walk to get to them, two days' round trip. Once they did move out to the river, Gary and I went back in there and showed the people where to build an airstrip so we could just fly in.

Over the next two years we made repeated trips in to help them work and to try and keep them encouraged. Gary and I would take turns going in. Reneé proved more than a match for the task and worked by my side day in and day out. The work was hard, because all they had to work with were axes and machetes, but they finished their airstrip. We had a difficult time getting permission from the government to use it, but praise the Lord, we finally got the needed authorizations and I was able to fly in with Kevin Swanson to check the strip out. You should have seen the Yanomamö faces when we came swooping in! For them, it was a dream come true.

Most of all, this airstrip represented medical help for them. So many times in the past they would send runners out to our village, asking for help. By the time they had run for three days, and then told us what was happening, and then we got ready and got back in to them, it was often too late. So many times all we found was a charred place on the ground where they had already cremated the body.

Just one year earlier, a good friend of ours from there had run out to get help for his father. Normally, it is a three-day walk from their village to ours. Because of the urgency of his mission, though, Casper had made the trip in one day. His feet bore the brunt of the punishment of the trip, and as we hurried our way along Casper had a hard time not limping too much. Even with sore feet he constantly urged us on to greater speed.

"My father was really bad when I left," he told us. "I am very worried."

Looking at him, I sensed he was not telling me the whole story. "What has happened?" I asked him.

Slowly he told me the story. I couldn't believe it. I knew the Yanomamö practice what is generally called *mercy killing,* but I didn't know it could be this bad. He continued telling me the story, his voice low, so as not to be overheard.

"My father had been very sick about two weeks ago," he told me. "But after about this many days [showing me four fingers], he began to recover. He was still weak, but he insisted he wanted to go to his garden. Nothing we would do could talk him out of it, so he went. A little later, someone passing by his garden saw him lying there. He had passed out in the hot sun. They called me, and I got him back to his hammock. I bathed him down like you all have taught us, and he opened his eyes and looked at me. He could not talk, however, and his body would shake uncontrollably. The witch doctor there decided it was because his spirit was already gone, and this was just some other spirit that was trapped in his body.

"'We have to let this spirit out!' he told everyone. I refused to let them touch him and guarded him fiercely.

"Finally, I got so tired. This was after a couple days of no sleep. I told my younger brother to watch him so that I could get some sleep. My father was much better, so I no longer felt we had a lot to worry about. I had just fallen asleep, however, when my brother began to call me loudly. I hurried over. There was a large commotion by my father's hammock. Running up to it, I was just in time to see the witch doctor tie a vine around my father's neck and pull it tight. Grabbing him by his shoulders, I threw him aside.

"'Get away from my father, you murderers!' I shouted.

"'No, no, this is not your father. You don't understand!' they yelled and yelled at me. But I untied my father. They already had his legs tied up and his arms bound to his body. The vine around his neck was the last vine. If I had not come running up, he would already be dead.

"I was furious. As I untied him, I shouted every insult I could think of at them. I finally told the main witch doctor I was coming to get you all, and if my father even just died in his sleep, I was going to kill him. That shut them up, but no one is very happy. I hope my father is still alive." His eyes filled with tears.

We hurried on down the trail. As we approached the village, my ears picked up the unmistakable sound of wailing. "Oh, no! We are too late!" Casper began to cry, and the rest of us stared straight ahead as we made our way into the village. A friend from the United States, Rick Johnson, was visiting, and had come in with me. We made our way to Casper's house, where the entire village had gathered to wail for the old man. Rick and I stood off to one side. We were so disappointed to be getting there too late. It seems it happens so often in the jungle. Travel is so difficult and time-consuming . . . and malaria can kill so quickly that mostly it is a race against time for us, a race that we don't win very often. Rick touched my arm and pointed at the old man's hammock.

"Mike, is he still moving, or what is going on?" he asked me.

I stared at the hammock, hardly daring to believe what I was seeing. The hammock was moving. The old man was alive. We quickly pushed our way through the crowd of mourners. Bending down, I took the old man's skinny arm in my hand and felt for a pulse. I could feel it faintly beating its erratic rhythm against my searching fingers.

"He is alive, Rick, but not by much," I told him. Rick quickly got out his medical bag and began to get a shot ready. The ol' guy was burning up with fever. While Rick got the shot ready, I called for some water to wash the old guy down with, to aid in getting his fever down. Every so often his body would jerk and twist with another convulsion. After Rick gave the shot, he began to try and get some malaria medicine down the old man's throat. How I wished we had some injectable malaria medicine, but we did not. Finally, Rick was able to work two pills down the old man's throat.

We felt we had better not push our luck, as we were afraid the old guy would quit breathing for good while we were working on him and his death would appear to be our fault. We did keep coming back and checking on him during the long night. Rick was concerned about how dehydrated he was, so every time we went back he tried to work a bit more liquid down his throat. While Rick was working on him, the old man opened his eyes. He looked right at me. Squatting down beside his hammock, I asked him, "Father, can you hear me? Do you know who I am?"

He blinked his eyes, as if to clear them, and nodded his head. "Yes, I hear you, Maikiwä," he whispered. I was thrilled. I felt we might be having a happy ending, after all.

"Maikiwä, I am really thirsty," he whispered again.

I jumped up to take the gourd that Rick handed me and held it up to the old man's lips. He took a couple of swallows and lay back in his hammock. We stayed there, monitoring him for a while longer, but were satisfied that this time instead of being in a coma he was in a good sleep. I looked at my watch.

Almost four o'clock! We made our way outside, back to where we had our hammocks hung. I was so relieved that the old guy was going to make it that I had no trouble falling asleep this time.

Suddenly someone was shaking my hammock. "Hey, get up, I am not sure what is happening, but it does not sound good," Rick told me.

I jumped up. Sure enough, the village was really wailing again. We ran over to the house, but this time it was for real. The old man was dead! I could not believe it. After all we had gone through last night, for him to have just died! It didn't seem fair. It seemed as if all we had done was give everyone a false sense of well-being, only to dash their hopes to the ground. I hung my head and Rick and I turned to walk back over to our hammocks.

Ramon was suddenly standing beside me. "We need to leave now," he whispered.

I looked at him. The look I saw in his eyes convinced me that he was not just fooling around. I translated for Rick and explained. "The Yanomamö do not do grief well. Our guys could be in danger. We need to get out of here."

Quickly we untied our hammocks and packed them in our backpacks. Heaving them onto our shoulders, we turned to leave the building. I at least wanted to say something, anything, to Casper. I found him still at his father's hammock, weeping loudly. I put my arm around him and told him that we were leaving. He looked up at me. Comprehension dawned in his eyes. "Yes, that is best," he told me.

I put my face next to his. "My friend, I am praying for you," I told him through my tears.

I left with the others, but although I was not there, I could see in my mind's eye exactly what the village was going through; I had seen it so often in other villages. I knew they would wail louder and louder as they made up the funeral pyre. Finally it would be time; they could put it off no longer. Grabbing up axes, they would dash to the place where the old man's body still lay in his hammock. They would smite the ground and the uprights the hammock was tied to with their axes to dislodge any spirits that might still be clinging to him. They would yell their war cries to psych themselves up to do this deed that defied thinking about.

Quickly they would untie his hammock and carry it between them out to the fire. The mourners would now be wailing at such a volume you almost could not hear yourself think. Approaching the fire, now at almost a run, the ones carrying the hammock would drape the body over the fire. Other guys would be standing by with lengths of firewood in hand. As soon as the body was on the flames, they would bury it under firewood as quickly as they could. The fire would shoot up, and with it the screams of the mourners would rise in intensity. Slowly, the fire would eventually die down. Gradually, the mourners, spent and exhausted, would get up and go to their own hammocks, still crying.

Only Casper and his family would be left by the fire. Finally his wife would gently lead him home. Two guys would stay by the fire to keep it burning until the last inch of firewood that had been placed on the pyre was totally consumed. With long poles they kept for this purpose, the fire would be turned to make sure the corpse was no more. Finally, with nothing more to burn, the fire would slowly eat away at itself until there was nothing left — nothing, that is, except a pile of still-smoldering ashes.

The next day Casper's two grandmothers and an old uncle would sift through the ashes carefully. They would sift out every last fragment of human bone they could find and place it carefully in a basket made for that purpose. Painstakingly, they would sift and sift until they were satisfied that they had gathered every piece. Wailing their grief, they would take the basket and set it down at the old man's hearth.

Walking back down the trail to home, I was weeping as well— weeping for my friend, Casper, as I knew the grief he was feeling. I could picture him sitting beside the fire, crying his heart out still. But I was weeping for myself, also. I had truly liked and respected the old man, and I took it as a personal failure that we had not gotten there in time to do more for him.

20

SNAKE

It seems that every time I am in Coyowä, the Yanomamö always pick up and head out on trek somewhere, leaving me to babysit a desolate, lonely, more-than-a-little creepy, empty village. If you think this is fun, think again. Not fun, and if you have any reason to be out at night, I'll tell you what, there is no place on earth spookier than an abandoned Yanomamö *shabono* in the darkness.

I don't know why I was thinking such morbid thoughts. This time was nothing like the last couple of times I'd been in here. This time I had my wife along, and there was another missionary couple on the base, and—guess what—without the Indians it was *almost* like being on vacation.

We sat over in our fellow missionary's house that night playing *Rook*. I think that was the only legal card game missionaries could play. Anyway, we were playing *Rook,* drinking hot chocolate, and eating popcorn . . . having a fine time. I guess that's what brought the memories back, because suddenly I remembered another time we had been in Coyowä, doing the same thing with another missionary couple.

Cochran and I were up there helping hold down the base, as the family that knew the language had to leave, and they didn't want the base left without someone on it who could speak Yanomamö. The Yanomamö in Coyowä were rough! We had gone in there at a time when the people were at war and were expecting a raid at any moment. Tensions were high. Finally, the nerve of the people broke and they decided to go away on trek to hide out for a while. So there we were by ourselves, bored out of our minds and wondering whether there really were raiders all around us.

The last thing the missionary who was leaving had told us was, "Don't go out to do any hunting; these people are at war, and I don't want one of you-all getting shot!"

Since getting shot was low on our own list of things we wanted to happen, we thought we would take him at his word this time. (This was the same guy, the one with the boat, whose advice we had once ignored, as you may recall.) So there we were now, about starving to death. We decided the Yanomamö wouldn't be out at night, so we started going out at night to try to shoot the rabbits and deer that would cross the strip to eat in the villagers' gardens.

The closest we came to bagging a deer was when Cochran was almost trampled by one: the crazy thing ran across the strip right toward his light. I never did figure that out. But I'll tell you what, it sure spooked ol' Cochran. Then we went back to the house to mooch a cup of coffee off the couple who lived next door. The wife made delicious chocolate chip cookies, and we figured she'd probably throw in a couple of them for us.

We got over there and, sure enough, they not only had some cookies and coffee, but they invited us to stay for a couple of hands of *Rook*. We should have said, "No, thanks," what with Cochran pumping about 90 percent adrenaline, but we agreed. As a matter of fact, by that time we were all pumping some adrenaline and, as I said, there is nothing spookier than an abandoned Yanomamö *shabono*. All during the night you would hear weird noises, as if there really were people or spirits or such outside watching you. After a while I would find myself looking over my shoulder more than in the direction I was headed.

In any case, we were into the second or third hand of *Rook*. I was getting sleepy and was just floating along. The bidding was between Fran and the missionary and was getting up there pretty high. Finally Fran gave in, and the old guy took the kitty to see what help he could get from there. I stared at his cards as I started to nod off. I never have been much of a card player, and I'm not much good at it. I don't memorize what cards have been played or what is still out. I guess I figure life is too serious to take cards seriously. Anyway, like I said, I was about half asleep at the time, and Cochran was still trying to massage his heart to get it to slow down from his encounter with the deer that had almost induced cardiac arrest. The caffeine in his coffee was not helping purge the adrenaline from his veins, either, as he'd hoped it would.

Suddenly, the old missionary (I'll call him Bill) who had gotten the kitty threw back his head and let loose the most blood-curdling scream I have ever had the misfortune to awaken to. I jumped up. Cochran was way ahead of me; I saw him climb down off the ceiling. We whirled around, trying to spot whatever had given our friend the fright. I was afraid to look at his back, as I just knew we would find one of those six-foot-long Yanomamö arrows sticking out of it.

"Are you OK? Are you having a heart attack?" his wife asked him. I looked back at him. The bug-eyed look he'd had when he'd screamed had been replaced by one of sheer ecstasy.

"I don't need a partner," he announced. "I am going to shoot the moon!"

"Shoot the moon?! What moon?"

Cochran explained it to me: "If you get enough of the right cards when you get the kitty, you can choose not to pick a partner but just go it alone. This way, he has a point advantage."

I'll tell you what, you would have thought the old guy had won the lottery! We slunk back into our chairs, whipped. That was just too much excitement for one night. Bill did win all by himself, and we shuffled back over to the place we were staying, happy to turn in and let sleep take us away from there.

So here I was back in Coyowä with the Yanomamö gone once again. We were playing the same card game and eating almost the same foods. The only difference was that we were with a different couple, and instead of Cochran I was with my wife, Reneé. We would be leaving in a couple of days, though, as we had to go out of the jungle for her to have our first child. She was already almost eight months' pregnant, and we wanted to get out to town to give us time to get settled in.

We finally said our goodnights and started to walk home. The moon was big. Now, instead of it feeling so spooky, with the Yanomamö gone, we were enjoying the quiet. I turned off our light and we walked across the airstrip to our house in the moonlight, holding hands. The night was cool and we could hear the whippoorwills calling across the landing strip.

We paused at our front door. The hair on the back of my neck was trying to get my attention. Suddenly I heard a whisper of sound down by our feet, almost like a dry leaf rubbing against another leaf. Instantly, with my arm I pushed Reneé behind me. I turned the flashlight on and shined it downwards. There, with its head back, ready to strike, and just inches from Reneé, was a large jungle pit viper. If I hadn't pushed her when I heard the slight sound, she would have stepped right on it!

These snakes are very dangerous; their bites probably account for the highest number of deaths from snakebite in all of Venezuela. I pushed Reneé farther back . . . and carefully moved backward myself. Shining the flashlight around, I found a handy stick lying on the ground. Picking it up, I killed the snake. Reneé and I went on into the house. She was pale with fright, and I was not in much better shape. *That was too close,* I thought, shooting up a quick prayer of thanks to God.

I was sobered to think how close I had come to losing her right then. In her condition, she probably would not have survived the bite of so large a snake—especially as far away from any kind of medical provider as we were. From Puerto Ayacucho, we were almost six hours of flight time away from the hospital. The unborn baby inside her most assuredly would not have made it. We thanked the Lord together that night for His constant love and protection over us.

21
HOVERING ON
THE ORINOCO

My *dream that one day technology may provide something to facilitate easier travel on the river just might be coming true,* I thought to myself, as I walked toward the watercraft that was not quite boat, not quite car, not quite airplane. I pulled the canopy back, then climbed in beside my mechanic and gave him the thumbs-up, starting the thrust engine. As it idled, I reached over and started the lift engine and couldn't help grinning as the craft slowly rose on a cushion of air. *This was the day! We were finally going for it!*

I looked at my watch. It displayed the date and time: January 25, 5:00 p.m. I slowly advanced the lift throttle to make sure I was hovering as high as possible, then gave the thrust engine a bit more gas. We moved down the sloping beach and ran out over the water. I turned the wheel and the craft moved sideways, its nose pointed toward the landing. I stood up and waved to the crowd of friends and interested passersby who had gathered to watch the strange new watercraft. *We were on our way!* I will never forget the day we pulled out of Ciudad Bolivar, on our way to Coshilowäteli, in our beautiful, homemade hovercraft.

I had spent the first part of the day getting Reneé and the boys on an airplane, which would fly them on into the village ahead of me. Meanwhile, I was embarking with a friend to take the hovercraft on its maiden Venezuelan voyage. It was too long a distance, and the craft was too experimental, to bring my family on this first journey. It would be a fitting test for our hovercraft, though, as we would be traveling most of the Orinoco River—the twelfth-largest river in the world. We knew, of course, that once we left port we would have very little chance of getting any help from others. We would also have no communication with anyone until we arrived in Caicara, about four hundred miles and about one-quarter of our trip upriver.

We had tried to be ready for anything. Well, we weren't. In fact, we were still within sight of the city when we noticed our thrust engine was running hot. *What to do? Do we go back . . . or just pull over?* I hated to go back with everyone still watching us, so we ran a bit farther to get out of sight, and then pulled over to see if we could isolate the problem. We decided that the overheating was caused by an air duct that we had added to the design. Out came the hacksaw and I started sawing. *Boy, that hurt!* We had spent a lot of time on that crazy duct.

Twenty minutes later we were off. *Or were we?* Something seemed to be wrong. We were up on hover, but not going anywhere. We zoomed around in circles for a while, then retired to the beach once again to see if we could find the problem.

"My word, we're caught in someone's fishnet," I exclaimed. After five or ten minutes of embarrassing work, we were off again. We thought about running after dark, since we had a good moon, but we soon found out—almost the hard way—that even up on hover there were some things that you couldn't go over. So, we found a nice beach (which wasn't hard to do on a river that was almost solid sand) and spread our blankets, planning to wait for morning to go on.

Have you ever slept out on a sandbar in the middle of a large river? If you have, then you know I am not exaggerating when I say that we woke up the next morning and had to dig our way out from under the sand. We were buried, and everything we had was buried, including a dish of rice left over from the night before that we had been going to eat for breakfast. Well, *Jim* was going to eat it for breakfast; I was going to have a bowl of glop. The wind that had buried us was still howling over the sand and it didn't look like it had any plans to quit. The waves were high; in fact, we had some mighty nice whitecaps out there . . . and you hovercraft enthusiasts should know that while little waves are nice, you can get too many in a hurry when the big ones start rolling in.

Now, rolling in they were — so big that we hadn't been out there too long before we felt like we'd been riding a roller coaster all day. The worst thing was that we kept having to slow down, because the waves were so high they kept smashing up through the lift venturi and smacking our lift prop, not to mention what all that extra spray was doing to the leading edge of our thrust prop!

Funny thing about something you don't want to mention: It keeps getting so much worse that before you know it, that's all you're talking about. We were more than just a little concerned about that prop. Here we were starting a 1,500-mile journey, give or take a few miles, and already our prop looked like it had come halfway across the Atlantic. I had visions of us sitting up on some lonely sandbar, waiting for Jim to finish whittling us a new prop.

Suddenly our prop wasn't so important — because our engines quit. Times like these make you really love your mechanic. "Can you start them enough to get us over to that sandbar, Jim?" I said. Believe you me, I really didn't have to motivate Jim to try this. At this point, we both had a boater's greatest motivator (especially if the boat happens to be out in the middle of the river, dead in the water): a leaky boat.

Come to find out, Jim was even more motivated than I was. He had believed and been contemplating all my piranha and croc stories (which, of course, were a hundred percent true!). In any case, we made it to shore, and while Jim worked on the motors, I pulled the bilge plugs and started bailing out the boat. By the way, our boat was leaking so badly because the night before I had made a less-than-perfect landing on a sloping beach, and the subsequent slide had ripped off one of the skids on the bottom. *Holes?* Yes, we had holes in that boat! Jim patched one of the smaller ones with one of my socks—the whole sock, that is! He would have patched more but the second sock fell all the way through the hole. Our problem with the engines was that water had seeped into the gasoline tanks, a problem that hounded us all the way. We had two built-in fifty-gallon tanks; one on each side, which had baffles in them. The only thing we could figure was that while the hovercraft was being shipped to Venezuela, it had sat so long in customs that the tanks got water in them.

We drained those tanks all the way upriver; yet every time the river got rough our engines sucked up water; so I think the water was trapped behind the baffles. Every time rough water shook the boat, it allowed some more water to get into our filters and finally into our engines. We must have used two dozen or more fuel filters.

Honestly speaking, except for the problem of the leaky boat, which was due in part to pilot error and the water in the gas, the hovercraft performed pretty well. There is absolutely nothing that can touch it in shallow water. That boat is incredible for going over sandbars, where no other boat has gone. We went where only the *minnows* could go, and many times when the sand would close us in we went where even the minnows couldn't come: over the sandbar itself!

Another thing that never failed to amaze us on this trip was every time we stopped, for any reason, within a couple of minutes we would have a crowd of people around. Where they came from I don't have the faintest idea. Most of the time there was not a house or a shack in sight. Then again, that was always the question they asked us.

"Where are you from? Oh. Ciudad Bolivar!? We thought for a minute that maybe you were from somewhere *up there*. You know, an extraterrestrial?" I'm not sure we convinced everybody that we weren't visitors from another planet, either, because this mode of transportation had never before been seen on the river.

We made it to Caicara, halfway to Puerto Ayacucho, which was also the city where we were going to make the decision either to continue or to discontinue our trip. Things were going pretty well, so after stocking up on more fuel filters and getting a nice, hot meal and a shower at the home of John and Judy Perkins (some missionary friends), we hovered on up the river. The most memorable incident on this leg of the trip happened at about 2:00 p.m. We were going up one side of a long island at the time. I had an aeronautical chart of Venezuela and was using it to pick the shortest sides of the islands in the river as we came upon them.

Anyway, we were about three-fourths of the way up this long island when we noticed a speedboat pulling out to meet us. As soon as I saw the dark-green color of the boat I knew we were in for it. It was the National Guard, and we were running in restricted waters.

"You are to stop!" a man shouted from the deck.

We stopped. What would you do with two or three machine guns (one more or less isn't going to make much difference) pointed at you?

"What are you doing? Where are you going? Why are you on this side of the island? Where are your papers?" he continued.

We're in big trouble, I thought. The guards were very upset. We had disturbed the turtles that were laying their eggs on the island, they said. I'm not sure why, but my aeronautical chart failed to mention turtles. I thought about asking why they had not had a sign or a person down at the lower end to warn people to stay away, but I figured we were in enough trouble. Also, remember, we were stopped dead in the water talking to the guards. I had forgotten this, but Jim hadn't forgotten. He was bailing two-forty!

Not understanding the trouble we were in, Jim interrupted us and told me to ask them if we could please go, as we were sinking. Meanwhile, I was still trying to keep us out of some obscure jail cell, so I wasn't about to interrupt these guys. Suddenly they really noticed the craft.

"Whose boat is this? Where did you get it? What is it?"

My head swam with this new deluge of questions. By the way, the bilge pumps were pumping their hearts out. Jim had taken to bailing with a much bigger bucket and we were still settling lower into the water every minute. Suddenly one of the guards came aboard. *Great,* I thought to myself, *they're going to tell us to follow the speedboat; we're detained.* Just then, though, one of the other guards pulled out a camera and they started taking turns posing on the hovercraft. I cleared my throat.

"Excuse me, *mi Teniente,* but we are taking on a lot of water as we have a large leak in our craft. I hate to bother you, but if we stay here much longer, we will not be able to leave; so, therefore, we will bother the turtles for a much longer time."

The guard stooped down and looked at Jim, who was now frantically bailing. He nodded his head. He then posed (as if he were driving) and I took his picture. With a wave, he climbed back over to his boat.

"Go ahead and keep going upriver," the guard official said. "We will not make you return and go all the way around. But don't bother any more turtles!" he told us. *Boy, talk about good news!* I felt like we had been pardoned from prison (which was not far from the truth).

The guards left and I started bailing alongside Jim. I sure didn't want them to change their minds! We finally got enough water out of the boat to get the craft up on hover again. We made it around the island and, as soon as we found a beach, pulled over and stopped to finish bailing.

The rest of the way to Puerto Ayacucho was great! We had a really nice cruise from there on in, seeing some of the prettiest scenery I'd ever seen, with mountains and huge rocks all along the river. We pulled into Puerto Ayacucho at about 6:00 p.m. The maps showed this to be our halfway point. Sad to say, it was there that I lost my mechanic, Jim, who had to go on to meet a prior commitment in the States.

We needed to find a way to portage our hovercraft almost fifty miles around some really wild rapids and waterfalls. So, since we had to take it out of the water anyway, we decided to try to repair the craft's bottom, at least temporarily, to make the last half of the trip not so hectic and dicey. We found a trailer, got it modified, and I was able to talk fifteen Yécuana guys into going to the river to help us lift the craft up onto the trailer (after first giving them all free rides on the unusual vessel). We took it into town and started working on the bottom. The next morning I said goodbye to Jim as he left for the airport. I sure was sad to see him go, because, while I can turn a screwdriver, I couldn't come close to Jim when it came to keeping that hovercraft up and hovering. Later that day a missionary friend of mine hooked the trailer to a pickup truck and we started the last half of our trip. Two Indian boys who needed to go upriver had asked to go with me, and I was glad for the company. We checked in with the National Guard at the port, cleared our papers to go upriver, put the craft in the water from the trailer, and then quickly drove it up on the beach. Yes, it still leaked, although not as badly. We then bedded down to sleep. One good thing was that the river was getting smaller now, and we didn't have so much wind.

We hit the river at around 6:00 a.m., and you should have seen those Indians as we started upriver. They had never before ridden in a hovercraft, so they were pretty worried as we went sliding sideways, making our way up the channel. But that was nothing compared to the way they looked as we came up to the first really shallow water. Now, to anyone who has spent time on the river, the deep water channel is very clearly marked, and those guys had spent just as much time on the river as I had. They knew what that long line across the river meant. It meant the water was too shallow to run a boat over, that's for sure! By the way, the line was getting extremely close to us by then—so close, in fact, that my two passengers decided it would be impossible to miss, anyhow, so they had better prepare themselves for the inevitable. They braced themselves as best as they could. They were so prepared that it was kind of a shame we didn't scrape bottom, at least a little. They opened their eyes to find that we were skimming over water less than an inch deep. Let me tell you, I had me some impressed passengers!

The little settlements along the river slipped quickly by: Raton, San Fernando, Santa Barbara, San Antonio, Quiratari. I was feeling really good. I was getting back into familiar territory again and, after a solid ten hours of running, the hovercraft had not had a lick of trouble. It had not even sucked in any water. This was at about 5:00 p.m. At the rate we were going, we would get to TamaTama around 6:15. I figured I would drop off my passengers, grab some petrol, and make it into Coshilowäteli by 8:30, because from TT it didn't matter to me if it was dark or light. That was my old stomping grounds, and I had the rocks down pretty good on that stretch of water.

In my mind I had already climbed out of the craft in Cosh and was kissing my wife when all of a sudden everything quit! Now, in a hovercraft when everything quits, you don't gently glide to a stop. I mean you *stop,* right now! The nose plows into the water, water shoots up like a geyser through the venturi, and, I'll be the first to tell you, you hit the water at a speed that is just a little bit unsettling. Yes, our old friend water was back, and both engines had now sucked in enough to keep us sitting there for a long time. By the time we got the craft over to shore and onto the beach, it was dark. I thought to myself, *I'll get up early, clean out both carburetors, and we can still get to TT by about 8:00 a.m. That should put me in Cosh by about 10:30.*

What a joke! Something had gotten stuck in the high-speed jet on the lift motor and I didn't have an Allen wrench to take the jet out. So, to make a long story short, we limped into Tama-Tama at about noon.

I got some gas, borrowed an Allen wrench, cleaned the carbs, and took off for Cosh. By that time it was roughly 4:00 p.m., but *talk about beautiful!* That river, as usual at that time of day, was smooth as glass, with the Duida mountain rising up as if out of the water. I'll tell you, I had some beautiful hovering. I soon came to the Padamo River (my exit point), then drove past the place where we get palm for the village houses. There Gary and Jerald and a boatload of guys came out to help me. Actually, I think they just couldn't wait any longer to see the hovercraft!

Then we're past Tedecai Yaji. Oh, I've got a passenger again: Gary got in the craft to ride the rest of the way with me. By that time it was getting so dark I had the canopy pushed back in order to see, but as we came around the bend Gary turned on all the lights, slid the bubble back into place, and we went screaming by that village like something out of a James Bond movie—or maybe something from outer space. It would be one and the same to these guys. *Praise the Lord, I'm home at last,* I thought, feeling very thankful and excited.

For the length of the trip we took, and the many miles we ran, the hovercraft did extremely well on the river. In my opinion, it more than adequately demonstrated the feasibility of this type of craft for this work. During the dry season, there is nothing on the river that can touch it. Although it still has a few bugs, with a bit of time to work these out and perfect our tweaks, there is absolutely no reason this craft could not be used as a vehicle to reach out to villages on rivers where travel, largely due to low-water sandbars, is such a problem.

22
LOST

"**I**f you-all don't get some meat for me to cook, I'll quit cooking," she declared. I looked up in surprise. I couldn't believe Reneé had actually said that. Those were the best words I'd heard spoken in a long time! We had been trying to finish our new house, so I hadn't taken time off to do anything but build. Normally, when I mentioned needing a break from it all and stated that I was thinking about going hunting, Reneé would hand me a to-do list that had to be finished first. All I had to do was look down that list for a while and all desire to go anywhere would quickly disappear. Why, if—in a moment of madness—I had assumed that I could complete her list and then go, I guarantee you I would still be working on that crazy list—and would only be halfway down it. So, normally, I just forgot about going and discarded the lists.

Now she was forcing me to go hunting, so to speak. Before she could come to her senses, I announced I would leave the next morning. Three or four Yanomamö men in the house heard me and we all began discussing where would be the best place to go. Finally we decided to go down to a mountain called

Tigre, which is the Spanish name for the jaguar. The mountain is called this because during a certain time of year, the way the leaves grow on the different varieties of trees makes it look like the face of a jaguar on the mountainside.

I have hunted on that mountain before and, to be perfectly honest, I never much cared for the place. I know the mountain's name is only derived from the jaguar face that seems to appear in the trees. During the different hunts we had made there, though, it seemed we had always had some kind of a brush with them—jaguars, not leaves! As far as I was concerned, the mountain was very well named and I would just as soon have gone up the Metaconi. Now, that is what I would call "Happy Hunting Land." I loved that river. The Yanomamö guys were right, though; it had been under an awful lot of pressure lately, what with the different villages having feasts and their men going up there to get their meat. So we made our plans to head toward the Tigre.

We left the next morning around 3:00 a.m. in order to get down to where we were going to start walking inland right around dawn. As close as we are located to the equator, that never varies much. By 5:45 it was getting light enough to start walking into the jungle. Once under the canopy, it was still pretty dark, but we could see better every minute.

There were seven of us: Yacuwä, Timoteo, Julio, Agustin, Däduwä, Lucas, and I. As we waited for Lucas to tie the boat, I looked at my watch. "We have to leave here by around 5:00 p.m. if we want to make it home before dark," I said. "Whoever is not here by then will get left."

I glanced at Däduwä. He was getting quite a reputation as someone who was forever wandering off by himself and getting lost. The last time this happened to him he spent twelve days out in the jungle alone with the entire village looking for him. He smiled now. "I'll be here; don't *you* wander off," he said, "or we will have to leave you."

I didn't figure there was much chance of that! I had never gotten lost before; besides, I had the only set of keys to the boat in my pocket.

We headed on out. Once again I tried to look at my surroundings through the eyes of someone who had not been raised there. Here I was out in the middle of the Amazon rainforest, walking single file through the jungle, hunting with a group of Yanomamö warriors. What a thrill!

The Yanomamö are unmatched in the jungle in their ability to track and call animals right up to them. I have watched them call monkeys to within arm's reach. The same with turkeys, toucans—you name it. They really are masters of their jungle environment.

We walked on, keeping our eyes and ears open. Normally it is the ears that first tell the Yanomamö there is something there to hunt, but I'm always fascinated to note, again, how well-developed their sense of smell is. They will stop and smell the breeze . . . or the odor of a particular animal will waft off the leaves along the way we are walking, and they will stop and investigate, just to see if it is something we want to go after.

Although we were still just heading out to our hunting area, everyone was quiet. Periodically during this walk, even though we were initially more interested in just putting distance between the boat and ourselves, different guys would take turns making the calls of the various species of monkey.

The spider monkey is considered prime game. If the Yanomamö had trophy walls, the spider monkey would command the most attention on them. Not only is the meat considered a real delicacy, but the animals are also difficult to hunt: that task requires a lot of skill and stamina. I have been on hunts where we started chasing the monkeys at about 10:00 a.m. and didn't quit running until noon or after. The interesting thing about this is that you are running through trackless jungle. No trail. You take your shots when you can get them. If and when you hit a spider monkey, you watch and make sure that he is not just wounded, but that he fell all the way out of the tree. Then you run to rejoin the hunt. What always amazes me is when the hunt is over the Yanomamö can retrace their route perfectly and retrieve all the monkeys. Let me assure you that the monkeys are not running in a straight line, either! Like I said, Yanomamö skill and ability in the jungle are nothing but amazing.

I recall one day that I was hunting with some of my friends. We were way up the Metaconi River chasing *basho,* or spider monkeys. We had killed a bunch of them and had stopped to rest before returning, slowly, to gather up the ones we had hunted. I suddenly became aware that the magazine that holds the bullets in my rifle had somehow fallen out. I was heartsick, as I didn't think there was any way in the world we could find it, and the gun was useless without it. Pablino noticed my growing sense of panic.

"Where did you last see it?" he asked. "Where do you think it fell?"

"I am not sure," I told him. "The last place I saw it was when I added bullets to the magazine, which was down on the other side of this mountain."

"Well, which way were you coming?" he insisted.

I described the way that I had been running and we took off in that direction. I followed Pablino as he slowly worked out my back trail. Getting to an area that was easier to track in, he verified with me that, "Yes, this was indeed the way I had been running"—then he set in to tracking *me* for real. To this day I have never been so impressed with anyone's expertise in the jungle as I was with him that day. We walked, with him tracking me up and down and around that crazy mountain. Every step I had taken we retook as he kept his eyes on the ground, first of all making sure he stayed on my trail, and second, searching for the lost magazine out of a .22 Browning pump. It was something that was approximately the size of your little finger (if you've got small fingers), and about ten inches long. It was a light copper, rust color. In other words, he was looking for something, in one huge pile of sticks and leaves, that would look just about like any other little stick in that big pile. And remember, we were not on a trail in the jungle: I had just been running through the trees behind the monkeys.

I didn't have much hope. I was awfully impressed that he stayed so faithfully on my trail, but still, to spot that crazy magazine was going to require an all-out miracle. We kept going. All of a sudden, he stopped.

"What does it look like again?" he asked me. I explained again.

"Is that it there?" he asked with a smile, as he pointed to the ground.

Sure enough, there it was . . . half-buried in the leaves of the jungle floor. I picked it up, wiping it off against one leg of my worn cutoffs.

"I honestly did not think you had one chance of finding it," I told him. He only smiled.

Woodcraft? These guys defined the word!

Back to our present hunt . . . We worked our way up the face of Tigre Mountain. Now we were hunting in earnest. Every fruit tree was examined for signs of animal activity. Our pauses were longer as the Yanomamö listened and sniffed. Every once in a while someone would slap a mosquito and the rest of us would jump at the sound.

On one of our pauses, Julio cleared his throat and began to make the call of the spider monkey. If I had closed my eyes, I would have sworn I was standing within three feet of one. We listened. Way off in the distance we heard a troop answer. Julio called back. Immediately they answered again. Judging from the way animals answer, the Yanomamö will say that they are either *shiumi* (selfish) or *shiöjöte* (generous). The *shiumi* ones will not come to you, but will just sit way off and holler back. The *shiöjöte* ones, on the other hand, will come running to beat the band. They are the best ones, because you can get prepared and wait for them instead of having to run right off like crazy to hunt them.

Thankfully, the ones Julio called up were *shiöjöte*. We waited for them to get to us. I was standing in an excellent spot because they had to pass on a small branch about fifty feet over my head. With the low noise of my .22 rifle, many times I could get off two or three shots before they realized what was happening. That morning was good. I was able to drop three monkeys without even having to run after them. Timoteo got one, too. It had only been a small troop, however, and the four monkeys we got were not enough to make us turn back toward the boat. By that time it was about 11:00 a.m. We began to bend our trail to make a large circle. If done right, we should arrive back at the boat by about five o'clock, which was the time we had to leave.

We came to a stream, and that is where we split up. Lucas and I were not carrying anything. I never take monkey meat home, as Reneé does not like it, and Lucas had missed his prey that day. While the rest of them were walking a small stream looking for alligator tracks, we decided to make our circle bigger and try to bag some turkeys if we could.

We had been walking for about two hours when there was a sudden cloudburst. The rain came down in sheets and the roar from the rain hitting the leaves was so loud I couldn't hear a word. Now, the wise ones in the jungle always stop in the rain, especially in such a cloudburst. First of all because of the noise; then there's the movement of every leaf from the rain, the trees shaking in the wind, lightning flashing, and the crash of thunder, which, taken all together, overwhelms the senses. What's more, the Yanomamö use the sun to navigate by (not consciously, but they do). So, when it is hidden during times of heavy rain or fog, it is incredibly easy to get lost. They almost always stop and let it rain itself out, then go on.

Like I said, though, we were trying to get back to the boat by five. However, we had gone farther away from the others than we should have, and now were worried that we weren't going to make it back in time. So, instead of stopping, as we should have, we kept going. The downpour stopped, but it never quit raining entirely. Instead, it settled into a slow drizzle, with the sky—what little we could see of it—a heavy, dreary grey. I was afraid it looked like something that had settled in for the night.

We were passing a large tree with some really wide roots. About an hour earlier we had passed another one of these trees. The root system was quite unique and I had stopped to examine it. Suddenly I realized it was the same tree.

"Lucas, we are going in circles," I told him. "We passed this tree a while ago." He stopped in his tracks.

"Are you sure?" he said, shocked at the possibility. "How do you know it is the same tree?"

Lucas paused as I explained my observations. "Let's get to higher ground so I can climb a tree and see if I can recognize something," he suggested. We headed higher up the mountain until he decided we were about as high as we were going to get without having to really work for it. Quickly he made the vine loop they put on their feet to help them climb and shinnied up the tree in less time than it has taken me to tell of it, then looked around.

"We are surrounded by mountains higher than we are, but I think this is the way," he said, pointing. "That way is generally sloping down, which is probably heading toward the river."

I looked at my watch. It was now a bit after 4:00 p.m. We were going to have to really bust a gut to get back to the boat by my own deadline. As soon as he got back down, we took off in the direction he had indicated, practically running. It was still drizzling and the ground was getting muddy. Suddenly Lucas stopped in front of me.

"Whose trail is this?" he asked.

I looked where he had pointed and it was obvious that two people had passed this way since the rain. We studied the trail and both arrived at the same conclusion: It was *our* trail. We were going in circles again! Suddenly, off in the distance, I heard the sound of an airplane. It was flying toward us low, under the overhanging clouds. I knew the flight plan for the airplane that week, so I remembered immediately that the plane was to go to Parima in the morning, back to TamaTama, and then on to Puerto Ayacucho.

"Listen," I told Lucas, "that plane is on its way back from Parima. All we have to do is run in the direction the plane is coming from and that will take us out to the river because the plane flies right across the Orinoco on its way to TamaTama." We listened until the plane flew right over us. We had taken some bearings off the line of the plane's flight path, and as soon as it flew over we took off. We weren't quite panicked yet, but we sure wanted to get out to the river before dark. Forget the boat; we just wanted to find the river.

Sad to say, what I had not realized was that the plane had not been in Parima. Bad weather had delayed it and now, instead of being on its way to TamaTama from Parima, it was on its way *to* Parima *from* TamaTama. We were running in the opposite direction of the boat! Oh, but we were convinced we were right!

I've often thought of this illustration when people tell me things like, "Oh, but as long as you really have faith in what you are doing, it is going to be all right. Just *sincerely believe* and it will work out. God loves you, and as long as you believe you are doing what is right, that is what counts." I tell you, we thought we were running as hard as we could run in the direction of the Orinoco River. But you know what? Our thinking it was so did not change *one bit* the fact that we were running as hard as we could run in the exact wrong direction.

Finally we had to admit it. Not only were we not going to get to the boat, we were not even going to get to the river, and it was getting dark fast. Once these afternoon drizzles set in and the clouds hang low, the night comes on very fast. By 5:30 it was almost too dark to see. We took stock of what we had. That didn't take long, since we had absolutely *nothing.* No matches, no food, no machete, no knife. Life was bleak!

We stopped. We were going to be miserable enough without wandering around in the dark and getting snake-bitten on top of it. We found a little spot that was a little less *baimi* (overgrown with weeds) than the area around it. We figured it was a large enough area to lie down in. We broke some palm fronds off and stuck them up in a circle to give us a bit of protection from the still-drizzling rainfall but, more importantly, from anything wandering around in the night.

I worked myself deeper under one of the big fronds we had stuck in the ground to try to get away from a persistent dripping of rainwater. The wet ground was hard and cold under me. I knew it was going to be a long night. The leaves we had woven above us helped a bit but not enough to write home about. Did I mention the mosquitoes? They were so thick above us that they were flying in holding patterns. One flight would take off, then another horde would land, seeking to gorge themselves on our quivering flesh. And I was cold! I once was up in Minnesota in the wintertime when they experienced record-breaking cold weather. It was so cold that the fuel froze in our truck's fuel tank. We had one-inch-thick ice on the inside of the cab with the heater running—but I was not as cold then as I felt here, shivering, huddled under those miserable palm fronds in the cold, tropical rain. Honest! I could feel Lucas shivering beside me. He was wearing less than I was (a pair of swimming trucks), and I was only wearing a pair of jean cutoffs and a sleeve-less tee shirt.

Sometime during the never-ending night I must have fallen asleep. I woke up with a start. Lucas was snoring beside me. *Snoring!* I woke him up quickly.

"Stop snoring! What are you trying to do, get us eaten by a jaguar?"

We both lay there in silence, quietly contemplating that thought. Suddenly I noticed that the jungle had gone deafeningly quiet. We both knew what that meant. There is only one thing in the jungle that will quiet everything from crickets to bullfrogs. We listened in the night, hardly daring to breathe.

Then I heard it. Not quite a growl but, rather, a low-pitched moan, almost seeming to make the ground tremble. The moans were then replaced by the low coughing sounds made by a hunt-ing jaguar.

"Be very quiet," I heard Lucas breathe. Boy, as if I needed to be told that! I did get my .22 ready, easing a shell in and hold-ing it in the direction from which I heard the jaguar coming. We had killed a couple of jaguars with this gun, but to do so you had to be dead on target. *How in the world can I shoot, when I can't see my hand in front of my face?* I wondered. And believe me, my eyes were bugged out so badly trying to see that it's a wonder I ever got my eyelids to cover them again!

But now I could hear the jaguar coming. It was obvious he was following the trail we had made in coming to this spot. I could hear the soft "puft, puft, puft" of his paws. He would sniff and snarl and moan quietly, almost to himself, as he came nearer and nearer to us. He was right outside our leaf shelter now. My head nearly swiveled off as he paced around and around. As I sat there in silence I wondered what we must look like to this great cat. Two guys cold and wet, sitting up now with humon-gous, caricature-like ears and huge, bugged-out eyes, straining to see into the darkness. I also wondered if the jaguar was going to do like Joshua of old and try and make the leaf wall that was protecting us fall down by walking around us seven times. I hadn't been keeping count, but I knew he must have been getting close. It was difficult trying to keep the barrel of the gun pointed right where I figured his head was, as I kept trying to pivot around silently each time I heard him move. I was afraid to make any sound at all, lest it cause him to jump into our leaf hideout.

Then, suddenly, absolute quiet! One minute we were listening to him "puft, puft, puft" around our leaf wall, as we wished he would go away, and the next minute it was just absolutely quiet. Not a sound. No moan, growl, or faint rustle of a leaf. Just *nothing!* I swear I think even the mosquitoes had gone away out of respect toward (or fear of) the jaguar. *Where was he?* Of course, in my mind, he was sitting about a foot from my face, staring me right in the eye, waiting for me to blink. It was utterly pitch-black. The blackness of an overcast jungle night is a blackness like the inside of a cave. No light at all. I determined not to blink or breathe, and it seemed like I held my breath for hours. I know it was just minutes, but an eternity seemed to pass during those minutes. Still nothing! *Where in the world was that crazy cat?* I had thought it was bad listening to him pace around our little palm barrier, but this silence was just about enough to make me scream.

You won't believe what happened next—of course, as it could only happen to me. I had to go to the bathroom . . . in the worst way! Still, I was determined not to move. Finally, my discomfort got to the point that I decided something was going to have to give. If I moved, maybe the jaguar would get me. If I stayed as I was, I would drown or burst for sure. I whispered the bad news to Lucas.

"I have to go to the bathroom," I said.

"*Sheeesh,*" he hissed back. "Quiet! It is probably crouched right there."

I sat there for maybe another fifteen or twenty minutes, which seemed like that many hours and more, or maybe days. Finally, I could take it no more.

"Be ready," I told him. Taking aim with my rifle, I shot about ten shots out into the jungle as quickly as I could pump and pull the trigger. Nothing moved, so I jumped up and out of our little leaf barrier, "went" as fast as I could, and almost *dove* back in behind our little leaf wall.

Amazingly enough, I then fell asleep. The next part sounds so weird that I have not told this to many people. Even now, I only tell it as it was to me: a dream.

I woke up from a deep sleep. There was a man sitting there. He handed me a small package of food. "You need to eat," he told me. I took it from him and ate what he gave me. The taste of that dream food tingles at the edge of my subconscious, even to this day. I can never quite place that taste. I then fell back asleep. The same man woke me up much later and gave me another package of food. Again I ate the entire amount. The next time I woke up, it was getting light. The long night was over.

I puzzled over my dream. The similarity of my dream to what had happened to the Prophet Elijah was unmistakable. I guess in my very hungry state my mind jumbled what I knew had happened to him into a dream in which I played a principal part. The funny thing was, I had gone to bed half-starved. We had not eaten anything the day before, and we had gotten out of the boat very early. Neither of us had been carrying food. Either Timi or Julio was carrying the food package the last time I saw it. We had been going to eat it at the next good creek we came to, but then we'd gotten separated. So, Lucas and I never got a crumb of that food. I thought it was funny that, for whatever reason, I was no longer hungry now.

I have gone without food before, and during those times I always feel light-headed and a bit dizzy. I felt none of that now. Lucas, in contrast, was really complaining about being hungry.

We spent the first hours we were awake with him trying to find some fruit to eat, finally finding some *edeweshi* palm fruit. He knocked some down.

"Come, eat up, so we can try and find our way home," he told me. "I do not want to sleep out here again."

"You know what? I am not hungry," I told him, relating my dream. He listened intently.

"The least you could have done is woken my dream-person up, and fed him, too," he told me solemnly. The Yanomamö look at dreams differently than we do and, as far as he was concerned, if I had eaten in my dream, then I should not be hungry. I apologized for not waking him. To me it was still just interesting, no more than that. I figured as soon as my stomach woke up, it would be one very upset organ. But no, all during that long, long, *long* day, as we drudged up one hill after another and swam across more swamp than I care to even think about, not once did I ever even feel the least bit hungry.

When the sun came up, it at least told us which way was east. This in turn gave us our bearings to get back to the river. In our panic runs the day before, we had really covered the territory. We started walking southeast and held that course all day. Again I looked at my beautiful jungle, but not with the admiring eyes of the day before. My jungle had turned against me. It was no longer friendly.

Now we felt closed in by enemy trees. They loomed over us, catching us as we tried to walk by. They used their roots to trip us up and their smaller branches waited for the slightest chance to come back and smack us in the face. The trees were thicker and more malicious this day. Almost everything had thorns or something with which to cut us. The trees were so closely interwoven with vines that it was almost impossible to see where we were going, let alone walk through them, yet we held to our southeast course, as if led by a tractor beam. We didn't even let a swamp deter us, so great was our interest in finding that river. As I said, though, we had covered a lot of ground, and we didn't realize that the section of the river we were now at was running at such an angle that we were almost paralleling it. We would intercept it, eventually, if we lived that long, but not today.

At this point we were getting a bit desperate. We had come to the swamp at around 2:00 p.m. and had decided it could not be that big. In the jungle, though, one's view of one's surroundings is so limited. Many times I could barely see my companion, Lucas, who was only a few feet ahead of me. Our world had shrunk to what we could see, which was not much.

"Let's just walk straight through it. It cannot be that long," he suggested. I agreed.

That thinking was coming back to haunt me. It was now about 4:30 p.m. and there was no end in sight. The last place in this world I wanted to spend the night was chest-deep in swamp water. Too many things live in swamp water—the least of which is the giant anaconda. Anacondas, I might add, that might have some kind of a grudge against me and want to get their own back. Sleeping in that water would have been a riot. But we had already talked and decided that since we didn't know where the swamp ended, we would stop at the next little island we came to and try to make a decent little house there to sleep in—something a bit more substantial than the broken palm fronds we had stuck in the ground the night before. Lucas was complaining more and more about being hungry, and I knew we would have to try to get him something more to eat.

Suddenly I heard the sound of a plane off in the distance coming our way. I strained my ears, to be sure. I knew it was Sunday, and the mission planes only fly on Sunday for an emergency. *Oh, no! What has happened?* I thought. *I sure hope Reneé and the boys are OK. I sure hope they're not the emergency.*

The plane came on, a little to the west of where we were, then passed us. How I longed to be sitting up there with the pilot, looking down at the jungle with the calm detachment that only comes when you are flying over it at over a hundred miles per hour, not a care in the world. As for the two of us, the last thing we were was calm. We were full of cares and wants. We were up to our armpits in swamp water, and might even be looking at our giant water bed for the night, in a literal way. Believe me, we were not calm. I kept listening to the sound of the airplane, and I realized it was turning and coming back toward us. It passed overhead and continued to fly parallel to the direction it had been coming from. Although I could still hear it disappearing in the distance, we could tell from the sound it made that the pilot was once again turning and heading back our way. Suddenly I realized that *we* were the Sunday emergency!

"Lucas, that plane is flying up the river. Listen! Reneé must have called and told him we were lost. They know about where we were, so they are flying up the river. If we hurry, we can make it." That was all we needed! We took off, and this time (thanks to the guiding sound of that plane flying up and down the river) we knew we were going to make it. I remember that on one pass the plane flew directly over us. Looking up, I caught a brief glimpse of it through the trees. *What a sight!*

At about 6:30 it was starting to get dark. We were really rushing now. Finally we came to the edge of the swamp and started making better time. I heard a motor working its way slowly up the river, which we still could not see.

Hey, if we hurry, the people in that boat can take us home, we both thought at the same time. Adding another burst of speed, we sprinted the last fifty or sixty yards until we came out to the edge of the river. I looked across. There, over against the far bank, was a small dugout canoe with about a 15-horsepower engine on it. With the noise that engine was making there was no way anyone could hear us yelling. I took my faithful .22 and, making sure the barrel was not clogged with swamp muck, held it about a hundred yards in front of the canoe and shot it three times. Even a little .22 rackets pretty loudly across an open body of water and, believe me, that got their attention.

They swung over toward us. They could see it was us while they were still a good distance away. Quickly they came on in. It was my brother-in-law, Jerry Lee, and some of my friends. They had been helping search for us.

"What in the world are you all doing way up here?" was their first question. We had come out about twelve or fifteen miles farther upriver from where we had left our boat. I'm not sure what we said, but I think we babbled something about being happy to see the river!

They took us back downriver to where we had left our boat. Pulling in beside it, we discovered that almost the entire village of Coshilowä had come down to help in the search. They had tracked us that day to where Lucas climbed the tree, and then they found the place where we had slept. They had seen the jaguar tracks around our little shelter, and every one of them clutched his weapon tighter. They had continued tracking us, but had finally lost our trail in the swamp. We hadn't realized it, of course, but if we had walked only about a hundred meters to our right, we would have gotten out of the swamp. It was a long, narrow swamp and we were walking right down the middle of it. I shivered again, remembering that if the plane had not flown over, we would still be out there in it. Once we got a bearing on where the river was from the sound of the plane, we turned and headed across diagonally, coming right to the edge of it, and got out. I was so thankful!

Everyone was, of course, very happy to see us, but certainly no more than we were to be seen, I can assure you. It was so late that many of the guys had decided to sleep there, as they had made some nice shelters and had their hammocks ready. I wanted nothing else but to get home and see my wife and kids, so we took off up the river. It was a much prettier night than the night before; instead of the overcast and drizzling rain, there were stars hanging in the sky—so close, it seemed, that I could have touched them. We had driven that section of the river so much that it really was not that big a deal to travel at night, and we arrived home, most happily, about 10:00 p.m.

I gave Reneé a big hug and had to awaken each of the boys and give them hugs, as well. Reneé told me how worried they all had been and how each of them had prayed for me. She told me they had especially prayed for protection against snakes and jaguars, and that I would not get too hungry. I smiled when I heard that and told her my dream and about the jaguar walking around us in the night. We thanked God for His protection.

"How did you find your way home?" she asked. I answered her question with one of my own.

"Did you call Rolland Trempert and have him fly the river?"

She nodded, "Yes." She explained, "I didn't know what to do. The guys you had gone with got home really late last night and said you two were lost. They went down this morning and I waited around all day to hear something. I was frantic, then, all of a sudden I remembered Mission Aviation Fellowship wives' talk on the radio every Sunday at 2:00 p.m. When I thought of it, it was just a bit after two. I ran and turned the radio on. They were still talking. I waited my chance and asked to speak to Rolland. After I explained what had happened, he offered to fly the river."

"Did it help?" she asked me, once again flashing that smile of hers. I gave her another big hug by way of an answer.

"Well, you may have saved our lives; I don't know," I told her, "but one thing I *do* know for sure: You saved us from having to spend a very miserable night in the middle of a swamp."

I explained to her where we had been when we first heard the airplane above us. "I could have cried when I heard that plane and realized it was flying there for us," I told her. "I was so thankful you had called us in as an emergency," I added, as I hugged her again.

Another thing I was thankful for was that Reneé was so happy to see me and to have me home that she didn't even notice that I had come home empty-handed from the hunt. The funniest thing, too, was that it was at least two days later that I even became hungry again. That *dream food* was pretty good stuff!

23
MYSTERIOUS WHISTLER

RUBEN
PINTOR

We were out hunting one day a good distance up the Metaconi River. We were on the trail of a herd of wild pigs, and you could feel the mounting adrenaline in the hunters as the tracks got fresher and fresher. Suddenly we froze and listened. Sure enough, off in the distance we could hear the squeal of the pigs and the clashing of boars' tusks. Those boars were more than dangerous with their large tusks: They could rip a man or a dog to shreds in one or two quick swipes of their huge heads.

We ran forward more quietly now. It was imperative that we surround the herd before the animals became aware of our presence. If they got wind of us before we were in position, they would be gone, and I mean *gone!* A herd of pigs can really cover some ground quickly!

We communicated with whistles until we were all in position. By this time I was in an excellent place. I could see about twenty or more pigs rooting around beside a small stream. Pablino was right beside me. I had my Browning pump .22 ready. It was about the best thing for hunting pigs, as it was so quiet that the sound of it firing rarely startled them. The Yanomamö said it must sound like a pig chomping down and breaking a *caleshi* nut. Anyway, Pablino was with me, and he had his arrows. I was going to let him shoot first, and then I would try and get as many pigs as I could before they really took off. Once everyone started shooting with shotguns, it was pretty much a free-for-all.

Pablino took careful aim and let fly his arrow. As soon as I heard his pig squeal I started shooting. I ran forward and shot again and again. Somehow in the melee I lost track of Pablino, but, figuring him to be somewhere off to my right and just a bit ahead of me, I continued running. I paused just long enough to get off another shot. I was breathing so hard from running that I held my breath while squeezing the trigger. Making sure the pig was dead, I stopped long enough to listen to see if I could get a bearing on the herd. I knew I had shot seven pigs, but with a village the size of ours it would take many more pigs to really count for anything.

Suddenly I heard a whistle off to my left. I hadn't realized that anyone was over that way. The whistle was strange, and I couldn't understand it. I whistled back to let whoever was over there know I was here and to ask him to repeat his order. Again the whistle came, this time with a sense of more urgency. *Who in the world is that?* I wondered. I began to slowly make my way over there. Something about the whistle bothered me, and I was cautious, making my way as quietly as I could.

Where in the world is Pablino? I wondered. I whistled again, this time asking, "What is it?" with my whistle.

The unknown whistler did not answer again. I decided to head back to where I had left my last pig, and from there to try and locate Pablino and the rest of the hunters. I was honestly getting a bit spooked by the mysterious whistler. I retraced my way and came to where I had left the large boar. I then looked at the spot in disbelief. The pig was gone! I knew I was in the right place, because there on the ground was the large pool of blood and the indentation on the ground where it had lain. Now I was really spooked. I whistled as loudly as I could the message that means, "Where are you?"

Faintly and far away I heard someone answer, with what sounded like a real whistle. I answered back and started making my way in the direction from which I had heard them answer me. After a bit I could hear the hunters talking and laughing as they made their way in my direction. I called them over to where I was. Everyone was happy, as it had been a very successful hunt. Finally, I asked them about the mysterious whistle.

"Hey, who was over that way?" I said, pointing in the direction where I had followed the whistle. They looked at me blankly.

"No one," Ramon assured me. "We all followed the pigs downstream. The group you were following was just a small bunch of them that was separated from the herd. None of us was over that way."

Pablino nodded his head. "Yes, that is right. As soon as you started shooting I started running, and it was not until I finished shooting all my arrows that I realized you must have run the other way."

"Well, someone was over there whistling, and when I went over there to see who it was, they came back and stole one of my pigs," I told them.

They stared at me in disbelief, but by this time we were back at the spot where the pig had lain, and it was obvious to all that indeed a pig had been dead there, and just as obvious that it was no longer there. It did not take the Yanomamö long to work out the trail, but I was surprised to see them become very nervous and put up their guard as they worked it out. After about five minutes, they left the trail they were working on and we made our way back to where the hunt had started, gathering the pigs we had killed as we went. The laughter and excitement of the morning was gone, and in its place was a quiet watchfulness that mystified me. I knew it must have something to do with the missing pig and the strange whistler I had heard, but I was perplexed as to why this should have made everyone so nervous.

We finally arrived back at our camp, tired and bloody from carrying the stinking pigs. That was the only bad thing about hunting pigs. They were fun to hunt, but packing them out of the jungle was a little too much like work. They were heavy and stinky, and by the time we had the pigs tied up with vines so we could carry them, the adrenaline of the hunt had left my bloodstream, leaving me jittery and tired. I flopped the pig I was carrying down in the pile and continued on to the river to get a much-needed bath.

I made my way back up to the lean-to shelter we had made, where my hammock was hanging. Gratefully, I sank into it. I listened to my friends continue to work, preparing the meat to be smoked. As always, I was impressed with how long they could go and go. Their endurance was impressive. Personally, I was bushed. I had only carried one pig out, and to lighten it I had cut its head off. Ramon had not only carried the pig's head I had thrown off, but he had carried two other pigs with it! And still there he was, directing the job of butchering all the pigs and building a smoking rack big enough to handle the weight of all the meat, as if he had just been out for a walk in the park all day!

As I lay back in the hammock I overheard Ramon telling the older men who had stayed in camp about the pig that had been stolen. I listened as they whispered about who might have taken it. Ramon wondered if it could have been the same people who had gone through their camp on a previous trip to the same area, leaving the smell of burning tobacco leaves. The Yanomamö do not smoke tobacco, but chew it, yet they know the smell of burning tobacco. Yacuwä's uncle was there, quietly listening to them all talk. After a couple of questions he said, "I thought all those people were dead." He said this almost more to himself than to the others. The work area quieted down as he finished talking.

"Who are you talking about?" we all wanted to know. "*Who* were all dead?" He stared into the fire.

"It was a long time ago, and probably not the same ones because, yes, I am afraid we did kill all of them. It is something I really do not like to think about, and most times try and convince myself that maybe it never happened. But the screams . . ." his voice trailed off as his mind took him back to something that had happened long ago. Slowly the story came out:

The old man looked up angrily as the large clay pot they were cooking in tilted and tipped over. He jumped up to try and stop its fall, but he was too late. With a crash, it fell over on its side and smashed into pieces.

He was furious, but there was no one to blame but the fire, and it did not care how angry he was. He fussed and fumed, regardless. This was the last large clay pot his village had. Now they would have to make the long trek over to where the clay bank was, where they got the clay that they made the pots out of.

Preparation was quick. It consisted of getting what food there was in our gardens that was almost ripe, making a few cakes of cassava bread, and bundling it all up. A few days later found the whole village on the trail over to where the stream was. It was a long walk. With the women and children along, having to stop and forage for food for them, it normally took about four days of travel to get there. But it was the dry season and food was plentiful. We were all in a festive mood, just to be away from the cares that overwhelm us so often in our daily lives. We did, however, maintain our guard, as one never knew when an enemy might show up. And there were always the spirits one had to be constantly on guard against.

"Don't call your little brother's name!" I heard my mother tell my sister. "What are you trying to do? Don't you know that the *shaboli* [witch doctor] across the mountain would like nothing better than to hear your names so he can work his curses on you?! Don't ever use his real name!"

Guarding the village against spiritual attack was the job of the *shaboli*, or witch doctor. In our village there were two main ones . . . along with a couple of younger apprentices. I was the younger of the two apprentices working under Guajaribo, the most powerful shaman in that whole area of the jungle. His fame as a healer was widespread, but his fame as a killer of men with black magic was even more widespread and was discussed only in whispers. Grown men feared his name, and a mother had only to hiss it at her children to make them instantly obey.

There were few things we could take for granted in the jungle. Safety was not one of them. We had to guard against all kinds of natural dangers, but the worst to be feared were the attacks against our village by the shamans of other villages. These attacks could be in the form of causing a big wind to blow trees down on our party, or they could send snakes to lie in wait and bite us, or they could send the *Öla,* the jaguar, to take his unsuspecting prey.

We also had to guard our *noleshi,* or mirror spirit. Every man and woman has one. For the men, it is the majestic harpy eagle. [They truly are the lords of the jungle. Flying high above the upper canopy, searching for their prey, you only knew it was around when you heard its shrill hunting cry echo throughout the jungle. The Yanomamö hold these birds in awe. To kill one is to kill the man that is this bird's mirror soul. In the same way, to kill the man was also to kill the bird that corresponded to the man. The Yanomamö are sensitive to this, and the bird is treated with respect and dignity. When the Yanomamö killed one, they went through the same cleansing *unocaimou* rites they used when they killed a man because by killing the bird, they had killed the man.]

The mirror soul of the woman is the *jajana.* [This is a small, elusive, wild doglike animal that is almost impossible to ever see. It runs in packs, and with its sensitive ears hears someone coming long before they are close enough to see it, and it vanishes into the deepest cover in the jungle. You hear them at night, so you know they are out there, but even most Yanomamö have never actually seen one. Because of their elusiveness, the descriptions you will get from the Yanomamö are varied and for the most part farfetched.] But the *shabolis* know what they are, and what they look like. . . .

For some reason, the *shabolis'* closeness to the spirit world gives them an affinity with animals that is difficult to explain. Most of the time the *shaboli* is the best hunter. He comes back with animals across his back when the rest of the hunters in the party come back with nothing. I have asked them about this phenomenon and they tell me that the animal just comes to them. "Here I am, shoot me," it will say to the *shaboli*. But the animal will show himself like this only if the witch doctor is alone. For this reason, most of the shamans are loners.

Yacuwä's uncle continued.

On the fourth day we came to the stream with the big clay bank that was the ideal clay to make our pots. After setting up our makeshift lean-to shelters, the men went right to work clearing off the bank in order to get down to the clay that was soft and pliable. This was time-consuming but fun work. The children splashed in and around the men while we were working. Every so often we would pause to watch the children splashing and tumbling down the bank. After a while some of the men even joined in the fun. The longer it went on, the more of them joined in the entertainment. The clay was slippery and before too long they had a mud slide from the top of the bank down to the stream below.

The next morning we got up early and went right to work digging out the clay. We piled it up on leaves and tied the clay up in bundles that the women could carry back to our village. The clay was heavy, so care had to be taken to make sure the leaves would hold it and that it would not fall out as they walked the long way home.

During the time most of the men were digging some of us kept guard against a surprise attack. We scouted up and down the stream, making sure we did not see the tracks of the dreaded *Onka*. These are the lone killers of the Yanomamö. They kill by getting close enough to someone to blow the magic powder called *alowali*. This is blown through a small blowgun. The *Onka* leave their villages and go out to kill. They spend months out on these trips, and they have been known to lie in wait for days until the one they wish to kill gets into the right position for them to blow their

powder on him. They become as deathly silent as the jaguar
. . . and just as dangerous. They live only for the kill, like
the jaguar.

On one of my scouting trips I went further upstream
than I had ever gone before. I was surprised to come to
a clearing beside the stream. This was the same stream
my people were down getting the clay out of, just a long
way further upstream. I looked around. There, sitting out
in the sun to cure, were some of the most beautiful pots
I had ever seen. Across the stream I saw where whoever
had made them had gotten their clay. The bank was high
and, judging by the size of the hole in the bank, whoever
had made these pots had been coming here making them
for a long time. From the deep shadows of the jungle I
continued watching until I was satisfied that the clearing
was empty. Carefully I edged out in order to get a closer
look at the pots. They were incredibly well-made and were
of a design that I had never seen.

You know our pots come almost to a point at the bottom.
We have never figured out how to make a pot flat across
the bottom, and still be strong enough to hold the weight
of the meat and the water needed to cook it. So we have
the pot come to a point, as the rounded end is stronger.
We take care of the problem of the pot tipping over by
carefully balancing it, and then propping it up with three
or four short poles from the top of the pot to the ground.

But these pots were flat on the bottom, and they sat
there in the sun perfectly balanced. I rubbed one with my
finger to try and judge its age and whether it could be
carried. I was surprised to feel a hardness in the clay that
I had never felt before. This clay was hard as rock, and I
noticed scorch marks on it, as if it had been baked in a
fire or something. Making sure I was still unobserved, I
made my way carefully back out of the clearing. I ran back

to join the group that was digging out the clay. Quickly I told them of my find, and they hurried back with me to see. The pots were still there; more than the fingers on both hands. Looking around, we each grabbed a pot and disappeared back into the jungle from where we had come. Hurrying back to where the women and children were waiting, we broke camp and left back for our village.

We did not keep our new treasures long, however, as we Yanomamö cannot be stingy. It is the only thing that will send someone to *shobali wacä* [the pit of fire]. We know that when they die they will start down a trail. Somewhere they will see something or someone. It might be a sick old woman or a malnourished little kid; maybe even a mangy dog. Anyway, it will be something you normally would not help. This person or thing will ask you for something.

Now if, in this life, you have habitually been generous, you will just out of habit stop and listen and give whatever this thing or person wants. If, on the other hand, you have not habitually been someone who has trained himself to be generous, you will just blow by without stopping to listen or help. The thing is, this person knows where the secret trail branches off to get to *Yalu's* [Thunder's] house. It is a beautiful land where the women are all gorgeous and there is always food. If you help him, or her, or it, you will be shown the trail. If you blow by without stopping, you will not be shown the trail, and as you walk along, all of a sudden the trail will fall out from under you and you will find yourself in a huge lake of fire. So, we have to practice being generous.

Well, as I said, because of this fact the pots did not last long, as every visiting village that saw them wanted one, and we could not say no. So, before too long we found ourselves all out of pots again. We had given the last one away, and it was time to go back and get more clay. We all secretly hoped that the strange pots would be there again.

Once again I made my way back up to the place where I had first seen the pots. I carefully scouted all around. There were tracks, but they were all old. I made my way to the clearing and was surprised to see another row of pots just like before. I ran back to tell the others. Not even stopping to dig any clay out for ourselves, we ran back and grabbed the pots and started on the long trek back to our *shabono*. These pots lasted us for a while, but once again we were out, and it was time to make the long trek back.

Again the pots were there. Not believing our luck, for a third time we grabbed them and made our way back to the village. But this time after the pots were used, everyone who had eaten or drunk anything out of the pots got very sick. Our stomachs were on fire and we could not keep anything down. We got sicker and sicker until most of the village was too weak to walk. No one died, but the whole village was very angry. We knew the makers of the pots had poisoned them. We vowed revenge.

After the men recovered, we got ready to go and avenge ourselves. We got our arrows ready. The best trackers were sent out ahead. Carefully we worked out the trail from the place where we had been getting the pots. We tracked them for days and days. Many of the younger men wanted to stop and go home, but the older men insisted we keep on working out the trail. Many times it would just disappear, and it was only through the skill of the best trackers that we could stay on it at all. But finally the trail got bigger and more obvious. We knew we were getting close.

Now we were all edgy. The main flank of the party stayed back and only two of our best warriors went on ahead to slowly work out the trail and make sure we were not ambushed. Tensions were high. Suddenly Guajaribo motioned for me to stop. He pointed. The trail we were following led right up to a large cave beside a small stream. It was obvious that this was the dwelling of the people of the pots, as there beside the mouth of the cave were a couple of the pots. It did not look as if the people were expecting any trouble. We could see no guard posted anywhere.

Listening carefully, we could hear the soft murmur of voices of people talking inside the cave. I heard someone say something in a language I had never heard before, and I heard someone else laugh. Carefully we backed away. We made our way back to where we had left the main party. Quickly explaining what we had found, we moved back into position.

The old guy paused in telling his story. The pain on his face was obvious. I edged closer, not wanting to miss a word.

"I do not remember whose idea it was," he whispered, "but someone mentioned we could smoke them out like we do the armadillo. That is what we did. We blocked the cave mouth with firewood and quickly built up a roaring fire. We could hear the screams of the trapped people in there. They screamed and screamed, but none of them got out. When the fire had all died out and the smoke cleared away, we went in to look. These were people that looked different than the Yanomamö. They wore their hair differently and wore different ornaments. I have often wondered who they were. But they are all gone now. We killed them all because they made us sick over our stealing their pots. Now I do not know who you could have heard whistling or who stole the pig, but in the morning we will leave and go to another area where we do not have to worry about strange people whistling."

That night, as I struggled to go to sleep, I wondered who those people might have been who had all been killed in the cave. I also wondered who could have whistled at me. I tried to remember exactly what the whistle had sounded like. It had sounded familiar, yet different enough that, even hearing it during the heat of the hunt, it had made me stop and listen. I wondered where they could be living, these hidden people. But I know the jungle is so dense and so uninhabited that it would be easy to lose a whole army in here. It seemed funny to think that maybe just a few short miles away from where I was trying to sleep, there might be another young guy also not able to sleep, wondering who had shot the pig his people were eating that night.

I tossed and turned in the night. I kept thinking back to the old man's story and remembering the pain on his face as he told it. The guilt he felt even after so many years was obvious to see. Some people would like you to believe that these people are innocents, that they live here in the jungle without the knowledge of right or wrong, so they have no guilt.

"It is only after missionaries come in with their talk of sin and hellfire and damnation that the people begin to feel guilt and the fear of punishment," they will say. I told this to some of the Yanomamö in our village, and everyone had a good laugh.

"What a crazy idea!" was the consensus. "If I had not known what stealing was, and that it was wrong, I would have gone out in daylight and taken anything I wanted from anyone's garden. Of course I knew it was wrong to steal; that is why I had to sneak around so I would not get caught. Because the owner also knew it was wrong, he was very angry when his stalk of bananas was missing," Ramon said with a smile.

"If I really had no idea of sin and guilt, why did I sneak around to have an affair with someone else's wife?" someone else volunteered. "We did know it was wrong, and we were always in many fights because of it."

"The guilt we felt for murder, even before we had ever seen or heard about a missionary or about a God that says, 'Thou shalt not murder,' was such that we had a cleansing ritual that went on for days and sometimes weeks before the person felt cleansed and guilt-free," nodded Bautista. "The last act we did to finish our cleansing process was to take our bow and arrows, hammock, and anything else that was appropriate and tie them to a tree out in the jungle in a ceremony that transferred our own guilt to the tree. Actions like this are not consistent with a culture that does not know sin and guilt," he concluded, eloquently.

24

ALONE AGAIN

Yacuwä, now known as Jaime, cleared his throat and started speaking slowly into the microphone. He was the narrator for the group's translation of the Jesus Film Project.

This was the pet project of my good friend, Rick Johnson, who had raised the money for the translation of the *Jesus* film into Yanomamö and set the whole thing up. Rick was now here in Cosh, along with a friend, with all the equipment necessary to start getting voices on tape that would make all the characters in the *Jesus* movie speak in Yanomamö instead of English. It was a big job! Yanomamö is not like English at all, so it was difficult to make their spoken words fit the time frames in the English version. It was even harder to get the Yanomamö we had picked for each of the parts to relax enough to say their pieces. But, slowly, we got through scene after scene. The women found it especially hard to relax enough to speak their parts. Eventually, though, as they saw the whole thing come together, they all got into the spirit of it and we all had a good time. We certainly had a lot of laughs trying to find Yanomamö words to fit specific scenes in Galilee during the time of Christ!

Our greatest hurdle had been trying to make them understand we could not destroy the film if one of them died. When
a Yanomamö dies, everything he had or was involved in is
destroyed by fire when they cremate his body. So, when we
started talking about doing the translation, I sat down with the
group who were going to be the voices and explained to them
that this project represented a lot of time and expense. If one
of them died, it was going to be difficult to burn the entire
Jesus movie just because their family did not want to hear their
voice any more. They listened quietly, and then nodded. They
and I knew that all the nod meant was that we could go ahead
and start, because if one of them died they would not be able
to control what their families wanted to do or did.

So, we began. Even before we started work on the project,
we had decided not to use any non-Yanomamö voices, but then
we came to the place where Jesus tells His disciples to feed the
multitudes. It was really late at night and we wanted to finish
that section before we quit for the evening. I'm not sure why,
in the movie, they gave that part to a woman, because in one
of the gospels it mentions that it was Andrew, Simon Peter's
brother, who brought the boy with the five loaves and two fishes
to Jesus. In the movie, though, one of the women who was with
them says, "There is no food. We only have these few fish and
some pieces of bread." It was a really short line and we didn't
have any Yanomamö ladies close at hand, so we talked my wife,
Reneé, into doing the piece.

This was the last thing on my mind a couple of months later,
as I got ready to head to a missions conference in Puerto Rico.
I had been invited to come and share what the Lord was doing
among the Yanomamö. I was excited to go, but also nervous.
Reneé had decided she was going to stay behind and keep the
boys. We had even argued about it. I really wanted her to come,
but she insisted on staying, as she never liked to leave the boys
behind.

The plane landed, taxied up to our house, and then stopped. I carried my bag out to the airplane. Turning to her as she walked beside me, I said, "Last chance, honey. Why don't you come with me? I know we can even get a couple of extra days and take a break on the beach." (My sister Faith had promised to look after the boys.)

"No, I don't feel right leaving the boys. It's hard enough to see you go; please don't make it harder," she begged me.

I gave her a kiss and a big hug. "That's OK," I told her. "You can plan on meeting me out in Puerto Ayacucho next week." I gave each of my boys a big hug and told them to be good, then threw my bag into the pod of the airplane and climbed in.

"I love you, hon," I told her through the open window. "See you in a week!" She flashed me her brilliant smile.

"That's a great idea about the boys and me meeting you in Puerto Ayacucho," she told me. "We can take a few days' break and then come back home together."

The pilot started the engine and I waved to my beautiful wife, who was standing beside our three sons as we started taxiing to the end of the grass strip to take off. What a beautiful picture they made standing there in front of our house! I wish I'd had a camera to capture it at the time, but that picture is forever burned into my mind.

I flew on out to Puerto Ayacucho. Even before we landed I started to feel like I was coming down with a case of malaria. I thought about canceling the trip, but when I got there, there was a letter with my tickets and a schedule of meetings.

I hesitated. What kind of a testimony would it be if I canceled just because I didn't feel well? The next day I flew on to Caracas and caught the afternoon flight to Puerto Rico. That night we had the first of a series of meetings. I felt terrible. I knew I had a high fever. The church had such a desire to learn more about missionary work among the Yanomamö that they kept me up on the platform for an extra hour after I spoke, answering questions.

I could tell the three Tylenol I had taken were wearing off, as I felt a bit light-headed coming down. As soon as we got home I took a cold shower and three more Tylenol, then tried to get some sleep. I hoped it was just *Vivax* malaria, as you can walk that kind off. The dangerous kind is *Falciparum,* and it is almost epidemic in our whole area.

Little did I know that Reneé had her hands full with Stephen, our youngest son. He had gotten sick as soon as the plane taking me out had left. To this day I have never understood why Reneé did not call me back. We had gone over this issue many times. I have seen so many young children die with malaria that this has always been one of my fears. I would leave on a trip, one of the boys would get sick, and before I could get back they would be dead. I did not want her coping with this by herself, so I had always told her: "If one of the boys gets sick and I am reachable, I want to know."

For some reason, this time she did not call me back. Honestly, as bad as I was feeling, I would have loved the excuse to come home! As it was, I just kept getting sicker and sicker.

Thursday night, and then Friday night, I went through the same thing—in and out of cold showers and just living on huge doses of fever-reducer in an attempt to get my high temperature down. Then, in the evening, going and speaking at church, answering questions about the Yanomamö.

Finally, on Saturday, after I had been speaking and answering questions for more than two hours, a man walked up to me and introduced himself as a doctor. "What's wrong?" he asked me. "You seem feverish. Your eyes are way too shiny," he explained. I told him I was fighting malaria.

He felt my forehead and immediately demanded that I go to the emergency room with him. By that time I felt bad enough that I didn't even argue, but went with him meekly. I was kept there until early Sunday morning when my fever got low enough to permit me to head back to the place where I was staying. The doctors told me I would be called as soon as they had the results of the lab test to determine what I had. I knew I had malaria and was kicking myself for having left the village without a treatment, but the hospital had to have positive results from a blood smear before they would give me the treatment. There is something about malaria that once you have had it, you just know when you have it again, but that wasn't good enough for the doctors. They had to be sure.

Back in the village, Reneé was still up with Stephen. By this time she was feeling the effects of missing sleep and trying to take care of him and also keeping up with two other little boys. Joshua was eight, Ryan was six, and Stephen was four. She was really starting to feel dragged out. Two of my sisters, Faith and Sharon, went over to see how she was doing.

"Reneé, do you feel OK?" asked Faith. "You look really tired."

"I'm OK, but you're right. I *am* really tired. Stephen isn't sleeping at night and I haven't gotten any sleep for the last two nights," she answered.

"Well, tonight you will. Sharon and I will stay over here with you and stay up with Stephen so you can rest a bit," Faith told her. Still, Faith was worried. Reneé just did not look good.

She mentioned it to my brother Gary, who came over to check on Stephen. He looked at Reneé. "I think you should take the treatment for malaria, Reneé," he told her.

"I think I'm just tired," she said. "I don't feel like I have malaria; I'm just really tired. I hate to take the medicine if I'm not sure I have malaria. The last time I took the medicine it really caused my heart to speed up and I felt like it was going to jump right out of my chest," she told him.

Gary wished that he had the microscope that we used to have for reading malaria slides, but it had burned up in the fire that had destroyed his house just two months earlier. With the microscope, he could have taken her slide and let his wife, Marie, read it so that he could insist that Reneé take the medicine.

But without the microscope, there was no way to be positive. He felt better when Faith and Sharon told him they were going to be spending the night with her. This was Saturday night. The next morning Reneé felt a bit worse.

"Maybe I *am* getting malaria," she confided to Faith. "I guess I might as well take the medicine." She was now over at my mom's house, so Faith could continue watching Stephen.

"Reneé, here's the medicine. I'll bring you some water to take the pills," Faith told her.

Reneé lay back in the hammock while Faith went to find some water. Stephen called her and Faith ran to find out what he needed. He was having a hard time keeping anything down, and by the time she was done with him and walked back to where Reneé was lying in the hammock, she noticed that Reneé was asleep. *Poor thing, she is just exhausted,* Faith thought. *I'll give her the water later.*

A little later she went back to where Reneé was in the hammock. Something about the way she was lying in the hammock bothered Faith. She decided to wake Reneé and make her take the pills. It was only then that she realized Reneé was not asleep, but unconscious!

Quickly she called the rest of the family. My sister Velma and her husband, Paul, were there on their way back from their mission station in Brazil where they were working with the Yanomamö. While Gary and Paul began administering what medical assistance they could, others tried getting in touch with anyone out in Puerto Ayacucho by radio. It was Sunday, so none of the pilots was on duty. Repeated calls went out all the rest of the day, but they could not get in touch with anyone.

Reneé lost consciousness at about 11:00 a.m. on that Sunday. At about 2:00 p.m. everyone heard a plane fly over. They rushed back over to the radio, frantically trying to get in touch with the pilot flying the plane. For some reason the pilot never heard them. (The pilot told me later he'd had to fly an emergency flight to Parima that morning, which took him right over Cosh on his way home.)

"I looked down and thought I should drop in and have a cup of coffee with the Dawsons," he'd thought. "I honestly almost landed, but then I remembered it was Sunday and you-all probably were trying to get some rest . . . and I really needed to get back and spend some time with my own family. If only I would have known how badly you all wanted and needed that plane," he told me with tears in his eyes.

That night, at 7:00 p.m., they were finally able to get a radio message out and let everyone know there was a medical emergency in Cosh. Reneé was still unconscious and Stephen was not doing well, either. The pilot assured them he would take off at first light.

That Sunday morning I felt too sick to go to church, so I canceled the meeting engagement I'd had and stayed home with Axel, a local friend who had invited me over. My fever continued to mount and the medicine the hospital gave me didn't seem to be helping. They told me I had a kidney infection. I was still positive I had malaria. I have seen cases where it can take four or five blood smears before it shows up, but even with continued examination, they did not see it in the slides they took, so they weren't about to give me any medicine.

At about seven-thirty that night, I received a call from Eric Johnson at our office out in Puerto Ayacucho, telling me that Reneé was in a coma and was going to be flown out the next day. My tickets were for the following Wednesday, but Axel called the airlines and got me on standby for the next morning.

We got to the airport and Axel explained to the airlines what was happening. They told us LACSA Airlines had an earlier flight, and suggested that if we wanted them to they could see if we could get on it. I jumped at the chance. Less than an hour later found me flying back to Venezuela. I landed at the International Airport and somehow made my way down to the National Terminal.

We landed at 10:00 a.m., but the Puerto Ayacucho flight did not leave until about 2:00 p.m.

By this time I was basically out of it. My fever was really high and I was in a haze. I checked in and walked down to the gate to wait for the airplane. I kept drifting in and out of consciousness as I sat there, and I was so afraid that I was going to miss the flight. I would come to with a start and jump up, only to realize that just a couple of minutes had passed since the last time I had jumped up. People were starting to look at me as if I were on drugs. I sat back down. The next thing I knew, I was being shaken awake.

"Michael, Michael! Are you going to Puerto Ayacucho?" I looked up. It took me a minute to realize this was not a dream, but that a missionary friend was really shaking me, trying to get my attention.

"Yes," I answered him, struggling up.

"Well, you had better hurry!" he said. "They've just called the last call. I was running to catch the plane and just happened to pass you sitting there asleep. Come on; they changed the gate. We have to hurry!" We took off running and barely made it before they shut the door.

I remember nothing about the flight to Puerto Ayacucho. I was grateful to see my sister Susan and her husband, Jerry, waiting for me upon arrival. We drove straight to the clinic where Reneé was admitted. I got down, stiffly, and followed them inside toward Reneé's room. She was still unconscious. My heart stopped when I saw her motionless body lying there on the bed. Time stopped for me as I stood there looking down at her.

She is not going to make it, I thought. *Oh, God! Please help!* I held her hand while my sister-in-law Marie brought me up to date on what was being done. I was shocked to hear that Stephen was also in the hospital. They took me to his room. I looked down at his little body, wracked by fever with the tubes in his arms and could not help but cry; he looked so small there.

Thankfully, there was an empty bed right next to him. I sat down on it and that was the last thing I knew for a couple of days. I woke up, noticing the tubes in my own arms. I also found out that, according to the blood smears for malaria, I had *both* types of malaria, *Vivax* and *Falciparum*. *No wonder I felt so bad,* I thought!

They told me Reneé had regained consciousness. My sister Susan was sitting with her at the time, and they'd talked way into the night. Reneé had been surprised to hear that I was also in the hospital and that Stephen was, as well. She asked about Ryan, as she kept hearing the sound of his crying. Susan explained to her that it had been three days since she was brought out. Ryan and Josh were with Gary and Marie here in town and were fine. Reneé fell asleep in the early morning hours and Susan went home to get a bath and change her clothes. By the time she got back, she was surprised to find that Reneé had taken a turn for the worse again, and had sunk back into a coma. By that afternoon, the decision was made to call for an ambulance jet and "medevac" Reneé and myself up to the capital city of Caracas. Stephen was responding well to the medication, and was going to be released from the hospital that same afternoon. They drove us out to the airport in separate ambulances, and I was already in the jet when they brought Reneé out, with all the life support equipment she needed.

"Oh, God," I prayed, "what can I promise You to make You give me back my beautiful Reneé?" My eyes were so blurred by tears I could barely watch as they strapped us in for the flight. All my life we have lived on the edge. Time after time I'd watched as God did the impossible for us. This time just felt different, yet I could not help but remind God of all the other miracles He had done for us. When we were kids, Sandy once drank a good shot of kerosene. Dad and Mom got her to the hospital more dead than alive. All night they'd fought for her life. The doctors told them later that he hadn't believed she was going to make it—but she made a complete recovery! Then the time Gary fell out of the tree climbing after that *ilo,* a howler monkey.

"God, if you could keep Gary alive through all that long walk being carried by Bautista, and then for the forty hours' trip downriver in a dugout canoe, surely you can heal my beautiful Reneé," I begged.

I looked around. All my life I have wanted to ride in one of those fancy business jets. When I finally got my chance, I was too miserable to even think about it. When we arrived at the airport in Caracas, it was obvious that Reneé was the most seriously ill, as I was virtually forgotten there while they made sure she was ready for the ambulance ride into the city clinic. Finally, they came for me. My arm hurt badly where the IV needle was stuck into it. Even in Puerto Ayacucho, every time I gained enough consciousness to complain, I would try and get someone to look at my arm, always with no luck. I looked down at my arm and was surprised to see it swollen and discolored! Finally, in Caracas, I was lucid enough to demand that someone do something.

"You pull it out, or *I'm* going to," I told the nurse.

"Let me go and check," she said. She finally came back and pulled it out. You should have seen her face when she saw that the needle was bent almost into a U-shape!

Reneé's mom, Naomi Pintor, along with Reneé's older sister, Debbie, and Debbie's husband, Ken, flew down from the States to be with her. I felt so sorry for her mother and, yes, even guilty as I lay there in the bed, too sick to take care of myself, let alone take care of her daughter. I had promised to take care of Reneé, and now look. I remembered a conversation I'd had with Reneé's father before we had returned to the field barely six months before.

"Look," he had told me, "you all have given enough. It is someone else's turn now. You all need to stay here now. Let someone else go down there."

I had tried to explain the burden we felt for the Yanomamö and how we were in a unique position to really reach them with the gospel. Although he was not there in person, I felt the burden of the responsibility I had to take care of his daughter.

"Oh, God," I prayed, "please help." My words echoed in the silence.

They told me on Saturday that if I felt better they would take me up to see Reneé. She had actually improved a bit and they felt a visit would do us both good. I still couldn't shake the feeling that she was not going to make it. Saturday finally came and I waited all day to be taken up to the floor where she was located in the intensive care unit. I waited and waited. They never came. I kept asking the nurses when they would take me up, and they kept telling me they were waiting for authorization from her doctor. That had to be one of the longest days of my life. I waited and waited.

Mrs. Pintor, with Ken and Debbie, along with Gary and Marie who had come up from Puerto Ayacucho with us, waited throughout the long day with me. They jumped up every time someone came into the room. Finally, the next day, they did let Mrs. Pintor and Debbie in to see her. Debbie told me Reneé kept trying to tell her something. She had the life support tubes down her throat, so she could not talk. Finally Debbie understood her to be saying she was going home. Thinking she was talking about her home in the village, Debbie agreed.

"Yes, as soon as you are better, you can go home."

Reneé then asked about her boys.

"Your boys are fine," she told Reneé. "Stephen is OK and is out of the hospital. They're waiting for you in Puerto Ayacucho. You'll see them in a few days . . . when you go home."

"No, no," Reneé insisted. "I am going home *now!*" She looked around the room as if wondering that Debbie could not see what she was seeing. I've often wondered exactly what she was seeing or, should I say, *who* she was seeing, because since then I have talked with a lot of people and it seems that when a child of God goes home, God sends His angels to usher them into His Presence. I am positive she was looking at the angels God had sent to escort her.

Dad and Mom and most of the rest of my family were still in Cosh waiting to hear any news. The Yanomamö believers kept coming in and praying with *them,* trying to encourage them. Normally it was *us* sitting up waiting with them and trying to pray with them, but now they were the ones who kept reminding Dad and Mom that God is always in control.

Late Sunday evening Dad was over in the church by himself praying for Reneé and me. Suddenly he looked up in surprise to see her coming in the door. She smiled that beautiful smile that Reneé was known for and waved goodbye to him. Without a word, she turned and walked back out the door of the church and was gone. Dad stared after her with his mouth open.

"Oh, God, please give Mike strength," he prayed, because from that moment on he knew he would never see Reneé again on this earth. Slowly he walked back over to the house. He did not know whether to share what he had seen, or not. The next evening word came over the shortwave radio that Reneé had indeed gone home to be with the Lord, and we were all flying in the next day to have the burial service there in the village.

Officially her death is listed as June 22, 1992. That was a Monday, but Dad will always believe that she went to be with the Lord on that Sunday night when she waved goodbye to him there in the church. The doctors may have kept her body alive longer, but she was home with the Lord on that evening.

The doctors argued harshly against my leaving the hospital. Finally I told the head doctor my decision: "I am going. I have three boys who don't yet know they do not have a mother. I have to be the one to tell them that and to comfort them. I have to go! Either you tell the nurse to pull this stuff out of my arm or I will pull it out and walk out. But I am leaving tomorrow morning."

He looked at me. Something he saw in my eyes must have convinced him, because with a sigh he nodded affirmatively to the nurse.

The rest of the time is such a blur. I was still so sick myself. I remember finally getting to Puerto Ayacucho and hugging my three little boys. I held them tightly as I tried to tell them in words a four-year-old could understand that their mother was not coming home anymore. She was with Jesus now. One step at a time we made it through the next days—days when it seemed I was too sad to want to go on at all. The Yanomamö brothers were so special during this time. They tried so hard to comfort us.

About a week later I packed up the house, took the boys, and went back to spend some time with Reneé's folks. How they suffered! During the funeral I had watched Bautista hugging Mrs. Pintor and thanking her for allowing her daughter to come down there to help reach them for the Lord. But now they were back in the United States and I felt we needed to be with them. Still, the pain was a huge hole that it seemed nothing could fill.

We had driven over to have a talk with our pastor in Berwyn and I had told the boys that we could stop at McDonald's on the way home. We ordered our food and all of us just picked at it, not really feeling like eating much. There was a large group of kids a couple of tables over and they were all laughing and having a great time. Ryan looked over at me. His eyes were huge, brimming over with tears.

"Don't they know my mommy died?" he asked me with such a mournful look that it was all I could do to choke back my own sobs and try to help him understand that *no, they did not know.*

After a couple of weeks we finally gave up and went back to Cosh and I tried to bury myself in the work. Now, though, it seemed like a chore, and it felt like there was nothing really worth doing. Day turned into day, and days finally turned into months . . . and time was a long, dark hole that stretched endlessly on. The only thing that kept me going was the boys. I knew they were suffering as much or more than I was.

Those have to be the hardest two years I have ever spent. I didn't think I would ever get over Reneé's death. I kept a journal for a couple of months at the time, and I include a few excerpts from it here. (Because this journal was kept for my own purposes, and during this time I was doing a lot of reading, I know I included thoughts and phrases from some of the books I was reading. I have made an attempt to remember and give credit for thoughts that were not original, but as I look back over this, I am having a hard time remembering which were only my thoughts and which I took out of books. I so appreciate all the different authors whose books the Lord used in mighty ways to bring me comfort, and I have tried to give credit for them. If somehow I have missed something, please know that it was not intentional, and I only leave this section in trusting that if there are others going through this type of pain in their lives, the Lord might use these words of mine as He used the words of others in my life.)

My Journal Excerpt

In the ebb and flow of living as we wander through the years,
We're told to listen to a Voice we can't hear with our ears.
They say to live by something that you can't see with your eyes.
Is there really any purpose to this foolish exercise?

—MICHAEL CARD

September 2, 1992: I am back in the village . . . and the house. It is really hard to be here, but I am glad to be home. The boys say they never want to travel again. Josh is waiting for his friends to get out of school so he can go fishing. Ryan is out riding bikes with his friends. Stephen is waiting for me to get off the computer so he can play a game. I still don't know what I'm going to do about school for the boys. I suppose it will come in time. . . .

It is good to be with the people. The house was full all day, with them telling me how good it was to have me home. Many of them said how much they missed Reneé and how hard it was for them to see me come back alone. One old guy, who always teased Reneé, told me he almost could not come into our house anymore. Poor old guy, he lost his twenty-six-year-old son a couple of days after Reneé's passing, also to malaria. He is really suffering. Another friend who lost his eight-year-old son the same day as Reneé, said that at least his little boy would not be scared or lonely because he would be with Reneé, and she would be someone in heaven that he knew. So, even though it has been very hard, I think it was right to come back.

September 3: I have been reading a book by Philip Yancy called *Disappointment with God.* It is really good. I had read it about a year ago, but at that time disappointment was so foreign to me (I was such an optimist) that most of it went over my head. So it was like reading it for the first time. One thing he said in it I really liked (maybe because I want to believe it). His quote was: "One bold message in the Book of Job is that you can say anything to God. Throw at him your grief, your anger, your doubt, your bitterness, your betrayal, your disappointment—He can absorb them all. As often as not, spiritual giants of the Bible are shown contending with God. They prefer to go away limping, like Jacob, rather than to shut God out. God can deal with every human response save one. He cannot abide an attempt to ignore Him or treat Him as though He does not exist. That response never once occurred to Job."

Although I would be the last to think that I was any kind of a spiritual *anything,* let alone a giant, I have been talking to God, even questioning Him. There have been times I felt guilty to even think some of the thoughts that I have thought about

God's fairness. But thankfully, God is so real to me that all I can do is stubbornly cling to Him, with all the faith that I can muster. I'm just too stubborn to give up. It takes so much more faith to hang on when God is silent, but no matter how distant God seems, I know I will never be abandoned. I guess it is just being "guided by that Hand I cannot hold."

In my life I had always longed for the closeness to God that men like Abraham, Moses, David, Daniel, and many others had. Now I realize that they had to go through some very difficult times themselves. Times when, I'm sure, they were disappointed with the silence of God. But the reason the Bible speaks so highly of them is that they stubbornly clung to God, even though He seemed to have abandoned them when they needed Him.

> *To hear with my heart, to see with my soul, to be*
> *guided by a Hand I cannot hold, to trust in a way that*
> *I cannot see . . . that's what faith must be.*"
>
> —MICHAEL CARD

September 7: Timi and Pablo and I were up in Timi's house, talking, when they suddenly started talking about Reneé and how much she had meant to them. They told me how much they had been praying for the boys and me. I didn't know it, but the whole Yanomamö community did not expect us to come back. In fact, they said everyone thought that everybody on the base would leave. They said how much they thanked God for the fact that even though I was obviously suffering, He gave me the grace to come back. Then Timi shared some verses from Hebrews, chapter 11. . . . What a blessing it was to me to hear him say that to him Reneé was one of the *heroes of faith,* one who gave her life so that they might hear. Now the desire of his heart was that he live his life in such a way that he be a true testimony for Christ, so that he could have the same impact on someone else's life.

I've been doing a lot of crying and thinking and really trying to see what God has for me. It is going to be so hard here alone. Everything reminds me of her. She had such a positive influence on my life. I'm just not sure I can make it alone. I am trying so hard to make Christ the reality in my life that He wants to be. I keep listening to that song by Michael Card. . . .

> *Lord I long to see, Your Presence in reality,*
> *But I don't know how,*
> *Let me know You in the now.*
>
> —MICHAEL CARD

I can see Reneé listening to that song and hear us talking about it—and now to actually know that she *does* really know Christ in all His perfection and glory, sometimes overwhelms me. She knows Him now! How come knowing that doesn't take away the pain I feel?

September 8: These days have been incredibly hard. I really want the Lord to use this experience in my life and allow me to be a testimony for Him, but I just can't seem to get a handle on my emotions. Maybe one day it will come for me.

I was thinking today that *it was easier for Christ to die because he knew that in three days he would rise again, whereas, for me, Reneé is gone for the rest of my life.* Then I thought of the fact that for Christ, His separation from God really started when He emptied Himself of Who He was and became a baby in Mary's womb. Who can know the loneliness that He felt? One Who had created the world, Who had inhabited eternity, to suddenly be trapped in time . . . knowing that at the end of His life He would be rejected by everyone . . . that even His Father would turn His back on Him, causing Him the greatest anguish any human heart has ever had to bear.

"My soul is overwhelmed with sorrow to the point of death," He said to His three closest friends. At one point He fell, face down, on the ground and prayed for any way out. His sweat fell to the ground in large drops, like blood. And God stayed silent. His cry of "My God, my God, why have you forsaken me?" haunts and shames me as I look at my situation and think I'm suffering for Him. Realizing what He went through for me, I cling all the harder to Him, even though He seems so distant and silent to me at this point in my life.

September 10: I have always loved the Book of Job, although I was always bothered by the first two chapters of it. I didn't like the fact that the interaction between Satan and God seems like just a wager, with poor Job in the middle. The more I've thought about it, the more I've realized what an honor it was for Job, however, to actually have God point him out, and ask Satan what He did: "Have you considered My servant, Job?" Of course Job didn't know anything about this, nor would he have felt it was an honor at the time.

How much did God risk when He allowed Satan to test Job? I have to believe there is so much more behind the scenes than we will ever know. If I were tested in that manner, could I say with Job, "Though He slay me, yet will I trust Him!"

I realize that most of my life I have been the kind of Christian that only wanted the life that the Twenty-Third Psalm talks about. Forgetting that before the Twenty-Third Psalm is the Twenty-Second. Philip Yancy says: "I have experienced times of unusual closeness with God, when it seemed every prayer was answered, and God seemed intimate and close." Now, I guess I am going through what he calls "fog times," when God stays silent and His promises seem glaringly false. Fidelity involves learning to trust that beyond the fog God still reigns and has not abandoned us, no matter how it seems.

A friend of mine wrote a song that says: "Though we walk on sinking sand, He is still the Rock."

Well, my mind is still full of an awful lot of mixed-up thoughts. I hope it gets better. I want to trust God so badly, yet I have to be honest and say that part of the time I feel like God cheated me. Reneé and I had gone through hard times together, living in little mud shacks and having hardly anything; that was part of our getting started in reaching the Yanomamö people. I had finally built her a decent house. She had just gotten it to the point where it was more than a house, but was really a home. Now she is gone. I sit and look at the house, and her things, and it is such an empty feeling. Reneé never complained when times were hard. As a matter of fact, she was half-embarrassed by our new house. She thought it was too fancy for missionaries. We had the best part of our lives before us. Now the future stretches out in front of me like one long, dark void. I was told I would have to trust God for my loneliness. One booklet I read said, "Give your loneliness to God as a gift."

Well, I've tried both, and neither has worked that well for me. Maybe it takes time, and even the unsaved say, "Time heals all wounds." *What difference has being a Christian made? Shouldn't I be able to handle this easier than the unsaved? Is it wrong to expect God to somehow comfort me, and take away my loneliness?* I see the Indians, who are suffering their own losses, and wish I could say something comforting, but my own loss looms so big that right now it is all I see.

September 12: I took Josh and Ryan fishing. We got up at 4 a.m. and went downriver. The fish were really biting. Josh caught about forty fish. Ryan caught about twenty. We also pulled in a 5-foot-6-inch catfish.

Anyway, we had a very good time . . . until Ryan said, "There's no one to show our fish to now." I felt so bad for him.

Josh is trying to be so brave and act like nothing is wrong. Poor little guy; so many times I have caught him crying. One day last week I was upstairs and he came up. I could tell that something was wrong.

"Are you OK?" I asked him. Next thing I knew he was crying in my arms; then we were both crying. Tomorrow is our Wedding

Anniversary. It sure is going to be a rough day. It is so hard to believe that twelve years could have gone that fast!

September 13: Well, it was about as bad as I thought it was going to be. It has amazed me how many memories there can be in such simple things. I see on the wall in the office, by Reneé's school desk, a plaque-like card that says, "Nobody Notices What I Do Until I Don't Do It." That card has just about haunted me. How incredibly true it is! Reneé and I always laughed about it. Also the one that says, "If Momma Ain't Happy, Ain't Nobody Happy. If Papa Ain't Happy, Who Cares?" I found a lot of our pictures . . . and several frames that Reneé had brought down to put the pictures into to hang. I took a day and put them all together. I found a wall plaque that Reneé had that says, "There's a Special Place in Heaven for the Mother of Three Boys." It really broke me up. I put that in a collage of pictures of her and the boys. We really have a lot of nice pictures of the two of us. Reneé was such a beautiful woman. I was so proud of her. I still am having such a hard time without her. To be honest, some days I wish I could just leave and never look back. To be in this house now is probably the hardest thing I have had to deal with in my whole life.

Pablo was talking to me today and asked how I was doing. I said I was thinking about leaving, that it was just too hard being here. He asked if I had regrets about deciding to be a missionary. I had to tell him that some days I sure wish I had stayed in the States *this* year. Timoteo preached the morning message and it was on the story of Christ raising Lazarus from the dead. He really spoke on the verse that says, "I am the Resurrection and the life; he that believeth on me, though he were dead, yet shall he live" (John 11: 25). He brought out the fact that if no one had come here and told them about this truth, they would have died in ignorance of that fact. How happy he was that someone did come! He said that Hebrews 13:7 says that they should remember the people who spoke the Word of God to them and imitate their faith. "Because of Christ we have hope that others don't have," said Timoteo. I felt that so much of his message was aimed at me. I really needed it, too, because I was *so* down.

September 14: One of the Missionary Aviation Fellowship pilots came by today. We are good friends, so if his schedule permits he always comes in and has a cup of coffee, or a cold drink with me. Today he came early and only had one more twenty-minute flight today, so we spent a couple of hours talking. He brought me a book called *Sacred Surprises.* I started reading it as soon as he left. A couple of thoughts really caught my eye: "The pain is too great for me to bear. I always thought I was a strong person. But now I know I have just been spared the pain that would have shown me how weak I am. I am broken, empty, shattered. I want to reach out to You, but I don't have the energy to even try. I need You now. Can You hear me? God, I know that this is just between the two of us. No one else can help me through this. I am alone except for You. And yet, I cannot see You or feel You through my suffering. I am too busy gasping for breath to call out Your Name. Will I survive this? And if I do, who will I be? Don't let me grow hard and cold, God. Don't let me go through this for nothing. Keep me open, God, even to the pain. Especially to the pain."

> *To all who've been born of the Spirit,*
> *and who share incarnation with Him,*
> *Who belong to eternity stranded in time,*
> *and are weary of struggling with sin.*
> *Forget not the hope that's before you, and*
> *never stop counting the cost,*
> *Remember the hopelessness when you were lost.*
> *There is a joy in the journey, there's a light*
> *we can love on the way.*
> *There is a wonder and wildness to life,*
> *and freedom for those who obey."*

—MICHAEL CARD

This was one of Reneé's favorite songs. We listened to it all the time. Lately I've really been asking the Lord to make it real to me again. I don't want to forget the hope that is before me, nor to stop counting the cost. We really did have a joy in our journey of service to Him. I hope I can get it back.

One night shortly after this I woke up unable to sleep. I tried so hard to stay angry at God, but down deep I knew and really believe that "all things do work together for good to them who are the called according to His purpose" (Romans 8:28)—but I just could not see it. As I lay there in the darkness, I relived our beautiful life together. Finally my mind came back to a time eight years earlier: A snake's head was poised to strike Reneé, who was then very pregnant with our first child. I pushed her back, just in time, before the snake could strike. I remembered how thankful I had been to have intervened in time to avert a possible tragedy. Both Reneé and I were convinced then that if the snake had struck her, I would, in all probability, have lost her that night. There is no doubt that she would have lost our baby. Suddenly I could almost hear God speaking.

"I gave you eight extra years," the Voice said. It seemed I could almost hear His soft whisper. I got up and wandered around the house, touching this and that. I went upstairs to the boys' room and stood there listening to the sounds of my three little boys sleeping. Josh was eight, Ryan was six, and Stephen was five. God really *had* blessed me with eight extra years.

Finally, I just could not take the house any longer! Every place I looked, everything I touched, had a memory attached to it. I was trying to swim through them, but the darkness had become too overwhelming. I decided to go away for a while. My sisters offered to keep the three boys in Venezuela, and I made arrangements with some friends to use a condo they had on the shores of Lake Michigan. While flying back to the United States I decided to read the whole Bible through, just as you would a novel. From Genesis to Revelation, just *read* it. Actually, what I was trying to do was figure out if God still had something for me to do. It seemed to me that by taking Reneé He had knocked me out of the work just as effectively as if he had let me die. Anyway, the point is that I was trying to figure out whether God still had something for me to do, and just what that was I now desperately needed to know.

I purposely selected a Bible with no helps or notes, as I did not want to be distracted in my search by human wisdom. I wanted just the Bible. I had a highlighter and anything that caught my eye I marked so that I could come back to it. What I wanted more than anything else was some kind of direction for my life. I felt as if I were drifting.

I read and read. I would start early and read until I just could not read anymore. I wanted to read the whole Bible in as near as one sitting as was possible in order to get the "big picture" of what it was saying. On about the third day, I was reading in the Book of Job. I came to the verse where Job talks about being *afraid* of the Almighty: . . . *therefore am I troubled at His presence; when I consider, I am afraid of Him* (Job 23:15).

Boy, that was heavy, because that is exactly what I was feeling. That *really* bothered me, as I didn't want that kind of relationship with the Lord. I didn't want to have to be terrified of Him. We had had a relationship that was intimate and close, and now I had to be terrified of Him? I looked up. It was about 11:00 p.m. and I had been reading for most of the day. I had started when I woke up at about 6:00 a.m., and had taken only a short break to get something to eat. I was tired, so I decided to go to bed. But this verse still haunted me as I tossed and turned, trying desperately to go to sleep.

Suddenly I woke up. I thought I had heard a Voice. I knew I was alone in the condo, however, and I was high enough in the building that the street sounds seldom reached me. I tried to imagine what had awakened me. I realized it had been a dream.

In this dream, someone was telling me something. I strained to remember what it was, and found that the words were still there.

"Those are man's thoughts," the Voice said. "The thoughts I have are different. I know the thoughts I have for you." *Where had I heard that before?*

The words did remind me of a verse in the Bible. I frantically began looking for it. Remember, I had a Bible with no helps— not even a concordance. I thumbed through the pages, trying to find a verse that talked about the plans God had. I thought it was in one of the Major Prophets. Loving the book of Isaiah, I started there. Nothing. Finally, in the middle of the book of Jeremiah, I found it. With tears streaming down my face I read the verse: "For I know the plans I have for you . . . plans to give you a future and a hope."

"Thank you Lord," I prayed. It was as if God had told me: "Job is man talking. But you do not have to be afraid of Me. For I know the thoughts that I think toward you, saith the Lord thoughts of peace and not of evil . . . to give you an expected end" (Jeremiah 29:11).

That was the turning point in my healing. After that, sure, I had hard times, but the Presence of the Lord was close and comforting. I still have no idea of *why* this was God's plan for me, or why He allowed it, but I can rest in the knowledge that "He does all things well." One day I will see the "big picture" and I will understand it all. Right now, it is enough that He knows best, and that I trust Him.

This was a sentence I found written in Reneé's Bible, the Bible she'd had when she'd started Bible school: "I am willing to be a missionary for the Lord, to suffer for His sake, the One who's so good to me. To serve Him because I love Him."

We'd gone into this job with our eyes open, and though the pain was hard to bear, I could not close them—or my heart— now. Reneé's words made me think of the last slide presentation, with musical accompaniment, we'd put together. We had used the second verse of that great song by Steve Green, *People Need the Lord.*

We are called to take His light to a world where wrong seems right.
What could be too great a cost for sharing
Christ with one who's lost?
Through His love our hearts can feel all the grief they bear.
They must hear the words of life that only we can share."

—STEVE GREEN

The cost is real, but in 2 Corinthians 4:17 we are told that our light affliction, which is but for a moment, worketh for us a far more exceeding and eternal weight of glory . . . for we walk by faith, not by sight (2 Corinthians 5:7).

25

"HE IS NOT A WHITE MAN!"

We were once again heading up the mighty Orinoco River by dugout canoe. (It seems the dugout canoe can define my whole life.) We were excited and exuberant, as we always were when heading out to visit a people we had never met. My brother Gary was with me, as were Yacuwä, Däduwä, and Ramon. We also had a friend visiting from the United States. We were heading up to the village of Jasubuwäteli. I had heard of the village often but had never made it that far up the Orinoco.

On my previous trips upriver, I had always turned off onto the Majecoto River and headed up to Coyowä. I had to smile to myself as we passed the mouth of the Majecoto, remembering the young man I had collided with running around that tree so many years ago. I wondered if he still told the story. I also wondered how big and how much uglier I had become in his many tellings of the story.

Actually, as so many Yanomamö have died in the years since that incident, I doubted he was even alive. Malaria is the big killer, but their culture has not helped them any. Since no death to the Yanomamö is a natural death, every death has to be avenged. So, when malaria kills someone, their shaman, through the influence of his drugs, contacts his spirits to find out who is responsible. After deciding who the guilty village or person is, their warriors leave in the predawn light to exact revenge. Sometimes the whole village participates, and then sometimes only one or two head out to find the guilty party. In the time I have spent with the Yanomamö, I would have to say that what scares me the most is when only one or two men leave quietly, with no fanfare.

When a large group leaves, the chances of one of them having a bad dream and turning the whole party around is very great. The right dream would be interpreted as foretelling the future, and if it tells of an unsuccessful raid or of one or more of them getting killed, they will turn around and wait until the signs are better. This could be any dream. Someone dreaming of crossing one of their pole bridges, for example, and falling in, could be interpreted that someone was going to get killed. Or, let's say one of them blunders into a beehive and gets stung. That is a very bad sign, as they would equate getting stung with getting shot with someone's arrow. The guy who has the dream or gets stung, or whatever, will want to go home. He will not want to return by himself, as that would be considered cowardly. So he will do everything in his power to try to convince the whole party to return home and wait for a better time.

But when only one or two go out, they are serious. Most of the time they return to the village having already begun their *unocai* ritual. They have been avenged! The bad thing is, though, that now they have to be on their guard, as the village where they just killed someone has to come and retaliate. Now *they* live in fear—such fear that they don't even like leaving the village to relieve themselves, but wait for nightfall so they can relieve themselves on a pile of leaves, which they will tie up, then chuck over the wall of the village. This is a hard time for them. Most nights the children cry themselves to sleep in hunger. The men's faces are haggard with fear and worry. They will only leave the village in a large group and are so touchy that if a twig is stepped on and broken, you will see the whole group jump!

You have to be impressed with how quickly they can get their long arrows notched and ready. When we were kids we used to sneak around and try to startle the men. I always thought it was so funny to watch them whirl around, contorting themselves to present as small a target as possible, and at the same time bring their own weapons into play. They, of course, failed to appreciate the humor and we always received a severe tongue-lashing for our antics.

We had started this trip for a specific reason. *National Geographic* had recently done a special on the Yanomamö of Jasubuwäteli, and especially on a girl from there who had married an anthropologist. Shortly after the film aired, the girl and her husband went back to the Jasubuwäteli for a visit. When it was time to leave, she refused to go home with her husband. Actually, I think it was more a case of two cultures not really understanding each other. A Yanomamö hates to leave her family, and her family hates to be left. If she did not make a huge issue of having to leave them, they would be offended. Americans, on the other hand, for the most part have an aversion to making anyone, especially a woman, do something she does not want to do. So when the girl did not want to leave, her family expected her husband to grab her and drag her screaming out of the village. But all her husband did was take the baby away from her and walk out of the village, leaving his wife crying. Personally, I think he thought she would not want to be without the baby and would come running behind him. But in Yanomamö culture, if a man is *really* throwing his wife away, he will take his children and leave. That is it. The marriage is over.

I had been in the United States and *National Geographic* called me, asking if I would be interested in going to this village to find out from the girl what had really happened. I had wanted to get up in that area anyway, so it was not hard to be talked into going. So, armed with one of their fancy cameras, we set off.

Every village we passed through on our way all told us the same thing.

"You are going where?" they would all ask, in disbelief. "Why, those people will shoot you on sight! Don't go up there; they hate the white man. They are expecting the white man to come back and get his wife back, so they will assume you all are helping him and will shoot you on sight!"

"We don't even know the man and have never lived in his village!" we told them.

They remained unconvinced. "If you insist on going, at least give us something to remember you by. Maybe a shirt, or pants, a machete, or fish line. That way when we hear you all have been killed, we will have something to mourn over you with."

Finally we arrived at the trail. At the last village before the trail we had talked some Yanomamö into taking us into the village. They were full of dire warnings, as well, but finally agreed to take us in, possibly figuring that if we met our fate up there, they could at least divvy up our packs. Besides, they had warned us!

We arrived at the trail about 3:00 p.m. I asked our guides if we could make it before dark, and they assured me the village was close. Actually, their exact words were, "Listen, you can hear the women fussing!"

I listened, but heard nobody. Having traveled with them all my life, I never put much stock in what they say about time or distance anyway. They always tell you exactly what you want to hear. If they think it will make you happy to think it is close, they will use words to describe distance like "the forehead of a tick." Well, for those of you who are not really familiar with a tick's anatomy, believe me, it does not have *that* long of a forehead!

Remembering all this, I slipped my mini-flashlight out of my pack and put it in my pocket. Good thing I did, too, because sure enough, it got dark on us. The rule of the jungle is that he who has the light goes first. Everyone else has to try and feel his or her way behind him. Well, we finally got to the village at around 8:30 p.m.; pitch-black 8:30 p.m. We could hear the witch doctors chanting to their spirits long before we actually got to the village, of course. We stood outside the village and made the whistles and yells that you have to do to let the people know that you are friendly. They answered back and we got ready to go in.

Gary and I decided not to let the people know that we were white. We thought we could keep our friend James enough in the darkness of the background that no one would notice he was not speaking. We felt this would give us time to feel out the situation and maybe find someone who knew us—or at least had heard about us. I turned my light off and stuck it back into my pocket. The entranceway into a *shabono* is just a small hole cut in the palm, normally blocked with firewood at night. Once the people inside had cleared the opening, we stooped down to crawl inside the village. Single-file, we stooped under the roof and were immediately surrounded by exuberant Yanomamö. They were smacking themselves and yelling, each trying to better the one next to him in greeting their visitors. To all questions we just replied we were from the village of Coshilowäteli. This satisfied our hosts. We were shown where we could hang our hammocks. It was difficult in the dark, but we had all agreed we did not want them to know we had a light. As we were all speaking Yanomamö, they just accepted the fact that we were all Yanomamö.

The next morning I was awakened by a shrill shrieking only inches from my face. It took me a while to figure out where I was and discover what was happening. The shrieking continued. An old man with his face only inches from mine was shrilling to wake the dead. He had my attention; I can tell you that! I guess he had wanted to be one of the first to talk to the visitors, so he had gotten up and decided not to wait for dawn. He happened to pick my hammock for his first greeting. It gets chilly in the predawn hours in the high humidity of the rainforest, so I had my blanket over my face. He pulled the blanket away and saw the unmistakable beard and fair skin of the white man! *Mercy!*

The shrieking continued. "He is a white man! Whites surround us! Defend yourselves!"

Like I said, he had my attention! And if that was not enough, here came the whole village running at us armed with every kind of weapon you could think of: machetes, axes, war clubs, bows and arrows—even two shotguns they had gotten from the anthropologist.

Däduwä, bless his heart, jumped out in front of us. "*No! No! No!*" he shouted, waving his arms. "He is not a white man!" *Boy, this is going to be good,* I thought to myself.

"No, he is not a white man," Däduwä continued. "His mother put clothes on him when he was just a little baby and his skin turned white like that and just stayed that way, but listen to him talk: he is a Yanomamö."

"Yes, yes! That is true!" I told them.

We finally got everyone quieted down, but we continued standing around, talking and laughing with them. It was obvious that we were white, but they accepted the fact that we were from Coshilowäteli.

Suddenly I became aware of an old man squatting on his haunches about twenty feet away from me. He was staring at me very intently. I could tell he was a shaman by the look in his eyes as he stared at me. I tried to ignore him by turning and facing away from him, but you know how it is when someone is staring at you: It gets harder and harder to ignore. Finally I could not take it any longer.

"What do you want?" I asked him.

"Who are you?" he demanded. He spoke very abruptly, with a lot of hostility.

Oh, boy, I thought, *this old guy is going to get everybody all worked up again.*

"I really am from Cosh," I told him. "My parents came across the great water before I was born. I was born here in the jungle and grew up in Cosh."

"No, who are you?" he repeated, just as abruptly. I could feel the tensions beginning to mount again behind me.

"Look," I told him again, "ask my friends here," I said, pointing to Yacuwä, Däduwä, and Ramon. "I grew up with them. Ask them who I am."

"No! Who are you?" he continued, unwilling to accept what I'd told him.

Boy, this is really getting old! I thought. "I do not know what you want me to say," I said, letting the exasperation show in my voice. "I heard you all were angry with a white man who used to live here. I do not know him. We are from Coshilowäteli. That is all I can say."

"No, no, no," he repeated. "Let me tell you. Last night when you all came into the village, I touched one of you. I think it was you. My arm still hurts from something that felt like the shock of an electric eel. My *jecula* (demons) fled, screaming, into the jungle at the shock. The few that were brave enough to return after everything quieted down were up all night long, throwing up. As far as I am sitting from you right now, my chest is beating like this." He demonstrated by taking his closed fist and beating himself rapidly on the chest. "I want to know who you are to affect my *jecula* like that!"

In all the time I have lived with the Yanomamö, I have never had an opportunity like that to present Jesus Christ. Gary and I took it with that old man. Squatting across from him, we took him from Who God is, to creation, to the fall in the garden, and all the way up to Calvary. He listened intently, sometimes nodding his head, other times clicking his tongue to show either his appreciation or his disapproval. When we were finished, he responded to us.

"I know the Supreme Being's land. I have seen it from far away."

Once again I listened as this old witch doctor told me about this beautiful land.

"But we cannot go there. The light is too unapproachable," he told us. "Besides, He is an enemy of the Yanomamö. Everyone knows he is *Yai Wanonabälewä* (the Enemy Spirit). He hates us Yanomamö. He steals the spirits of our infant children."

"No, no," we told him. "He does not hate you Yanomamö but loves you so much that He sent His own Son to become a Yanomamö so He could make a path to His Father's land . . . that all we who believe on Him might one day go there to live with Him," we told him.

He continued listening intently.

We were told that the girl in question was not in the village. Basically, the story we were told there only reinforced my belief that what had happened was mainly due to two very diverse cultures that had never quite gotten around to really understanding each other. I felt bad for the husband, as I had talked with him on the phone and I believe he really loved her.

We stayed there visiting for a while longer. During one of many conversations with the old shaman, he told me something interesting. "I know you. I have seen you."

"When?" I asked him, because I knew I had never been up here before and it was way too far for him to have ever made it to *our* village.

"I have gone to your village to *lämou,*" he told me in a low voice. He used the word that means he had gone to "lie in wait," like in an ambush. "I have seen you," he told me again. "I saw you sitting in front of a box with a light coming out of it."

I realized he was describing a computer. *How could he have ever seen a computer, in order to describe it so well?* I wondered. It suddenly dawned on me that he was telling me that he had gone after us in the *spirit world.*

I felt my face flush with anger against him. The raw wound of Reneé's death was too new for me to look at his statement objectively. However, God's Spirit calmed my aching heart and I breathed again those precious words: "Greater is He that is in us than he that is in the world." Regardless of where the old witch doctor had gone or what he thought he had done, God was still in control. Once again it was brought home to me that "we wrestle not against flesh and blood, but against principalities, against powers, against the rulers of the darkness of this world, against spiritual wickedness in high places" (Ephesians 2:12).

26

RIPPLES ON THE WATER

Have you ever stood by a pond on a very still day? The water is so smooth and shiny it looks like a giant mirror, clearly reflecting the sky, the trees, and anything else at a right angle to the water. Then, have you picked up a rock and chucked it into the water? First there is a splash, and then the ripples start going out in ever-widening circles away from the point of impact of the rock. I am fascinated by the way the ripples just keep going and going away from the point of impact. Some people are like that. They have an impact on others that is greater than life itself.

It has been ten years since Reneé died. As I look back, I see ripples still traveling out from her life. So many lives continue to be touched by hers. Just to name a few:

Don Shire was up at Silver Birch Ranch the summer I worked up there with her and I showed my movie. Remember the movie Paul Bramson helped me make in Bible school? Well, I was still showing it. Don is a professional trumpet player, and he did the music before I showed the movie. I loved his playing so much I couldn't wait to try to talk with him after the service.

"Don, you have to come down and play for the Yanomamö. They have never seen a trumpet before and they would love to hear you play," I told him.

"Well, if I come down, will you take me fishing?" was his response. We shook on it. Honestly, I never thought I would see him again. This was in August. Reneé and I were married in September, and by January we were in Venezuela. Six months later we got a letter from Don.

"Were you serious about wanting me to come and play my trumpet?" he asked. "Because if you were, I want to come down with a friend." We assured him we were quite serious about our invitation, and in December of that same year Don came down with his friend Mark Ritchie. Don and Mark have since become best friends of ours and are very engaged in the work. They still come for visits, and Don brings at least two short-term work groups down to Cosh every year now. Because of a girl most of his groups never got to meet, they come down, are blessed, and return a blessing. Many of them are down for (at the most) ten days. But the impact they have had and many of them continue to have is unbelievable—an ever-widening ripple.

Mark Ritchie went on to write *Spirit of the Rainforest: A Yanomamö Shaman's Story.* On subsequent book tours to some of the most prestigious universities across the United States, Bautista and Gary, along with Mark, have spoken at these universities. On one of these tours, during a question-and-answer time, someone asked Bautista a question.

"You keep talking about your people needing change. Just what kind of change do your people need?"

Bautista answered: "First of all, I want to make it very clear that any change apart from the gospel of Jesus Christ will not help my people."

One of the professors stood up. "I know you have been brainwashed by your friend there," she said, pointing toward Gary, "because I have a good life, and I have not had to convert to

Christianity to get it. My parents immigrated over here to get away from the fighting in Lebanon when I was just a little girl. I am at peace, yet I have not had to change my religion or culture to have that peace."

Bautista was silent for a moment, then spoke. "While out in the jungle, if I notice a storm approaching I grab my machete and begin to build a lean-to shelter. Working quickly, I cut the poles and palm leaves I need. I then run and pull some vines to tie the whole thing together. I build my shelter and get under it before it starts raining. Now, if you come running up right before the storm breaks and I let you come in, you are just as dry as I am, although you have done no work. You are dry because you are under my shelter. I submit that that is what you have done here. My friend here has told me how this country was founded by people coming across the great water because they wanted to serve God. They built this country great by having the shelter of God's Word over them. You can live a life of peace here because you are under the shelter that they built. You have done nothing to deserve this life, but you are enjoying the benefits of their labor. Now my people, on the other hand, have no shelter. So that is why I say the first and only change that will really help my people is to have this shelter that is Jesus. We have no other hope."

Slowly the professor sat down. Bautista looked around, bewildered at the standing ovation he received from the student body.

Mark has received numerous letters and e-mails from people all over the United States saying how their lives have been changed by his stories of the Yanomamö. Many tell of how the Lord used *Spirit of the Rainforest* to show them their need for a Savior.

Others tell how the book was used to help them make their lives right with the Lord. I submit that this book would never have been written and these lives never touched if it had not been for Reneé's life . . . a short life, but the ripples from it continue to roll on even now.

EPILOGUE
JOY IN THE JOURNEY

We kept using the *Jesus* movie, and now my words to the Yanomamö came back to haunt me. When I told them about how they had to really start trusting God for their loved ones who pass on, and how we could not let someone dying stop us from using the tool the Lord was giving us in this movie, little did I know that just a few short months later Reneé would be dead of malaria, and that it would be *I* who would have to deal with listening to a voice with a void in my heart so big that it would come up and almost choke me. And I have to say it was very difficult listening to her voice on the film . . .

I guess I have spent too much time with the Yanomamö. All my talk about trusting the Lord was really put to the test here. Nevertheless, we continued to use the film in our evangelistic work. One night after showing it in the village of Maweni, an old witch doctor slowly got to his feet. Tears came to my eyes as he started telling us that he finally understood.

"I have heard all this before, but now I really understand just what Jesus went through for me," he said. After the meeting, when we had finished stowing everything back into the large waterproof boxes we carried the projector in, we went down to the river for a midnight swim before going to our hammocks. We were hot and sticky from the heat of the tropical night.

As I said, Jaime is the main voice on the *Jesus* film, as he is the narrator. This particular night he was quiet. Finally he asked me, quietly, "Does it bother you to hear Joshua's mother's voice?" He had his voice in the respectful whisper they use when they speak of someone who has died, and he referred to her through her kinship term, not her name. I was surprised to hear him say that much because since her death, very few of my friends had even acknowledged the fact that I had ever been married before. They never talked about her when I was around, but the different times I walked in and they all quickly quit talking let me know who they had been talking about. So, now that Jaime was asking about her, it took me a minute to think of what to say. Finally I spoke.

"Yes, it really does. But the only reason I can still keep going, even though it makes me sad to hear her voice, is that I am strengthened by reminding myself that although she has gone on to heaven, with her small part in the film, she can continue to serve the Lord."

"Look," I told him, "that old man that got saved tonight. *She* had a part in that!"

Jaime was quiet for a while, then he told me in a much louder voice, "I see what you mean. As soon as we get home, I am going to sit down with my whole family and explain to them what you just told me and tell them that even if I die to let the film alone so I can still keep working for the Lord."

What a time we've had! It has been ten years now and sometimes the pain is still so intense, but God has again blessed me with a loving wife, Keila, and two more children, Mikeila, and Mia. Our boys are now teenagers and are such a blessing as they work with us here in the village. Joshua is now nineteen, Ryan is seventeen, and Stephen is fifteen. In all three of them at different times, in just the way they might look or some gesture they make, I see their mom, Reneé, and I have to smile.

A long time remembered,
Are the memories we shared through the years,
The good times are cherished,
The bad times forgotten with the tears.
With friendship and laughter,
We've walked hand and hand along the way.
Yesterday's memories still linger in the memories of today.

Tomorrow's making changes,
Our lives aren't the same anymore.
But the echoing laughter's still heard from our open childhood door.
Time can't erase all the dreams that we shared along the way.
And we're making new memories
To add to the ones from yesterday.

For information or to contact the author, please write to:

Michael Dawson
715 Stockton Rd.
Front Royal, VA 22630

Or call:
540-635-5777

Or e-mail:
mdawson@metaconi.com

Visit the Web site for more information about
the Dawsons and the Yanomamö tribe:
www.missionpadamo.org